Ripple Effect

Ripple Effect is a clarion call to the church to let go of human thinking and human influences and step into a life of intimate, dependent, trusting, interactive relationship with Jesus. Jillian says, "It's time to pull away with God, tuning out all the voices until the only One you hear is His." This book opens the door into her own life, telling you how she did it, and how you can, too. This is for anyone who wants an authentic faith walk and is done with "playing church."

Brynn Taylor Ashford
Author of *Welcome to the Fresh-Squeezed Life Cafe*
and *Don't Get Stuck!; As Real As Apples*

A ripple effect by one person's definition is "a spreading, pervasive, and usually unintentional effect or influence." While that may be one definition, what Jillian shares in Ripple Effect, will have very intentional effects as the truth of God's word is applied to your life circumstances and mine. As Jillian Ahonen's pastor, I am confident that you will be challenged and encouraged by *Ripple Effect*. Her commitment to the transforming power of God's word literally jumps off of every page. As she states in the opening of the book, this is an "invitation." I invite you as she has, on a very intentional journey, with amazing outcomes available to you, that will affect your personal life, family life, vocational life, and most of all, your spiritual life.

Gary Jones
Senior Pastor, Crossroads Church, Temecula, CA

Jillian writes with passion and authority, as someone who has faced many hardships in life but has come through with a stronger faith and a powerful testimony. Her words will inspire you, challenge you and call you back to your first love, Jesus. Her natural teaching style turns the reader back to the Word of God as the foundation for everything we believe. Ripple Effect will help you to examine your life closely to discover cracks that only Jesus can fill. I was drawn in by Jillian's honesty and authenticity, challenged by her boldness to confront the lies of the enemy, and reminded that I don't have to live an "average" Christian life, bound up by anxiety and frustration. This is a great book for anyone who needs someone to come alongside and show us how to undo habits that are not honoring to God and patterns that are holding us back from the life God wants us to live.

Jaimie Bowman
Pastor and author of *Breathe: 31 Moments with God {for Moms}*

Our perception and understanding of life is formulated by the environment that surrounds us, both good and bad. As Christians, this world view should be seen and understood through God's revelation and not from man's limited wisdom. God has given us His paradigm for life through the biblical narrative and the Holy Spirit's revelation. In this latest work, Jillian has challenged us to ask the honest question; "Are we in line with God's world view or are we really just living according to man's world view?" If we aren't honest with ourselves we may fall into the trap of not seeing things clearly, so we often compromise God's truth to satisfy ourselves. She explores the traps we fall into and the ripple effect that inhibits our full experience of God's amazing grace! Thanks Jillian for helping us connect with the tough questions!

Reverend Kirk D Peterman
Founder of Red Oak Healing Ministry

Ripple Effect is infused with example after example of God's deep and intimate love for us. It is an important and timely reminder of how, as the body of Christ, it is crucial that we not only embrace God's love for ourselves but then release that love into the world around us. As always, Jillian writes with breathtaking honesty and vulnerable transparency.

Jennifer Miller
Author of *Finding Freedom as Daughter of the King* and *Bridal Bootcamp: 7 Keys To Building The Marriage You've Always Dreamed Of*

I met Jillian Ahonen over fifteen years ago and have personally witnessed how Jillian's life has changed dramatically by allowing Jesus Christ to impact her heart and overcome fears. In *Ripple Effect*, Jillian shows us how to overcome our fears by developing critical, biblical characteristics so we can confidently share the message of salvation with those we care about most ... In *Ripple Effect*, we learn to reshape our thinking and our hearts through the combination of journaling, Biblical insights, and the Holy Spirit. We learn how to love and develop spiritual insight which can have a powerful impact on our hearts through God's truths. *Ripple Effect* provides the right answers to many of life's tough questions ... we will learn to overcome our fears and live our lives the way God created us to live.

Raymond Cruz
Minister, Life Coach, President, Abide Reintegration Services, Inc.

A Transformational Journey into God's Heart
That Will Change You from the Inside Out

JILLIAN AHONEN

©2022 Jillian Ahonen

All rights reserved. This book is protected by the copyright laws of the United States of America. This book may not be copied or reprinted for commercial gain or profit. No part of this may be reproduced, stored in a retrieval system, or transmitted in any form or by any means—electronic, mechanical, photocopy, recording, or any other—except for brief quotations in critical reviews or articles, without prior written permission from the author. The use of short quotations or occasional page copying for personal or group study is permitted and encouraged. Permission will be granted upon written request.

Scripture taken from the Amplified Bible (AMPCE), Copyright © 1954, 1958, 1962, 1964, 1965, 1987 by The Lockman Foundation. Used by permission.

Scripture Quotations marked NLT are taken from The Holy Bible, New Living Translation, Copyright ©1996, 2004, 2007 by Tyndale House Foundation, Inc., Carol Stream, Illinois 60188. All rights reserved.

Scripture Quotations marked NIV are taken from The Holy Bible, New International Version, Copyright ©1973, 1978, 1984, 2011 by Biblica, Inc. Used by permission. All rights reserved worldwide.

Scripture Quotations marked MSG are taken from The Message, Copyright ©1993, 1994, 1995, 1996, 2000, 2001, 2002 by NavPress Publishing Group. Used by permission. All rights reserved.

Scripture Quotations marked TPT are taken from The Passion Translation, Copyright ©2017, 2018 by Passion & Fire Ministries, Inc. Used by permission. All rights reserved.

Please note that Jillian Ahonen's writing style capitalizes certain pronouns in Scripture that refer to the Father, Son, and Holy Spirit, and may differ from other publishers'/authors' styles. Take note that the name satan and related names are not capitalized. She chooses not to acknowledge him even to the point of breaking adopted grammatical rules.

Ripple Effect is available worldwide. For distributions worldwide.

Published by Marked Publishing

Official publishing Imprint of Jillian Ahonen Ministries

www.JilllianAhonen.com

P.O Box 872734

Temecula, Ca. 92589-2734

Cover and Page designs by Dineen Miller

Printed in the United States of America

Paperback ISBN: 978-1-7342080-5-4

Hardcover ISBN: 978-1-7342080-6-1

"All you thirsty ones, come to Me!
Come to Me and drink!
Believe in Me so that rivers
of living water will burst out from within you,
flowing from your innermost being,
just like the Scripture says!"

JOHN 7:37B-39 (TPT)

Dedicated to my Heavenly Father,

*Thank You for Your loving kindness,
Your mercy, and Your unending grace.*

*Thank You for setting me free
and empowering me with a testimony
that we've all been invited into
because of Your one and only Son, Jesus.*

*I pray my life is a continual
living testimony of all You are,
all we have in You, and through You.
Use the words written in this book powerfully.
Your will be done!*

Contents

Special Thanks	11
Introduction	13
How to Read *Ripple Effect*	19
Chapter 1: Revelation of Love	23
Chapter 2: Radiating His Glory	55
Chapter 3: Responding as a Child	93
Chapter 4: Restored Mind	129
Chapter 5: Rhythm of Grace	169
Chapter 6: Respond to Him	195
Chapter 7: Releasing the Kingdom	219
About Jillian	245
Let's Stay Connected	247
About *Life is Muddy*	248

Special Thanks

Special thanks to my incredible husband, Rolf, who lets me pull away and write out the words God places on my heart. You have been a vital sounding board through this project. Thank you for your love, constant encouragement, covering, and full support. I love you!

To my parents, Louis and Susan DiGerolamo: You both sowed into my life and laid the foundation I continue to build upon. Dad, you taught me the meaning of grace and life-giving words even when I would continually do the wrong thing. Mom, you showed me how to fiercely take a stand in my life over the devil and all his schemes! You both taught me more than you realize, firmly rooting your lives and mine in the Word. Thank you for all you went through to get me here. I know you paved the way.

To my grandparents, Joe and Mary Lou Santos: Your life and your story has set the foundation of an incredible legacy for our family. Your love for Jesus radiates in you, and through you, to all who know you. Your lives are a living testimony of what it looks like to love like Him. I love you both so very much!

Thank you to my amazing friend, Brynn Ashford: You are more than a friend to me, you've been a spiritual mother, a mentor, one who is readily available for my brain dumps and incredibly deep ponders, including how much you helped and came alongside me as I worked on this book. Words cannot express the love I have for you. Thank you for your time, love, and continued support.

Cheryl Montoya, my other mother, you've been a constant support, not just with this project, but in my life for a steady twenty-five years. Thank you for being you. I love you!

Dineen Miller, working with you on this project was an ease and an honor. Your talent is truly a gift! Your extra care with every detail shows on every page of this book. I especially cherish our friendship that has formed through this season. Thank you for partnering with me on this project and more! You are precious to me.

Alice Shepherd, the gem that brought this project to the final finish line. Thank you for taking so much time and thought reading through each page with such care. You have a gift and it's beautiful how God is using you in this season of life. I especially loved your additional comments and stories. Thank you for sharing parts of your heart along the way.

Introduction

I have come alongside men and women through ministry, casually and professionally through coaching, and I discovered that a large majority of the body of Christ is struggling on so many levels it's overwhelming.

I began to wonder . . . What's happened?

What are we missing?

Why are so many believers crumbling, struggling, depressed, anxious, stressed out, and secretly (or outwardly) falling apart?

Where is the peace and joy without end that we should be living out of?

Why does it seem like much of my family of faith is crawling their way through life?

How are we shouting and singing praises of the bigness of our God, quoting scriptures of Truth and promise while still internally battling fears—mind wars of doubt, disbelief, and insecurity, living with heaviness in our spirits and stress knots in our stomachs daily?

This is not the life we've been invited into.

Why are we accepting a life in opposition to what the Bible says is ours through Jesus and His Spirit within us?

Why are so many wrestling internally with emotions, shoving down or justifying what they are feeling, and missing out on the empowered life in the Spirit that Jesus paid for on the Cross?

There is a huge disconnect here.

God has not only taken me on a transformational journey that has completely changed me from the inside out (and continues to), He has also spoken into each of my questions . . . it's been revolutionary!

Many of us are not contending for what's rightfully ours: a life in rhythm with God's heart that transforms us from the inside out. Instead, we're living as captives, wearing chains that block our true transformation. It's causing too many of us to be caught living with a push and pull between what God's Word says and what we are experiencing, still living out of our old nature, with a broken view, and belief systems that have been shaped by circumstances and feelings that are attached to what we've been through. However, God's Word says we are set free, new creations with new garments—the power of the Holy Spirit is in us, and we have been given the mind of Christ!

The chains that kept us bound from living in this spiritual freedom have been unlocked and should no longer be present in our lives because Jesus died to break those chains. Jesus paved the way for us to live in complete freedom through the power and presence of the Holy Spirit, and this rhythmic life has already begun!

It's time to stop depending on our human understanding based on our experiences and line our beliefs up with God's Truth. We need to begin connecting the dots between our hearts and minds so we can recognize the areas where we are trusting our feelings over God's Word.

> *Trust in the LORD with all your heart; do not depend on your own understanding. Seek His will in all you do, and He will show you which path to take.* — Proverbs 3:5-6 (NLT)

It's right there, family: do not depend on your own understanding. Seek Him!

Oftentimes we are relying on our own understanding and we don't even realize it. Then, we filter life through our own belief systems and live from our worldview instead of God's; we even read His Word through brokenness and our own interpretation. When living from our worldview, we learn what it looks like to be a Christian rather than fully connecting with the Holy Spirit, letting the Spirit produce a new way of living in us and through us by walking in sync with Him. Rather than the

Spirit producing fruit in us, we begin to manufacture what appears to be "fruit" but find it's an exhausting standard to live by. We secretly struggle to "get there" and "do better" in order to have what Jesus says is ours.

We *know* we have to rely on the Holy Spirit, but we don't fully comprehend what that means or how this idea works. Depression and anxiety can set in, knots form in our bellies, and heaviness pounds our chests. We go down our spiritual checklist to make sure we are doing everything "right," to be better and do better, begging for God's help. But the help we're wanting is according to what we think things should look like instead of allowing ourselves to be empowered by His Spirit. All of a sudden that "burden-is-light-yoke-is-easy-life" feels impossible; we can't even wrap our brains around what that scripture is saying, but we sure can quote it.

Yikes!

When our Christian-life survival checklist does not eliminate our "burdens," we succumb to believing the burden is the "thorn in our side" (or our circumstances' fault), and we become roomies with the world's standard of living, not God's! Even our theologically sound doctrine and highly educated studies can keep us hindered.

We have complicated Christianity, and we are missing out on what it means and feels like to live life in the Spirit. This unnoticed reality is creating a perpetual cycle of discord in our walks with God and each other, and it's blocking us from living in the rich and satisfying life that Jesus died on the Cross to bring us!

Our Christian checklist of dos and don'ts can easily create a façade that we've arrived at a fullness of understanding, but that "understanding" does not transform us. It's head knowledge. We *believe* we are changed because we know the scriptures that tell us this, but inside we don't feel it.

> *Jesus returned to Galilee in the power of the Spirit, and news about Him spread through the whole countryside. He was teaching in their synagogues, and everyone praised Him. He went to Nazareth, where He had been brought up, and on the Sabbath day, He went into the synagogue, as was His custom. He stood up to read, and the scroll of the prophet Isaiah was handed to Him. Unrolling it, He found the place where it is written:*

> *"The Spirit of the Lord is on Me, because He has anointed Me to proclaim good news to the poor. He has sent Me to proclaim freedom for the prisoners and recovery of sight for the blind, to set the oppressed free, to proclaim the year of the Lord's favor."*
>
> *Then He rolled up the scroll, gave it back to the attendant and sat down. The eyes of everyone in the synagogue were fastened on Him. He began by saying to them, "Today this scripture is fulfilled in your hearing."* — Luke 4:14-21 (NIV)

"Fulfilled in your hearing," meaning received and believed, you are free. I think we have heard but are we truly listening? We have heard the message that we are free and received it through head knowledge, but we're not experiencing the heart transplant that comes from the Spirit, leading us to total transformation that can only happen through Jesus, and by getting our minds lined up with His.

"If anyone has eyes to see and ears to hear . . ." Jesus repeats this concept over and over throughout the gospels. We are not going to be free through our human understanding. Understanding what we have available because of Jesus should lead us to His power within us, and through Him, we experience His supernatural freedom and joy. Outside of His Spirit we lessen the power of the Cross and live out of a duty. Which is just plain exhausting!

You feel me?

The abundant life that is supposed to be rich and satisfying is now causing us to live the opposite of what Jesus accomplished through His time on earth, and on the Cross. Many are tired, weary, and burned out on religion.

> *"Are you tired? Worn out? Burned out on religion? Come to Me. Get away with Me and you'll recover your life. I'll show you how to take a real rest. Walk with Me and work with Me—watch how I do it. Learn the unforced rhythms of grace. I won't lay anything heavy or ill-fitting on you. Keep company with Me and you'll learn to live freely and lightly."* — Matthew 11:28-30 (MSG)

It's time we start living in the freedom and lightness that is ours, wouldn't you say?

Let's undo the religious checklist that so many of us are living from, recognize some belief systems that have complicated Christianity, and learn to live through the power of the Holy Spirit that's within us.

God is calling us to break free from the religious system that has created a false comfort, blocking us from living in the freedom and victory that Jesus paid for, leaving us feeling heavy and filled with the worries of this life. What's familiar to us and "the way it's always been done" is not setting us up to be more than conquerors in Christ Jesus. This familiar cycle is causing us to seek outside stability when our stability is truly found when our life is built on the Rock.

Are you ready to experience everything that the Word says is yours?

Are you ready to do away with check-list Christianity and live powerfully in everything that Jesus paid for?

Are you ready to undo your humanistic thinking and learn the unforced rhythms of God's heart to the point that what He's doing in you begins to naturally flow out, transforming the world around you?

Let's get away with Jesus, recover our lives so we can live out what we believe, creating a powerful ripple effect from the inside out!

How to Read Ripple Effect

To my Kingdom family,

We are all in different seasons in our walks with Jesus. You are not behind or too late, so be patient with yourself. Each one of us has more areas of learning and growing to uncover. Whether you've been walking with God for fifty years or fifty days, there is more to be discovered with Him. We can spend a lifetime being learners with Jesus, and there will still be more thresholds of faith to cross over, more revelations, and more breakthroughs to experience. The Bible says that we go from glory to glory, which means there is a continuum of levels of glory as we are formed into His glorious image. God wants to meet you where you are and take you deeper and further in your faith-walk with Him.

> *We can all draw close to Him with the veil removed from our faces. And with no veil we all become like mirrors who brightly reflect the glory of the Lord Jesus. We are being transfigured into His very image as we move from one brighter level of glory to another. And this glorious transfiguration comes from the Lord, who is the Spirit.*
> *— 2 Corinthians 3:18 (TPT)*

I've learned in my own personal journey with Jesus that my most powerful breakthrough moments were when I felt a jolt to my system or when a question popped into my mind from something I read or heard. Rather than arguing away the moment or getting defensive, I pressed in and asked God to help me connect with what I was feeling or questioning, allowing Him to speak into my internal wrestle. He began to shatter my belief systems and thought-wiring in ways I didn't know were available. Through this process, I've learned to continually surrender every single one of my preconceived thoughts, allowing Him to completely reshape my mind and heart.

With that being said, there will be moments while you are reading *Ripple Effect* that may cause a jolt, a nudge, a question, or even an emotional reaction. These are powerful opportunities to pause on your reading and invite Jesus to speak into each area.

Having your journal and Bible nearby are great ways to interact with this content and the Holy Spirit. Don't skip past these moments. Highlight the content that jumps out at you, write your questions down, even the arguments that pop up that make you want to disagree with what you've read . . . these are incredibly freeing moments where you get to invite the Holy Spirit to speak into what's being revealed to you.

Basically I'm giving you permission to mark the heck out of this book and use what's written to go deeper with God!

God is inviting each one of us into a powerful and interactive relationship, but it requires our participation by learning how to connect with Him. These pause moments are the nudges from the Holy Spirit desiring to take us deeper in our faithwalk where we learn to lean into what He wants to do in us and through us. Go to Him with your questions, believing He will answer through a quiet whisper and His Word, bringing His Truth to your heart.

Read *Ripple Effect* at your pace. This is definitely not a quick reading book.

Sorry not sorry.

But seriously, do not feel like you need to rush through these pages to get to the end. This is your opportunity to go privately before the Lord and allow Him to undo any belief systems that have kept you from living in the fullness and freedom that Jesus paid for. Ask the Holy Spirit to shatter any barriers that are in the way of receiving more of Him until you are walking completely whole and free.

Get ready . . . we're gonna go deep!

You are going to get breakthroughs in the areas of your personal struggle!

And here's what you can do—

When something jumps out at you, take the time to pause and talk with Jesus. Put a bookmark where you left off (even in the middle of a chapter) if you need to, and trust that the Holy Spirit is speaking to you personally.

We're gonna call these "pause and reflect" moments! You're going to learn how to access the Holy Spirit as your Teacher rather than relying on me and a pre-written Bible study.

Here are some great journal questions to start with when something written grabs your attention. These can be prayer points between you and Jesus:

1. What am I feeling? Connect with that feeling and invite Jesus to meet you.

2. What am I believing? Hold that belief up to God's Word and see if it lines up. Ask the Holy Spirit to show you if you have anything in your belief system that conflicts with Truth, and ask Him to rewire your mind until it is lined up with His.

3. What am I holding onto that needs to be surrendered so I can learn what it means to live by the Spirit?

Take time to process what is personally highlighting to you. Jesus is going to bring revelations, healing, immeasurable peace, comfort and incredible freedom as you trust Him with all it all. He is faithful.

Father,

I pray for a hedge of protection over each one who picks up this book and reads these pages. Protect them from the evil one. I'm asking you, Holy Spirit, to go both before them and beside them, removing any and all barriers that have been hard-wired into their belief system, blocking them from living in the fullness and freedom that Your Son paid for. I'm praying for an increase in wisdom and understanding by your Spirit to move in each heart and mind as you take them from Your ever-increasing glory to more and then some! Holy Spirit, soften hearts to receive more of You, more of Your love, more of Your power, increasing their spiritual insight. I'm asking You to take Your Word from their head to their heart until Your Truth is the only Truth they are living from.

May we all learn in greater measures what it means to live by the Spirit. Help each one of us connect with Your heart in ways we have never experienced before, and let each one of us come out of this season with a powerful testimony of Your transforming love, mercy, and grace upon grace. In Jesus' mighty name, amen.

Much love,

Jillian

Chapter One
Revelation of Love

I made a conscious decision in high school that I didn't really want to be a "Christian" anymore. Life outside of my church upbringing seemed way more attractive at the time. Looking back, I can clearly see where the enemy was twisting things, using situations to lead me away from Truth and into a lifestyle that was far from God's heart. The day I found out I was pregnant with my first daughter at just eighteen years old, I ran back to Jesus.

It was really that simple.

I believed that I would be received by Him and that the moment I ran back to Him, I was made right, forgiven, redeemed . . . a spotless bride!

I was met with His unrelenting love, and placed a purity ring on my finger without a second thought of reservation. My mom bought me a new one with my unborn baby's birthstone on it; a pearl for June. Looking back, I can see how God used that moment to solidify all I was taught—I was forgiven and the moment I turned to Him, I was reconciled. He gave me a brand-new life with promise. If Jesus came to restore everything, I was included in that restoration.

I didn't struggle with the concept of grace, mercy, and unconditional love.

I didn't question whether or not I was truly forgiven.

I didn't feel ashamed when I went to church.

When people gave me "looks" while we were out and about, I smiled, free and clear of feeling embarrassed. After all, I was barely nineteen. I knew I was being stereotyped, but I didn't care. I made countless mistakes, and God turned my life around with my baby girl in my arms. She was, and is, my undeserved gift from God.

The Word of God says that He will work my life out for good.

And I believed Him.

> *And we know that in all things God works for the good of those who love Him, who have been called according to His purpose. For those God foreknew He also predestined to be conformed to the image of His Son, that He might be the firstborn among many brothers and sisters. And those He predestined, He also called; those He called, He also justified; those He justified, He also glorified.*
> — Romans 8:28-30 (NIV)

I was predestined for destiny with Him.

I was called and justified so that He may be glorified in me and through me.

Not that being a teenage single mom was easy. I don't want to paint a picture that this course change was an easy one. I had to learn and grow through many challenges (I'm still growing and learning). But I believed and put my trust in God's unconditional love, and because of that, I was able to wholeheartedly run back to Him. This moment became the foundation that my new life was built upon.

Notice the key to unlocking this confidence was through believing what God says is true.

My belief system is simple: If God's Word says it, I believe Him.

For the last twenty-four-plus years, the Holy Spirit continues to take me to a deeper revelation of what it means to live confidently from His unconditional, undeserving, unwavering love. His love is not complex. It's simple, yet overwhelmingly powerful and beyond my human comprehension. I am continually in awe ... His love truly is my freedom.

However, what I've observed from so many who genuinely love Jesus is they can talk about God's love, sing about His love, yet wrestle internally with acceptance. Not just from God, but also with themselves and with others. The struggle is subconscious; it's a secret battle that is playing out and hurting the body of Christ.

I went to the Lord with my concerns, He said: "What you see is My children who need a revelation of My love. A love encounter with Me."

Simple truth: When we receive a personal revelation of God's overwhelming love, and that nothing can separate us from Him—we live differently.

When God's unconditional love syncs with our hearts, we begin to see everything and everyone, including ourselves, through His amazing love.

Through His pure, unrelenting, overwhelming, all-encompassing, empowering, fulfilling, life-changing, earth-shaking, breathtaking . . . I could go on forever and ever, l-o-v-e—LOVE!

His love changes the very chemistry of our internal wiring—we begin to think differently, act differently, see differently and what flows out of us looks like the love of Jesus that we read about in the Bible. His love is not supposed to be forced; it's natural. This natural flow of His unconditional love is where forgiving those who have hurt us (or think differently) comes straight from the throne room of Heaven, because we are not stuck in a conditional love that puts parameters on ourselves or those around us. We love because He first loved us, and from there we are empowered to forgive as Jesus does. Loving those who are imperfect (ahem, this includes your family members), or those who don't know Jesus, does not come naturally unless the overwhelming love of the Father is flooding our lives. This natural love is the effortless rhythm filled with grace upon grace that God has invited us into.

> *We know how much God loves us, and we have put our trust in His love. God is love, and all who live in love live in God, and God lives in them.* — *1 John 4:16 (NLT)*

Are you experiencing this effortless rhythm in your life or is your love toward yourself and others conditional?

Let's go deeper and a bit more personal . . . Are you loving your family and those closest to you through God's overwhelming grace and love, or is it more natural to unleash your anger and impatience on them once

> His love changes the very chemistry of our internal wiring—we begin to think differently, act differently, see differently and what flows out of us looks like the love of Jesus that we read about in the Bible.

you pull away from the church building?

God sees what many hide. Let's be honest with our hidden areas and get our hearts right before the Lord. We need the Holy Spirit and an infilling of His unconditional love to love ourselves and others well!

Maybe you're stuck on this idea that loving yourself is vanity and my mention of this doesn't sit right with you.

Here's a scripture to consider, one I've reflected on myself:

> *"Love the Lord your God with all your heart and with all your soul and with all your mind and with all your strength.' The second is this: 'Love your neighbor as yourself.' There is no commandment greater than these."* — Mark 12:30-31 (NIV)

What if we have self-hate in our hearts?

If we don't love ourselves well, we cannot effectively love others. In fact, we will end up judging them the same way we judge ourselves. With this being said, let's include ourselves in the love factor and realize that the measure of grace and love that we need from God is not just for those around us, it's for us as well. God actually wants us to love ourselves, the way He does.

What I've discovered through my own personal journey, coaching sessions, and as I do life with my family of faith, is a gap between knowing about God's love versus living from a place of unconditional love. The root problem is a lack of trust. Many of us are struggling to trust in God's unconditional love, not realizing the internal block. When we struggle to trust and simply receive His love, loving others remains a challenge.

Rather than being filled with God's unconditional love, we are empty and only have a conditional love to give. Then, we meet someone who is, well, prickly, causing a jolt to our system, triggering a negative feeling that causes us to pull back, withholding grace and love. Oftentimes we listen to those feelings and develop a judgment toward that person who rubbed us wrong, sometimes even going as far as to build hatred against them in our hearts. In truth, we are living from our feelings instead of from our new natures, which is to be like Christ, freely loving because He first loved us.

> *We love each other because He loved us first. If someone says, "I love God," but hates a fellow believer, that person is a liar; for if we don't love people we can see, how can we love God, whom we cannot see?*
> *— 1 John 4:19-20 (NLT)*

Yikes . . . whoever hates a brother or sister is a liar.

Sounds harsh, right!?

This is God's Word which is the lamp for our feet that lights up the path of life for us. So, we really need to take into consideration what may be going on in our hearts.

I get it.

> MANY OF US ARE STRUGGLING TO TRUST IN GOD'S UNCONDITIONAL LOVE, NOT REALIZING THE INTERNAL BLOCK.

Who wants to admit that there might be hate in their heart toward others?

It's ugly, right?

Avoiding what's stirring in our hearts is not going to get rid of it. The issue festers, creating barriers in our hearts, limiting the flow of God's love in us and through us, and we become ineffective—limited by our old nature.

The flesh.

Then we read the love chapter in Corinthians and try in our own strength to look like love while struggling with secret battles of guilt and reasoning because of the strong negative feelings that are weighing in. What are we left to do other than learn to work harder at covering up what we are feeling so we can look and sound like love? We end up leaving the Holy Spirit out of the equation, not even considering going to Him for help.

Now, many genuinely believe that reading God's Word and hearing the messages we've been given on love *is* asking for God's help, but is it?

We can do a heart check to see if we've allowed the Holy Spirit to genuinely help us in the love factor or if we are trying to look and sound like love in our own strength. It begins with being honest with ourselves, a willingness to evaluate what's going on in our hearts and our thought-life, and checking to see if what we are feeling and thinking lines up with the heart of the Father.

Here are some great journal questions to help you connect—this could be a good "pause and reflect" point for you ...

Do you feel a softness toward others, or do you pull back with harsh, unloving thoughts?

Is love truly running through you or are you creating a façade of love by saying all the right things, but feeling the opposite toward others?

Are there people that you have cut out of your life, maybe even your own family members whether the church body or your immediate family, and you are withholding love with your list of justifications and reasons?

Have you been hurt by someone and your thoughts toward them are strong and hate-filled?

Keep in mind I am not referring to a need for safety in abusive situations. That is a completely separate conversation. But we still need to check in with our hearts to find out if hate is stirring.

Looking at these truths will reveal the areas where we are struggling in our flesh, not living by the Spirit, and in need of a healing touch from Jesus.

I know I'm probably hitting some pressure points here. Please know that this is not to shame anyone, but an invitation for us to evaluate what's stirring in our hearts. We, as a church body, are struggling with the love factor big time, and many are faking love.

Yes—I am calling us all out right now!

It's okay.

Deep breath.

I have gone through seasons where I have struggled to see people through God's eyes and genuinely struggled to like them, let alone love them.

I know, shocker, right? (Insert eye roll here)

Upon recognizing my distaste, I acknowledged my hidden inner struggle, brought it to the light of God's presence, and asked my Heavenly Father to show me who they are to Him. I invited the Holy Spirit to help me see them through my Father's eyes, not my own.

> We, as a CHURCH BODY, ARE STRUGGLING WITH THE LOVE FACTOR BIG TIME, AND MANY ARE FAKING LOVE.

His love overwhelmed me for them.

I didn't shove away my inner struggle, justify or rationalize my flesh (giving myself a list of excuses and reasons), or even try to find something good about them (try doing that when all you see is their flaws, weakness, and mistakes). Instead, I acknowledged my struggle before the Lord and asked for help.

And He showed up!

I think we forget that we can go to the Holy Spirit for help in all areas of life. As I included Him in this personal struggle, He began to show me how my tendency to judge or criticize (usually in my head) was revealing brokenness or insecurity in myself that was not fully restored in Christ. These moments became an opportunity to invite Him into my places of brokenness and insecurity so I could experience His supernatural healing touch in each area of need. Not only did He touch my insecure areas and reveal a greater understanding of my worth to Him, He flooded me with a love toward someone that I was unable to love in my own strength. This was such an incredible experience, proving I didn't need to acquire anything or try to "get myself" to a more loving or accepting place in my heart. Now, when I find myself criticizing, judging, or withholding love, I quickly catch it and ask the Holy Spirit to give me His heart and eyes to see them the way He does. This moves me to a place of compassion and grace with an overwhelming love for them, rather than allowing a toxic thought-life to rip them apart in my head.

Hey, jus' being real here and calling those judgy, unloving, critical, not-walking-in-grace thoughts what they are . . . TOXIC!

This Holy Spirit-led prayer continues to be a powerful tool that I use regularly. Especially when someone I love hurts me. I wasn't consciously aware of what I was doing or following any type of step-plan. I just believe that God calls me to love and see others with a pure heart, and in my flesh it's impossible.

For those who really struggle with letting those negative thoughts go, justifying why it's ok to think (or speak) them towards any given person, realize you are grieving the Holy Spirit in you.

> *Do not let any unwholesome talk come out of your mouths, but only what is helpful for building others up according to their needs, that it may benefit those who listen. And do not grieve the Holy Spirit of God, with whom you were sealed for the day of redemption. Get rid of all bitterness, rage and anger, brawling and slander, along with every form of malice. Be kind and compassionate to one another, forgiving each other, just as in Christ God forgave you.*
> *— Ephesians 4:29-32 (NIV)*

It seems that those who are closest to us can hurt us the most, am I right?

That's because we've given them space in our hearts, and in their humanness, they are flawed just like you and me. Through our Father's eyes, we can see them through His unconditional love and that they are hurting individuals with brokenness themselves. This perspective moves our hearts to pray for them. While our hearts may hurt deeply, we can invite Jesus to come into that place of wounding for our healing. This new life in the Spirit causes us to soar with wings like eagles high above our feelings and painful situations.

When we surrender our hurts and struggles to God, we can love others like our Father in Heaven, as we become more like Him, seeing others the way He does, living in the supernatural flow of His heart.

Go ahead, ask the Holy Spirit to bring names to your attention right now.

Take the time to bring each person and each heart-hurt to the Father. Confess to Him where you have withheld forgiveness and unconditional love, and forgive those who have hurt you.

> *"And forgive us our debts, as we also have forgiven our debtors."*
> *— Matthew 6:12 (NLT)*

Invite Him into the pain these people have caused and believe that He will not only heal those wounds from the past, but He will also fill you until you are overflowing with His love!

You can do this each time something surfaces in your life that reveals where you have heart-hurt from a specific person that you need to forgive and where you need more of God's unconditional love filling you. Lean into what's going on in your heart, so you can unclog what's blocking you from God's transforming love, receive a healing touch from the Father, and get a breakthrough!

When we surrender OUR HURTS AND STRUGGLES TO GOD, WE CAN LOVE OTHERS LIKE OUR FATHER IN HEAVEN, AS WE BECOME MORE LIKE HIM, SEEING OTHERS THE WAY HE DOES, LIVING IN THE SUPERNATURAL FLOW OF HIS HEART.

Amen?

I have both observed fake love and have also been a recipient of my brothers' and sisters' "lack of love" so many times over it would shock you.

Or maybe it wouldn't.

Maybe it's been your story too, and the word "church" puts a sour taste in your mouth because the body of Christ has not loved you well, or worse, judged and excluded you.

If you have been hurt by the Church, by the family of God, or by your very own brothers and sisters in Christ—I'm sorry. I truly am.

That is not the love of the Father.

Their judgments come from brokenness in them that has not been fully met by His love.

Maybe your experience hasn't taken you so far away that you don't go to church. You do go, but with your heart guarded and a barrier that is subconsciously ready to cut anyone out of your life who triggers you. Paul shows us in 2 Corinthians that it is not always a lack of being loved well or right that keeps us from receiving love. It's because we've closed our hearts off from others. Love can't penetrate. We need to open our hearts wide in order to receive, but because "self" gets in the way, and we have an underlying fear of hurt or shame that our insecurities might leak out if we let people come too close, so we keep our hearts closed.

> *My friends at Corinth, our hearts are wide open to you and we speak freely, holding nothing back from you. If there is a block in our relationship, it is not with us, for we carry you in our hearts with great love, yet you still withhold your affections from us. So I speak to you as our children. Make room in your hearts for us as we have done for you.* — 2 Corinthians 6:11-14 (TPT)

There have been many times my love has been pure toward others, but barriers in their hearts from life's hurt had not yet been healed by Jesus, causing their love toward me to be conditional, making it easy to cut me out. Truthfully, the rejection I experienced was from a place of fear in them. When perfect love is moving freely through our hearts, fear gets pushed out and love keeps us connected.

Perfect love casts out—I know you finished the sentence for me.

Fear.

We, as the Church, know the scripture that says perfect love casts out fear, but we aren't really connecting with that reality; fear is messing with our walks with God and with others.

- Fear of being judged.

- Fear of being hurt AGAIN.

- Fear of someone noticing that we are insecure inside and it will mess with the image we are trying to project.

- Fill in the blank of what your fears might be.

Fear is manifesting through the body of Christ and it's hurting us, creating a negative ripple effect of disconnectedness from each other and even God. This fear factor is causing us to live in the chains of our old nature, robbing us of living in the freedom and unity that Jesus paid for when He tore down the divide that separated us from God and each other.

Fear is not the only dividing factor that is blocking unity and love in the body of Christ. For generations there has been a constant and clear divide among the church from theological opinions to the ways we "do" church, the way we worship, political views . . . you name it. Each position decides who is right and who is wrong, putting us at odds with one another, making it impossible to see our Kingdom family through love. Our attention is focusing on the wrong thing and behind the scene, is the enemy at work causing us to lose sight of what's most important.

> WHEN PERFECT LOVE IS MOVING FREELY THROUGH OUR HEARTS, FEAR GETS PUSHED OUT AND LOVE KEEPS US CONNECTED.

If our humanistic views and actions cause the type of division that makes people our enemies, the ones Jesus died for, you better believe that is a strategy straight from hell, the kingdom of darkness! These battles ARE NOT against flesh and blood, so let's stop waging war against one another.

> *For our struggle is not against flesh and blood, but against the rulers, against the authorities, against the powers of this dark world and against the spiritual forces of evil in the heavenly realms.*
> *— Ephesians 6:12 (NIV)*

How can we possibly love those we are called to love when we are making them our enemies based on our feelings and a worldly perspective?

The simple answer: we can't.

The Bible tells us to focus on the things of Heaven, not of this world . . . to not get hung up on earthly matters. Fear, heart-hurt, religion, and a lack of experiencing the Father's love pits us against one another. God knows what's going on in each of our hearts, so whether it's obvious to others or not, remember that nothing is hidden from God. When negative thoughts and emotions stir in our hearts and minds, or we have our list of justifications for our unloving thoughts that go unchecked, we don't turn to Jesus and get the healing touch from Him that's available to us. Instead, we withhold love, cut people out of our lives, blame, and demand justice rather than trusting God and loving those we are called to.

> *Fear is* MANIFESTING THROUGH THE BODY OF CHRIST AND IT'S HURTING US, CREATING A NEGATIVE RIPPLE EFFECT OF DISCONNECTEDNESS FROM EACH OTHER AND EVEN GOD.

Jesus died for all mankind.

All!

Even our perceived enemies.

Thought to consider: If we feel a strong need to demand justice from a person or people group, rather than releasing them to God, trusting that He is just and will take care of our defenses, reveals that we, ourselves, have not fully received what Jesus accomplished on the cross. We need His love to minister to our fears and hurts caused by the brokenness of man, and a greater revelation of His unconditional love. This is the benefit we have in Jesus. I promise you, when you are filled with His unconditional love, what once triggered you will lose all power over you.

I went to the Lord and asked Him why the body of Christ so often sounds and looks like the world in their actions and behaviors toward one another. Not just against the unsaved, but even toward their own brothers and sisters of faith, cutting off unity and love in their hearts, withholding forgiveness, and breeding a root of bitterness.

The Lord spoke to my heart, and it caused me to drop to my knees.

He said, "Many of My children have 'picked up their mat' out of a duty but have not come for a heart-healing touch from Me. They are walking through this life trying to carry a mat of religious obedience but are severely wounded. These heart wounds are continual triggers that cause barriers toward one another, and even Me."

Wow, my heart hurt hearing this. I have been praying for the body of Christ to have an encounter with the Father's love and turn to Him for heart-healing since; which has compelled me to write this book.

God wants us to experience the rhythm of His love, what it looks and feels like, so we are no longer bound by a false version of love that feels heavy and hard; as if somehow we still have to earn it. He is calling us all back to the beginning where love met us, and it's His desire for us to live from that place continuously. This place of living from love should not waver; it should only get richer and deeper over time.

When we are truly walking in an overflow of God's love, overwhelming circumstances and the heartbreak that life brings cannot give us a hardened or insecure heart. Jesus came here to accomplish everything that blocked us from living freely in His love. Because of His unrelenting love, we can boldly and confidently go to His throne room of grace.

> *So let us come boldly to the throne of our gracious God. There we will receive His mercy, and we will find grace to help us when we need it most.* — Hebrews 4:16 (NLT)

Let's take a look at this scripture in its simplest form. The word boldly grabs me every time. To be bold, by definition, means to be fearless and courageous!

Are you boldly running to Him?

Or—do you have fear and insecurity, maybe even areas you are struggling to trust Him with, holding you back from going to Him with boldness and courage?

He never said that we need to hold back any parts of us. He isn't holding back any parts of Himself. This includes His son and His Spirit!

Wow, right?!

Let this powerful reality sink in!

God did not want us to live apart from Him, so He gave up His Son, and then took it even further by putting His Spirit—His power—in us. Because of love we are now fused into the family of God, heirs to His throne, and the inheritance that is His is ours too.

> *Furthermore, because we are united with Christ, we have received an inheritance from God, for He chose us in advance, and He makes*

> *everything work out according to His plan. God's purpose was that we Jews who were the first to trust in Christ would bring praise and glory to God. And now you Gentiles have also heard the truth, the Good News that God saves you. And when you believed in Christ, He identified you as His own by giving you the Holy Spirit, whom He promised long ago. The Spirit is God's guarantee that He will give us the inheritance He promised and that He has purchased us to be His own people. He did this so we would praise and glorify Him.*
> — Ephesians 1:11-14 (NLT)

God gave up what is most precious to Him to give us a glimpse of how far, and how deep, and how wide His love truly is. He shared everything, holding back nothing.

God's love is so selfless, it will wreck your brain when His Truth goes from your head to your heart through His Spirit. We cannot comprehend this kind of love through our human understanding. While God doesn't hold anything back, our human nature, insecurities, and/or selfishness cause us to withhold ourselves or things that are precious to us, and because this is in our wiring, it's hard to imagine this kind of love.

Many of us are subconsciously living out of a belief system that has convinced us that we have to earn God's love by "doing" instead of just believing and receiving. We need the Holy Spirit to show us. Without a revelation through the Holy Spirit of His love, we have a subconscious belief that we still need to earn His love. So, we approach Him with extreme caution and awareness of self, or worse, we don't go to Him at all.

As a life coach, it's in my wiring to help people get free in their area of struggle. I wanted to identify the block and understand why so much of the church is struggling. If we don't identify what has established the block, we cannot undo it, or come out of agreement with the lie we may be living under.

You with me?

The Holy Spirit began to show me, beyond the lack of trust and fear, how the self-awareness movement in our culture has trickled its way into the church, creating a negative ripple effect in the body of Christ.

"Self" is one of the biggest barriers in the body of Christ, hindering us from living in God's love.

God doesn't want us to go to Him with an awareness of self, but with an awareness of Him, and in that we experience His love. The only "self" awareness that is required is that we realize who we are without Him, recognize our need, and turn toward Him.

Let me back up a minute and clarify what I'm bringing to the table so we can come together and move forward with full understanding.

> The Holy Spirit began to show me, beyond the lack of trust and fear, how the self-awareness movement in our culture has trickled its way into the church, creating a negative ripple effect in the body of Christ.

I am not referring to the idea that we skip evaluating what's going on in our hearts and checking in with our thought-life. We've already discussed this but I'm going to clarify in case there's an argument that's stirring in your mind. It is vital to our spiritual journeys to be honest and self-reflect, making sure our reflection time includes inviting the Holy Spirit to reveal any areas that need His help, where we need to grow in maturity, and/or where our thinking is not lined up with His Word. Staying aware of our thoughts and feelings helps us identify the areas we are living in conflict with what God says, and what strongholds may be blocking us from receiving God's unconditional love. Identifying strongholds and taking our thoughts captive will be discussed later. I just want to make sure we are all on the same page and clarify what I'm addressing: the difference between a godly self-reflection time that is vital, versus the cultural self-awareness movement that has subtly taken us off course.

Let's take a look at how the worldly self-awareness movement has created a negative ripple effect of twisted truth and confusion and has blocked us from simply and confidently living loved.

Self-awareness is exactly what it sounds like. It's self-focused, not God-focused, which means we are constantly focusing on our strengths (or weaknesses), our abilities (or lack of), our talents (or shortcomings), our position in life ... you get me, right? Self.

There are many ways that "self" has distorted our walks with God, but for now, I want to focus on how the constant state of self-awareness breeds shame, preventing us from freely running to Jesus, living accepted, and walking in His unconditional love.

This self-awareness movement is the "little leaven that has leavened the whole lump" (for all my KJV and NKJV friends) and it's time for us as the Church body to get our hearts lined up with everything God has invited us into.

"Self" was the first thing that separated us from God...

> *The woman was convinced. She saw that the tree was beautiful and its fruit looked delicious, and she wanted the wisdom it would give her. So she took some of the fruit and ate it. Then she gave some to her husband, who was with her, and he ate it, too. At that moment their eyes were opened, and they suddenly felt shame at their nakedness. So they sewed fig leaves together to cover themselves. When the cool evening breezes were blowing, the man and his wife heard the Lord God walking about in the garden. So they hid from the Lord God among the trees. Then the Lord God called to the man, "Where are you?" He replied, "I heard you walking in the garden, so I hid. I was afraid because I was naked."* — Genesis 3:6-10 (NLT)

Did you catch that?

"The woman was convinced. She wanted the wisdom it would give her (self-exaltation) ... At that moment, their eyes were opened" (self-aware) "and they suddenly felt shame in their nakedness." Then, they hid from God. It was a selfish desire to be exalted, which led to sin and self-awareness, causing them to feel shame and then fear set in.

The result?

They hid themselves from God.

I think many are living from this place without realizing it. We are not fully connecting that we live under a new covenant because of Jesus. We are no longer seen through our shame, brokenness, and humanness (our fleshly old nature), but through the righteousness of Christ, our new nature in Him, through God's perfect love. His perfect love drives fear out of our lives!

> *Love never brings fear, for fear is always related to punishment. But*

> *love's perfection drives the fear of punishment far from our hearts. Whoever walks constantly afraid of punishment has not reached love's perfection.* — 1 John 4:18 (TPT)

How often do we find ourselves bound by fears that prevent us from running to God and receiving His love?

Seeing God through our human understanding, and not through Jesus, has created a heartbreaking barrier that keeps so much of the body of Christ separated from His unconditional love. This is why it is so hard to love others and why there is so much division in the body of Christ. If we are seeing God through human understanding, then we see others in that same manner and not through His love.

When we live from a conscious awareness of self, evaluating ourselves through our own understanding, we naturally want to hide our insecurities and flaws. Because we are so aware of the areas where we fall short, and what we are not good at, we live with underlying feelings of inadequacy, causing us to feel ashamed of ourselves and unworthy of love. Shame wants to cover up and hide so that no one can see our shortcomings, subconsciously believing that God feels the same. We might know in our heads that God doesn't feel the way we do about ourselves, but because we are so focused on "self" and our own idea of worth, our eyes are trained to be on ourselves, not on God, and His love isn't syncing with our hearts. So, we live from a belief system that we are not enough until we've worked our way toward this idea of "good enough." In order to avoid feeling that sting of shame and unworthiness, we cover what we believe are our flaws, working harder at the appearance of godliness to prove we are worthy of love through a checklist of works. This idea that we have to do more to be accepted by ourselves, God, and others is not only wrong thinking, it's exhausting!

As soon as we fall short of our idea (human understanding), fixating on where we've missed the mark, weariness sets in. What's written in the Bible becomes such a foreign concept, we don't realize that our belief system has formed around our human understanding, feelings, and experiences instead of around God's Word and upon the foundation of His unconditional love.

This is the cycle that many believers are living in.

Who we once were is dead. And because of this Truth, we are directed to "put off" the former ways of living and thinking so we can walk in our new natures, to be like Christ. Because of Jesus we are pure; blameless; holy; redeemed . . . we are fully loved; the righteousness of Christ and THAT is how God sees us.

Many do not simply believe and receive that God sees them through the righteousness of Christ, fully accepted and loved by Him.

Life here becomes a battle to get to a place of acceptance, never feeling good enough, not fully living in the total fulfillment and richness of God's love, or seeing ourselves the way He sees us. Because of this, we have a vacancy in our hearts that needs to feel loved and accepted, and without realizing it, we put that need on those around us rather than going directly to God to get this inner need met. We find ourselves giving a fabricated (or conditional) love to those around us without realizing that it's with a subconscious desire for love to be reciprocated. When we don't feel love in return, we feel even more insecure than we were before, pull back from the hurt, and a barrier forms in our hearts.

Our love remains conditional.

Bottom line, we are not loving to give; we are loving to get a need met because we haven't fully received our fulfillment from God. If we do not feel loved by others, we naturally pull back and withhold love. A negative ripple effect takes place when the flow of God's unconditional love is not present in our lives.

If you think about it, this could explain why so many leave relationships, churches, and even marriages . . . if we aren't getting the love we think we need from people, misunderstanding that we get this need for love met through God, we are incapable of loving those around us effectively.

When we receive God's unconditional love, it's easy to love others whether they deserve it or not. We don't need love from them, we are already so filled

> *Because of Jesus*
> WE ARE PURE; BLAMELESS; HOLY; REDEEMED . . . WE ARE FULLY LOVED; THE RIGHTEOUSNESS OF CHRIST AND THAT IS HOW GOD SEES US.

with a supernatural love that is more powerful than the worldly concept of love. Wordly, selfish love says to love only those who love you back. God's unconditional love says, "love because I have first loved you."

The awareness of self can also affect our walk with God by creating a barrier of pride in our abilities or achievements. We become puffed up with knowledge (even the knowledge we've received from God). From there, we view ourselves "higher than we ought" while looking down on those who, from our perspective, aren't on our level. This is where we can end up tangling our identities apart from God, and, instead, form our identities through our human achievements, even our spiritual anointing can become our pride barrier.

Honestly, this negative cycle is easy to get caught up in because we live in a world that measures personal value using ladders of success. We have social economic tiers, positions, pay grades, and we automatically begin to judge others (and ourselves) through humanistic standards.

> When we RECEIVE GOD'S UNCONDITIONAL LOVE IT'S EASY TO LOVE OTHERS WHETHER THEY DESERVE IT OR NOT.

Identity through achievement is hardwired into us because it starts when we are little. We get awards (unless you are like me; I never got any awards) for everything we accomplish, and our grades tell us if we are good enough (or tell us how not good enough we are. Mine). We are disciplined by our parents when we do something wrong (All. The. Time. Just being real) and rewarded when we do something right. We then develop a belief system that says everything must be earned and subconsciously believe God works in the same manner. We see God through our human understanding rather than through His Son's love, which doesn't require any achievement. Honestly, I believe a gauge to measure ourselves makes us more comfortable, so I do understand how easy it is to get caught up in this way of thinking.

However, the Bible clearly shows us to love unconditionally, forgive freely, and not judge one another by a worldly standard. Pride based on our successes blocks the flow of love.

I mean, let's be real, how can we love from a pure heart if we secretly think we are better than someone else based on our human achievements and/or knowledge?

Truth bomb: we can't!

The Bible clearly tells us to think of others above ourselves. This opens our heart to receive God's overwhelming love, and then naturally give out an abundance of His love because we are not caught up in thinking all about ourselves, our needs, our feelings, demanding our own way—living the complete opposite of Christ.

> *Be devoted to one another in love. Honor one another above yourselves.*
> *— Romans 12:3-10 (NIV)*

We will discuss our values and identities in greater depth in the next chapter. I just wanted to bring this to the table and tie it in with the love factor in hopes you can make a connection with a potential area of struggle.

Are you following me?

If you think about it, this sounds a lot like the self-righteous Pharisees we read about in the Bible, doesn't it?

This pharisaical mindset is robbing us of living in the unconditional love of the Father's heart.

What I mean by pharisaical is a religious mindset that has a checklist of dos and don'ts that many are living from, and we call it "righteous living." But is a self-made checklist the righteousness of Christ?

If we are the ones "getting there" through our own efforts, that is not the righteousness of Christ, that is self-righteousness.

See?

Back to self.

If we are evaluating ourselves through our human efforts, we can very easily lead ourselves into deception. We feel false comfort when we justify our flesh, convincing ourselves we're "good" based on accomplishing an external checklist of outward works, forgetting to check in with our hearts.

Many of us genuinely seek to honor God with everything in us, but without realizing it, we have reduced our Christianity to living from a pretty standard Christian checklist. The Holy Spirit started to show me how the well-meaning list has slowly taken His place, leaving His love and power out of the equation, and it's keeping us crippled, blocking us from true transformation.

This pattern is understandable because our world conditions us to feel like we need the step plan listed out. In order to be good or successful at anything in our culture, there is a "5 Ways to . . ." article for just about everything. But many are left feeling heavy and inadequate with a deep desire to feel worthy, accepted and loved.

Here's an example checklist many of us follow:

- Go to church
- Take a test that determines strengths and weaknesses to understand how I fit in the body of Christ
- Find a ministry to serve in
- Bring my kids to Sunday School
- Tithe my ten percent
- Sign up for a meal train
- Read my Bible Daily
- Go to a Bible Study
- Have the right scriptural answer
- Have scripture memorized and even be able to tell others the historical context of what was going on. Extra bonus if you know the Greek words and their meanings!

Many of us GENUINELY SEEK TO HONOR GOD WITH EVERYTHING IN US, BUT WITHOUT REALIZING IT, WE HAVE REDUCED OUR CHRISTIANITY TO LIVING FROM A PRETTY STANDARD CHRISTIAN CHECKLIST.

Does this sound familiar?

Check, check, check, right?!

Let me clarify real quick . . . there is nothing wrong with anything on this list. We should absolutely be plugging our children and ourselves in with a community, tithing, etc. Realize though, much of this list is doable in our own strength, apart from God, not truly connected to the Vine.

And that's the problem.

This disconnect has created a false idea of what being a Christian looks and feels like.

Are you *doing* all the Christian things, but still find that you are internally unchanged?

Maybe you haven't even connected with your disconnectedness to God and this concept is a lightbulb moment to you.

Maybe this idea is coming in sharp because it's hitting a cord that you weren't expecting . . . don't worry if you are feeling this poke in you that might be revealing what's been festering in your heart. You are so dearly and deeply loved by God, and He is not mad at you. He knows "self-awareness" and checklist Christianity has slipped into the body of Christ in such a subtle way, and His heart is hurting for His children to know of His authentic and rhythmic love. Let's disarm any defenses and just get real. Allow the Holy Spirit to speak to you personally as you continue to read.

Okay?

Let's undo some beliefs that are blocking you from living from a direct overflow of God's overwhelming love. This is a one-foot-in-front-of-the-other journey that we all get to walk out with Jesus as He takes each of us in His hands.

Let's keep going here—we're gonna connect it all and experience the "more" our hearts genuinely desire.

In 2 Corinthians Paul shows us what it looks like when we are filled with God's love. Let's take a look:

> *For Christ's love compels us, because we are convinced that One died for all, and therefore all died. And He died for all, that those who live should no longer live for themselves but for Him who died for them and was raised again. So from now on, we regard no one from a worldly point of view. Though we once regarded*

Christ in this way, we do so no longer. Therefore, if anyone is in Christ, the new creation has come: The old has gone, the new is here!
— *2 Corinthians 5:14-17 (NIV)*

It's the love of Christ that compels us to no longer view anyone (including ourselves) through a worldly lens. His unconditional love is the new driving force that we live by, seeing ourselves and others through the heart of our Heavenly Father. Our old self-centered ways have died. This place of living through His unconditional love cannot be accomplished in our own strength, it's not in our human wiring. It's supernatural.

When the Holy Spirit unlocks God's unconditional love in our hearts and minds, we are moved to reconciliation in the church, cultivating unity in the body of Christ. Living in this continual flow, we can see ourselves and others through His unconditional and sacrificial love. God's love helps us see and think differently toward ourselves, and it becomes the push toward a positive ripple effect to how we see others. This includes those who we believe to be our "enemies." Rather than making enemies with those who think and believe differently than us, we see them through the heart of Jesus and are reminded that His painful death on the cross was for them too. If we are truly walking in the Father's love, then what comes out of us towards others will look like Him. The love of God should have a powerful and influential effect on our lives that transforms us on the inside and then ripples out, impacting the world around us.

If we continue to judge ourselves and others through a worldly, self-awareness lens, then the outcome is what we see today: A quick-to-judge and lack-of-love attitude that leads to heartbreaking division in the body of Christ. There is a lot of "stone-throwing" and "spec- removing" going on both loudly and secretly and it needs to stop.

"Do not judge, or you too will be judged. For in the same way you judge others, you will be judged, and with the measure you use, it will be measured to you. Why do you look at the speck of sawdust in your brother's eye and pay no attention to the plank in your own eye? How can you say to your brother, 'Let me take the speck out of your eye,' when all the time there is a plank in your own eye? You hypocrite, first take the plank out of your own eye, and then you will see clearly to remove the speck from your brother's eye."
— *Matthew 7:1-5 (NIV)*

When we decide to withhold love based on a worldly or humanistic perspective, we make ourselves enemies to the very ones we are called to bring the good news to. We cannot truly help anyone get free, pointing them to the love of Jesus, if our lens is blocked from loving and seeing others through the Father's heart. This is a religious plank that needs to be removed from our own eyes first.

> *The Love of God* SHOULD HAVE A POWERFUL AND INFLUENTIAL EFFECT ON OUR LIVES THAT TRANSFORMS US ON THE INSIDE AND THEN RIPPLES OUT, IMPACTING THE WORLD AROUND US.

Think about it . . . we can't change anyone. We need to stop getting hung up on what we see in others' lives and allow the Holy Spirit to transform us through love. From there, a well of God's life-changing love, straight from the throne room of Heaven, will spill over from our lives into the lives of others. That love that changed us carries the power to change them too.

Too many are justifying in their own hearts "why" they are judging, withholding love, and making enemies with people, creating a wrong ripple effect that is in complete opposition to God's Kingdom. We have moved away from the basic principles of Christianity, justified our flesh on so many levels, and we desperately need to recognize this. Whether it be in a casual conversation or through a coaching session, I hear more often than not an excuse as to why someone won't forgive, and would rather judge, argue, and refuse to love. I call this the "yeah but" syndrome. The Bible clearly shows us to love unconditionally, forgive freely, and not judge one another by a worldly standard.

There are no exceptions or "yeah buts" in the Bible.

If we have a tangled belief system that says we are followers of Jesus based on our religious checklist, but have a bad habit of criticizing others, we've become judges of the very ones we are called to love. This subconscious disconnect causes us to become selective in what we hold ourselves accountable to in accordance with God's Word. We end up spending more time giving ourselves excuses and permission to remain judgemental instead of truly following Jesus, and walking in the supernatural flow of His unconditional love.

We are justifying the flesh instead of crucifying it.

When we crucify the flesh, we are choosing to disagree with the humanistic reaction toward a situation or a person and, instead, we yield to the Holy Spirit, invite Him into the situation and ask Him to help us love like Jesus.

Too many are living by their flesh, not asking for God's help, mindlessly going down their Christian checklist, believing they are on track.

Bottom line—we are not denying ourselves so that we can truly follow Jesus.

> *Then Jesus said to His disciples, "Whoever wants to be my disciple must deny themselves and take up their cross and follow me. For whoever wants to save their life will lose it, but whoever loses their life for me will find it." — Matthew 16:24-25 (NLT)*

This is affecting the body of Christ as a whole. Rather than allowing the Holy Spirit to fill us with the supernatural ability to love unconditionally, we lessen God's standards for ourselves and cut people out, deciding we don't have to love them. When we lessen God's standards for ourselves, we are also lessening the power of His Spirit within us because we are not relying on His strength to help us in our weak areas.

Do you see how all of these cycles have created a negative ripple effect that has been causing us, the Church, to be ineffective?

Imagine the heartbreak of our loving God who so desires for us to see ourselves and then others through His loving heart.

Love has been cut from the Source, and what we have replaced God's unconditional love with is a conditional one that has created division instead of unity causing many to fake Christianity.

Yeah . . . I said it!

We are *doing* church, not *becoming* the Church in Her purest form.

Can we be brave enough to handle this kind of talk?

We are JUSTIFYING THE FLESH INSTEAD OF CRUCIFYING IT.

> **When we lessen God's standards for ourselves, we are also lessening the power of His Spirit within us because we are not relying on His strength to help us in our weak areas.**

I don't believe this is intentional or even a conscious, calculated reality. But it's happening, and we need to realize the blocks and barriers in our own lives so that we can receive a greater depth of God's love, and freely give it to those around us.

Yielding to His Spirit versus faking Christianity has a powerful exchange. When we find that our flesh disagrees with what God says (hint: the flesh is our human nature and will always conflict with the Spirit), we have an opportunity to go to the throne room of grace and get God's help.

Meaning, we go directly to Him through the power of prayer and invite His presence to reign in the situation. We have access to His throne room where His presence is real, powerful, and full of the grace we need to change.

> *For we do not have a high priest who is unable to empathize with our weaknesses, but we have One who has been tempted in every way, just as we are—yet He did not sin. Let us then approach God's throne of grace with confidence, so that we may receive mercy and find grace to help us in our time of need.* — Hebrews 4:15-16 (NIV)

This scripture is not symbolic; this is real. From there His love meets us, heals us, and we can then remove the "plank in our eyes" that caused us to see those around us through a conditional love. All of a sudden, we are filled with a love so powerful, we can clearly see through the Father's heart, not through humanistic views and feelings that toss us around like the waves of an angry ocean.

Going confidently to God, asking for His help, and allowing Him to fill us with His supernatural and unconditional love creates the natural ripple effect that God intended us to live out.

So many are struggling to receive or understand the love of God. Some have a subconscious belief system that He is still holding a high expectation over them. Others see Him as distant or angry all the time. We have to read God's Word and invite the Holy Spirit to undo all false belief systems that are keeping us from receiving the fullness of God's heart.

Then, there are those who will receive love from Jesus, but not from God, the Father. If that's you and you desire to know of the Father's love, study the life of Jesus. He is God made flesh. Nothing He did was outside of what God had Him do. So, when you see the Son, you see the Father.

> *He is the divine portrait, the true likeness of the invisible God, and the first-born heir of all creation.*
> — *Colossians 1:15 (TPT)*

> *Jesus gave them this answer: "Very truly I tell you, the Son can do nothing by Himself; He can do only what He sees His Father doing, because whatever the Father does the Son also does."*
> — *John 5:19 (NIV)*

> *"If you really know Me, you will know my Father as well. From now on, you do know Him and have seen Him." — John 14:7 (NIV)*

We are DOING CHURCH, NOT BECOMING THE CHURCH IN HER PUREST FORM.

Our view is everything!

When we identify our wrong belief system, we discover which areas need God's help so we can know Him and His heart in greater measures. Jesus bridged the gap between us and God so that we could fully know His love.

When we get a revelation of the overwhelming love from God, it cannot be contained or remain hidden in our human shells.

It's too big!

When His love fills us, it becomes a powerful force that has to come out of us, impacting the world around us, pushing out darkness as the light of His love takes over.

Think about it, when people were touched by Jesus, they RAN back to tell others what He did for them. It was a natural response to a supernatural experience. Even when Jesus said, "don't tell anyone," they did anyway.

Why?

Because when Jesus' love touches our lives, we can't stay silent! We become true disciples, learning to walk connected to the Vine and what it means to live by His Spirit.

Unfortunately, with very good intentions, discipleship has been reduced to that how-to checklist that we try to accomplish in our own strength. Our God encounters either seem to fade to the back of our memory or become just an occasional experience rather than a constant flow straight from the Source.

Throwing off our old nature seems like a painful and overwhelming process that needs constant ministry and prayer when we constantly look at all we've done (or where we've fallen short), rather than remembering what Jesus already did on the Cross. We keep trying to throw off the "old self" in our own strength instead of simply yielding to His Spirit, walking in His Truth and grace, continually filled with His love and power.

Please don't misunderstand the perspective I am coming from. Prayer is vital and ministries can be helpful, but oftentimes we are desperately asking for prayer and ministry for the flesh that we need to crucify so we can walk in the Spirit, saturated in God's overwhelming love. This love frees us from the chains of our flesh so we can access life in the Spirit. Where the Spirit of the Lord is, there is freedom.

> *But whenever someone turns to the Lord, the veil is taken away. For the Lord is the Spirit, and wherever the Spirit of the Lord is, there is freedom. So all of us who have had that veil removed can see and reflect the glory of the Lord. And the Lord—who is the Spirit—makes us more and more like Him as we are changed into His glorious image.* — 2 Corinthians 3:16-18 (NLT)

This scripture is not something to read and brush off as a nice idea. This spiritual freedom is supernatural, and it empowers us to live in hard situations without being in bondage to the circumstances or our human nature so we can actually go from glory to glory.

We either believe God at His Word or we don't.

Our responses in hard situations will reveal what we believe and become an opportunity to get our hearts lined up with His. We are supposed to be living in this rhythm, where we are literally (not figuratively) reflecting the glory of God.

It's time to live confidently from God's amazing love and freely run to Him. Let's stop hiding the parts of ourselves that need changing in fear that God will reject us and live accepted. Let's get honest with ourselves and with God.

Prayer is vital AND MINISTRIES CAN BE HELPFUL, BUT OFTENTIMES WE ARE DESPERATELY ASKING FOR PRAYER AND MINISTRY FOR THE FLESH THAT WE NEED TO CRUCIFY SO WE CAN WALK IN THE SPIRIT, SATURATED IN GOD'S OVERWHELMING LOVE.

Jesus came to walk this earth, fully man, releasing the Kingdom of Heaven and then sacrificing Himself so He could take back the authority Adam handed over to the devil and give it back to us. Jesus came to restore what Adam gave up because God loves us that much!

Because of love, Jesus came to fulfill the law so that we are no longer bound to an unrealistic checklist that NO ONE could live up to WITHOUT His power. God put His Spirit in us, empowering us for a life like Jesus lived.

Freed from our sinful nature.

Filled with His grace and power.

We are born again, the righteousness of Christ, all because of love.

Christianity was never supposed to be a religious checklist. It's an invitation to a life-changing relationship with the Creator of all things who loves us passionately. When we ditch the checklists and learn to live in God's amazing love, our attention is off of what we've done wrong, (which leads to shame and condemnation), or right (which leads us to pride and self-righteousness), and our full attention is on everything He's done to make all things right all for the sake of love!

From there, it's a natural desire to get into His Word daily as we sit

Let's stop hiding THE PARTS OF OURSELVES THAT NEED CHANGING IN FEAR THAT GOD WILL REJECT US AND LIVE ACCEPTED.

at the feet of Jesus. We aren't doing it to prove anything to anyone or even ourselves. It's coming from a deep longing to live as Christ, connected to the Vine at all times.

It's not a duty.

It's a deep burning desire that cannot be quenched otherwise.

This opens us up to receive a love that cannot be measured by our human understanding because it is so vast no one can fully understand it. Self-awareness becomes unimportant because we are now focused on all that God gave up for us. It breaks the need to measure ourselves against one another, which in turn empowers us to freely love others unconditionally, the way Jesus did. A selfless, overflowing, unconditional love that we can't hold back!

There is an urgent call for the Church to know the depth of His love.

A love encounter is what we, the body of Christ, so desperately need.

When we turn to Him wholeheartedly, His love fills us, becoming a constant well that naturally flows out of us. Our new lives in Christ becomes a direct effect of what we have through our Heavenly Father as His immeasurable love changes us from the inside out.

A supernatural force of love, straight from the throne room of Heaven, that has completely changed our view of ourselves, our old way of seeing and living has died. We unashamedly run into His arms as He saturates us with more of Him.

When His love is in us, we are truly free.

When we are free, we have an uncontainable desire to go out and love so fearlessly it's effortless and natural.

Unconditional love is now freely running through us; forgiving others, loving our enemies, and praying for them is no longer a jolt to our system, a painful duty, or avoided completely. There's an ache that has birthed in our hearts that longs to see captives and slaves fully free. All of a sudden, we can hear the whispers of our Father's heart toward others, and from there we are pouring out from a well of love without end.

No checklist is telling us to do this.

No religious spirit is weighing in telling us to act like a bunch of robots trying to love better …

We are love!

> *Christianity* WAS NEVER SUPPOSED TO BE A RELIGIOUS CHECKLIST. IT'S AN INVITATION TO A LIFE-CHANGING RELATIONSHIP WITH THE CREATOR OF ALL THINGS WHO LOVES US PASSIONATELY.

And what comes out of us oozes from that overflow, our cups are continually running over, we can't help but drench the world around us.

This is the ripple effect of the Father's heart.

> *I pray that from his glorious, unlimited resources He will empower you with inner strength through His Spirit. Then Christ will make His home in your hearts as you trust in Him. Your roots will grow down into God's love and keep you strong. And may you have the power to understand, as all God's people should, how wide, how long, how high, and how deep His love is. May you experience the love of Christ, though it is too great to understand fully. Then you will be made complete with all the fullness of life and power that comes from God. Now all glory to God, who is able, through his mighty power at work within us, to accomplish infinitely more than we might ask or think. Glory to him in the church and in Christ Jesus through all generations forever and ever! Amen. — Ephesians 3:16-21 (NLT)*

Chapter Two
Radiating His Glory

In chapter one we dove into a greater depth of God's unconditional love and identified some barriers that have blocked us from living loved. In this chapter, we're gonna go deeper and connect how the Christian checklist and cultural idea of self-awareness have negatively affected our value system, blocking us from the Spirit-empowered refining process. Broken trust, fear, self-awareness, and the checklist have caused too many of us to "work" to feel worthy and of value by "doing" instead of remaining connected to Jesus, and allowing the Holy Spirit to help us become that refined, purified image of God.

Some of the methods and structures that have been put in place to "help us" have actually hurt us and are blocking us from living as new creations in Christ. These well-meaning concepts have pushed us to rely on ourselves, instead of Jesus, and the power of the Holy Spirit that's within us.

Remember to keep your Bible and journal by your side. Write down your 'aha' moments as well as your questions, even the arguments that arise as you're reading. I promise you, some of the things I have written about in this chapter will stretch and challenge you in ways you were not expecting. Be open to what the Holy Spirit might want to relay to you personally, and trust Him.

Jesus left His Heavenly throne, walked the earth fully man, and died a painful death on the Cross for you and me because we are of high value to Him.

That's it.

Our value is already marked by our Maker. Our value cannot be earned, increased, or decreased; we are a highly valued treasure designed by God.

We are much like a diamond when first discovered, dirty and uncut with minimal shine. But like a diamond, our worth is already secured. Once the diamond is discovered, it goes through a rigorous process. That process starts by evaluating the diamond to decide which cut will keep the maximum value intact. From there, the dirt and debris are removed and the stone gets polished until it beams. The diamond purifying process does not create value just because the stone looks better. The process to make it shine brought forth what was already there. This is the way God sees us, fully valued, ready for a process, empowered through His Spirit so that we can shine, bringing forth what He's already put in us. This understanding creates a positive ripple effect in us as God works through us until we are radiating His glory.

As long as we are living on this side of Heaven, there will be more work for God to do in each of us. He is faithful to complete the good work that He began at the time of our surrender to Jesus. That's all it takes. Understanding our value is not in what we do, but in who God says we are to Him, and then a surrendered heart that desires to obey God over the cravings of the flesh, with a willingness to get our "old self" out of the way.

When our old self is out of the way, we become empowered to live by the Spirit.

If our old self is still our lead, and not the Spirit, then the feelings of our flesh dictate our responses to life, and we block ourselves from experiencing everything Jesus paid for us to have here and now: A life empowered through His Spirit!

> *Our value* CANNOT BE EARNED, INCREASED, OR DECREASED; WE ARE A HIGHLY VALUED TREASURE DESIGNED BY GOD.

My personal journey has been hard and painful, but one of high value and worth; I would choose this path all over again.

Well, for the most part.

There are definitely moments where I would go back and make

better decisions, but then again, I learned from my bad decisions and they have sharpened my discernment. This process of "dying to my old self" to be more like Him has catapulted me into a confidence and freedom that is mind-blowing!

> *We know that our old sinful selves were crucified with Christ so that sin might lose its power in our lives. We are no longer slaves to sin. For when we died with Christ we were set free from the power of sin.* — Romans 6:6-7 (NLT)

I have literally, not figuratively, been on such a crazy stripping-of-self journey, and as I continually press into God, He shows me that everything I experience and go through is an opportunity to root myself deeper in what He thinks and says. Even while being torn down by others or by life.

And let me just tell you—there's been a lot of tearing, trust me. Your girl ain't got the perfect set up . . . I just got the perfect peace from my Heavenly Father moving through me no matter what.

I took God's Word to heart and learned to crucify my flesh. I realized that in order to access the supernatural and live by the Spirit, I had to stop feeding into my thoughts and ideas that were keeping me locked into my old nature, and starve them!

When we begin to starve our own feelings, and what we believe about ourselves, feeding our souls by meditating on the Word of God and what He says about us, a powerful transformation takes place. God's Word carries the power to transform us, and we become firmly rooted in who God says we are, no longer wavering in our beliefs about ourselves. Our confident trust becomes firmly planted in God's Truth and from there we grow in spiritual maturity, becoming more like Him.

The body of Christ should be allowing God's transforming power to bring us from glory to glory as we walk securely in who we are to Him. When we know our true value, we embrace the refining process that God wants to take us on, and the sting of crucifying the flesh doesn't break us. We are secure and recognize that to get to a place of purity and spiritual maturity, we agree with Him that we have to remove some debris in our lives and belief systems that are in contradiction to His.

The self-awareness movement is keeping us in tension between our old self and our new nature in Christ. We are not supposed to be improving our human nature and flesh (unless we are talking about our physical health, but that's for a whole other book topic, wink-wink), which is exactly what the self-care, self-examination, self-awareness movement focuses on.

We are new creations in Christ Jesus, called to live by the Spirit.

We are born again.

Our new life has begun!

> *This means that anyone who belongs to Christ has become a new person. The old life is gone; a new life has begun!* — 2 Corinthians 5:17 (NLT)

I realized THAT IN ORDER TO ACCESS THE SUPERNATURAL AND LIVE BY THE SPIRIT, I HAD TO STOP FEEDING INTO MY THOUGHTS AND IDEAS THAT WERE KEEPING ME LOCKED INTO MY OLD NATURE, AND STARVE THEM!

Many of us are trying to get to a place of confidence, unsure how to walk out who we are by design as new creations in Christ, rooted in our already established worth. Our culture tells us that we need to develop "self" confidence.

Let me explain how this idea has created confusion—our human tendency is to compartmentalize our faith in one box, our duty as a believer in another, and then way over in another box is this idea that we must develop self-confidence. Culture's way of cultivating self-confidence is through our own evaluations, our hard work, our successes, and our personal self-talk. We engage with those components, allowing our work and our accomplishments to define us, placing our value system through our human understanding. If we are honest with what we think about ourselves, we find our self-esteem is determined by how good of a day we had, what we've accomplished, our successes, and/or by what other people think of us. This idea is putting us in conflict with a constant internal feeling of "not enough," leading us to try and perform even better (or give up altogether). Our self-confidence is limited to how much we feel we've accomplished based on our personal evaluations, leaning on our own understanding.

This cycle reveals that our confidence has been formed through human perception, not grasping that God's value system doesn't work that way.

> *Trust in the Lord with all your heart; do not depend on your own understanding. — Proverbs 3:5 (NLT)*

We are directed through the Word of God not to lean on our human understanding, for very good reason, and to trust God with all of our hearts.

Our thoughts, feelings, and evaluations of ourselves cannot be trusted. They waver and fluctuate too often and are not built around a Kingdom perspective. Rather than taking God's Word seriously and going straight to the Bible to understand how valuable we are to Him, we've mixed the two, adopting a worldview in with God's view, which has created continual insecurity through the body of Christ.

Our worth is found through our Maker and what He says about us. Mixing a worldview (humanistic perspective) with God's view has led us to a constant inner struggle in our personal walks with Jesus.

Can you relate?

Let me put this into simple terms . . . if you identify yourself as a Christian, then your identity and value are found in Christ.

That's it.

The word Christian means "to be like Christ."

When you come into a relationship with Jesus, you are to strip yourself of all your old ways and allow the Holy Spirit to mold and shape you to become more like Him. He is the Potter, and we are the clay. If we haven't fully surrendered every part of ourselves to God, we will continue to be molded and shaped by something, whether it be our upbringing, our situations, others' opinions, our experiences in life, our feelings, even our successes or failures. If it's not God, then it will be something else that will shape us into who we are today.

Many of us have been shaped by life, not by God.

We've formed our value through an ungodly perspective.

Rather than taking God's Word seriously and going straight to the Bible to understand how valuable we are to Him, we've mixed the two, adopting a worldview in with God's view, which has created continual insecurity through the body of Christ.

I know that sounds harsh, but seriously, anything outside of God's value system is ungodly. Let's start calling things what they are so we can put each idea and thought into its proper place. When we confront things in full honesty, without sugarcoating or minimizing, we naturally have a stronger desire to acknowledge and uproot anything that opposes what God says to be true.

His Truth is the only Truth that truly sets us free.

If we are paying attention to our thought-life, again, this is where self-reflection is vital, we usually have an excuse to undermine what God says about us because of how we feel about ourselves.

Check in with your thought-life regularly, and invite the Holy Spirit to reveal to you what you really think and believe.

- What do you tell yourself throughout the day?
- What thoughts do you have about yourself (loudly or secretly)?
- Do you find you have more critical than loving thoughts toward yourself?
- How about when you look around at others, are you checking to see where you measure up against them to decide your value and worth?

Our thoughts determine our true belief system. When we are looking at ourselves through our own belief system, what we find is a flawed individual with strengths and weaknesses. Self-awareness causes us to want to fix our flaws in our own strength, or cover up what we don't like, projecting an image of what we feel will make us look good to others, putting our "best self" forward.

Not always, but often.

Some just feel completely unworthy and wear "garments" that match how they feel. Bottom line, self-awareness causes our focus to be on what we think and believe about ourselves (which wavers), not who God says we are (His unwavering Truth).

Then, when we read what the Bible says about us, we feel a push and pull in our thought-life because our thoughts, feelings, and emotions have been given too much power, making it humanly impossible to see ourselves the way God sees us. We have become too self-focused, not looking to God to see ourselves through His heart, struggling to believe Him at His Word.

When we are struggling to recognize these Truths, or the inability to receive what God says, we resort to self-talk which is not always beneficial. Self-talk usually puts the emphasis on our human understanding. And for many, self-talk is spent beating ourselves down in our head (or trying to build ourselves up) instead of allowing the Word of God to build us up according to what He says. This creates a constant frustration in our minds and hearts because we do not feel the way God does about us. Trying to change our own mind is not only mentally draining, but as soon as we fall short in any given area, we go back to our default belief system (human understanding) and feel this pressure to measure up in order to feel good enough. This can easily lead us to depression and discouragement.

I want to introduce a powerful difference between self-talk and God-talk.

Self-talk can change based on our circumstances and the feelings that arise. God-talk is through the power of the Holy Spirit, built on His unwavering Word that will not change, even when circumstances, thoughts, feelings, and emotions do. This is why we must build from God's unchanging Truth, not our own

When we confront things in full honesty, without sugarcoating or minimizing, we naturally have a stronger desire to acknowledge and uproot anything that opposes what God says to be true.

version of the truth.

God-talk makes the decision that what He says about us is the only thing that carries value, placing the emphasis on His thoughts about us; our attention is on Him and off of ourselves. God's Word must carry a higher value to us over all humanistic thoughts, feelings, and emotions. From there, we get to invite the power of the Holy Spirit to come and help us rewire our thinking until it lines up with His value system. In order to do this, we have got to get "self" out of the way, so we can clearly see who we are through our Maker's eyes. This is where being rooted in God's love becomes vital. We need to know the love of God that helps us recognize the high price that was paid for us, and that we are seen through the blood of Jesus.

His righteousness.

We are the righteousness of Christ.

We cannot earn our way to this place of confidence.

It's already been secured through Him.

I have a very practical and simple rule for myself. I call thoughts and words that create a dialogue in my mind that conflicts with God's heart and Truth "toilet talk." If it doesn't line up with Him, it gets flushed.

My belief system is shaped through God's Word, not through my feelings. From there, my perspective lines up with the Kingdom of Heaven. I've had to train myself to willingly and consciously choose to remove those ideas and thoughts from my mind and mouth!

Period.

We have the choice in what we tell ourselves. Too many are giving themselves permission to fixate on wrong thoughts.

I want to dive into some more ideas and undo some belief systems so we can get our value intact according to God's value system.

Are you ready?

Let's keep going . . .

The self-awareness movement causes us to see ourselves through what *culture* determines is good enough. We have been measuring ourselves by the world's standards and ideologies, not through the Kingdom and many of us aren't even aware of this reality. This has been such a struggle in the body of Christ for so many generations which is why, with good intentions, we have adopted resources outside of the power of the Holy Spirit and brought them into the church.

> God-talk makes THE DECISION THAT WHAT HE SAYS ABOUT US IS THE ONLY THING THAT CARRIES VALUE, PLACING THE EMPHASIS ON HIS THOUGHTS ABOUT US; OUR ATTENTION IS ON HIM AND OFF OF OURSELVES.

For example, the personality tests the church has embraced, including a trend being preached from pulpits to "help" us better understand ourselves and others, are causing many to live by a test-result number versus seeing ourselves the way God sees us and seeing others through His heart.

Now, before you build your defense and cut me off, please hear what my heart is trying to relay. By the end of this chapter, I truly believe you will understand what I'm bringing to the table for us to digest.

Rather than defending the resources that we have adopted into our spiritual journeys, we should be tackling a bigger truth head-on: we are struggling to see ourselves through the righteousness of Christ because we are too hung up on what we see, believe, and feel through our human understanding. We are desperately searching for the confidence the Bible describes that we are welcoming anything to help us.

Please understand, I am not writing these things to condemn or shame anyone who has placed high value in the self-awareness, self-evaluation, or identity-tests tools and tips. I'm just bringing awareness to my Kingdom family that if we dig deep (self-reflect), we will most likely find our inner confidence still wavering, and we've subconsciously built limits for ourselves around the tests framework.

Have these tools brought true breakthroughs that lead to lasting transformation?

Are you seeing yourself through what God says about you to the point that negative situations (or people) no longer cause you to feel insecure?

Did taking the test help you live as a new Creation in Christ, unlocking life in the Spirit?

More often than not, you are still struggling, trying to remain focused on the strengths the test helped you discover, convincing yourself you're good, but you don't feel good inside, and you're not living confidently free.

Embracing these tests in the church is actually counterproductive and complicates the work of the cross, blocking us from the simplicity of going to God and allowing Him to show us who we are to Him, living from His perspective, not our own. These tests focus on how we see ourselves, instead of learning to see ourselves through God's eyes. We are building our confidence around the results of a test instead of remaining confidently rooted in God's Truth.

Rather than **DEFENDING THE RESOURCES THAT WE HAVE ADOPTED INTO OUR SPIRITUAL JOURNEYS, WE SHOULD BE TACKLING A BIGGER TRUTH HEAD-ON: WE ARE STRUGGLING TO SEE OURSELVES THROUGH THE RIGHTEOUSNESS OF CHRIST BECAUSE WE ARE TOO HUNG UP ON WHAT WE SEE, BELIEVE, AND FEEL THROUGH OUR HUMAN UNDERSTANDING.**

Honestly, I believe they're keeping us limited to our flesh, teaching us to rely on our "natural" human strengths, instead of tapping into *His strength* within us that is beyond our human capacity.

We are trying so hard to get this "Christian thing" right, desperately trying to live out what the Bible says about us. When *we* can't "get there," we welcome tools outside of what God has already given us through the power of the Holy Spirit and His Word.

His divine power has given us everything we need for a godly life

> *through our knowledge of Him who called us by His own glory and goodness.* — 2 Peter 1:3 (NIV)

Boom!

Mic drop ... it's right there!

We have already been given everything we need so why are we clinging to tools and resources outside of His power?

These tests, without realizing it, actually makes us want to hide our flaws or in our own strength "fix" them, or worse, give ourselves permission to remain with those weak areas, making excuses for ourselves instead of allowing the Holy Spirit to do His work in us and through us until we look like Him.

Example conversation that I've had with many of my brothers and sisters: Well, I'm a (fill in the blank number) that's why I respond that way. I know I should work on that but....(enter in the excuse).

What's wrong with that?

Well, the test pointed out the weak area, and the pressure is on the person to "fix" it, try harder ... do better, but when a hard situation blindsides them, the natural human responses come out, and they respond out of the weak area. Not the power of the Holy Spirit. Then, they use the test result as their "why" they can't grow in their area of weakness.

We are not supposed to limit ourselves through a test to find our strengths and abilities. We are supposed to lean into God, trust Him with our weak areas, invite Him to show up in all areas of our lives, allowing the Holy Spirit to make us more like Jesus.

Becoming like Jesus is our goal.

This is scriptural.

The goal is to radiate Jesus in every area of our lives.

Looking like Him is what we should be pursuing.

The tests will tell us our strengths and weaknesses of our flesh! We are no longer bound by the flesh; we are born again by the Spirit and we are taught through the Word of God to get our thinking lined up with

His.

> *You were taught, with regard to your former way of life, to put off your old self, which is being corrupted by its deceitful desires; to be made new in the attitude of your minds; and to put on the new self, created to be like God in true righteousness and holiness.*
> — Ephesians 4:22-24 (NIV)

The test results and the self-awareness movement are not only creating a belief system that makes us feel unworthy and not valuable, but it's also keeping us locked into our old nature. We are left trying to make our old nature godly instead of "putting it off" so we can "put on the new self, created to be like God . . ." If we continue basing our worth on our human understanding, we will keep ourselves limited from becoming like Christ.

We are new creations in Christ.

The old is gone and the new is here!

This is our invitation as we enter into a life in rhythm with our Father's heart. We need to walk in this simple, but powerful, Truth and allow the Holy Spirit to shape us into the image-bearers that God designed us to be.

As believers, we do not need more tools. What we need is to actually trust God, and allow the Holy Spirit and His Word to penetrate our minds and hearts. We have to stop arguing with God's Truth and smash the parameters of our self-made belief system until our thoughts are lined up with what He says.

We are no LONGER BOUND BY THE FLESH; WE ARE BORN AGAIN BY THE SPIRIT AND WE ARE TAUGHT THROUGH THE WORD OF GOD TO GET OUR THINKING LINED UP WITH HIS.

I've heard some say that taking a personality test has helped them love someone they were struggling to love.

The truth: When we are filled with God's unconditional love, we don't need an identity quiz to help us love better. If we are struggling to love, it reveals where our value system is not lined up with God's and proves that we are not functioning by the Spirit through His unconditional love, we are still stuck in a love that is conditional.

Think about it, the Spirit doesn't need to understand everyone's strengths and weaknesses in order to love. The flesh does.

When our value system is intact, knowing who we are and what we have through Jesus, we begin to see others through His heart as He shows us who they are to Him. We become empowered through the Holy Spirit and our response toward others is from a place of wholeness and confidence. From there, we can see the broken and lost through grace and compassion. When we see the mess in others lives, rather than seeing them through a critical lens that measures through judgment, our hearts will desire to see them healed and free.

> We have to STOP ARGUING WITH GOD'S TRUTH AND SMASH THE PARAMETERS OF OUR SELF-MADE BELIEF SYSTEM UNTIL OUR THOUGHTS ARE LINED UP WITH WHAT HE SAYS.

God's value system calls us higher; we need to respond to His call and acknowledge that we need His help and the power of the Holy Spirit to live this way. This is why we must crucify the flesh and make sure we aren't coddling it, petting it, and making sure it's comfortable.

Sounds kinda ridiculous and gross, right?

If we are still living by the flesh, then our love remains conditional. We don't need to beat ourselves up for those feelings or shove them away either. We need to acknowledge the feelings and negative thoughts and confess them to the Lord. From there, we can ask Him to give us His eyes and heart to see that person the way He does.

Remember what I shared with you in chapter one when I'm struggling to love?

Go back and read that section for a refresher if you need to. God is love, and when His unconditional love is filling us, we see people through His eyes, despite their personality (flaws, strengths, and human nature) which empowers us to see their value and worth through His heart and love them the way He loves us.

We love because He first loved us. — *1 John 4:19 (NIV)*

Let's stop complicating the work of the Cross.

We shouldn't have to work hard to see how valuable someone is to the Kingdom of God in order to love or try to find something good about them so it's easier to. We need to connect with God's value system that is beyond our humanistic way of thinking, and it all starts with knowing how much we are all loved by God, and from there, our value system is built around His. When we experience His unconditional love, we can see our value through our Heavenly Father, and from there we can see others through His eyes. We can see how He has woven unique strengths into each of our designs, and that we all have a valuable role in the body of Christ. Learning to walk in God's unconditional love, placing His value system over ourselves and others is part of the refining process that makes us more like Him.

When we are living by the Spirit, He reveals to us who we are to Him and what He made us for as our identities in Christ take form, naturally and effortlessly. When we walk with Him, remaining connected to the Vine, we produce lasting fruit.

> *"I am the sprouting Vine and you're my branches. As you live in union with Me as your source, fruitfulness will stream from within you—but when you live separated from Me you are powerless."* — *John 15:5 (TPT)*

The real power to becoming more like Christ is not in a man-made personality quiz.

It's not by outsourcing, trying to find "new" or uncovered man-made tools to become Christlike, or through this idea that we need to talk ourselves into feeling confident. We already have all the tools we need through the presence and power of the Holy Spirit: We need to learn to access them!

When we find ourselves in situations where we are rejected, and it causes us to feel angry or insecure, these moments reveal to us that our confidence and value as a child of God is not intact. It's in our wiring, a deep longing in all of us to be accepted. What we are missing and struggling to believe, and remain in, is that in Him we already are highly favored and valuable. We will never feel rejected when we are living accepted.

The dying-to-self-journey that God has taken me on has been ridiculously hard, and sometimes very isolating where I didn't have much outside support. This brought to the surface a high need to find support from others in hopes they would encourage me, and when I didn't get the encouragement I felt I needed, my feelings led me to a thought-life that was far from God's Truth.

I started to feel sorry for myself.

This revealed to me an underlying need for acceptance and encouragement from others instead of confidently knowing God's encouragement is enough, and I'm fully accepted by Him. From there, I had to choose to get my thought-life in sync with His Word until my mind was in accordance with what He says, not what I felt I was lacking. This confidence continually propels me forward no matter what season I find myself in.

When I was blasted or misunderstood for my heart, or judged harshly, I learned that going around and telling everyone who would listen to me did not bring peace to my soul or heal me. I was still left feeling betrayed and broken by the one, even if twenty others encouraged me. I learned there was a greater value in going quietly to God and sharing my heart-hurt with Him. This dates all the way back to my ex-husband lying about me and what actually happened in our marriage (and after our divorce) to make himself look like the victim, leading people to believe I took his kids away from him so, "he just gave up."

This was furthest from the truth.

Trying to counter his accusations to clear my name was exhausting.

I had to learn to rest in a confident trust that God knows what really happened and at the end of the day, what He thinks of me is all that matters. In order to be in that place of confidence, my worth and value had to be secured with God, and God alone. I had to be so anchored in a confident trust with Him, I didn't need to get my value in what others thought or said about me.

We already HAVE ALL THE TOOLS WE NEED THROUGH THE PRESENCE AND POWER OF THE HOLY SPIRIT: WE NEED TO LEARN TO ACCESS THEM!

> **We will never feel rejected when we are living accepted.**

Had I not walked through what I did and only relied on people as my support system, I wouldn't have learned to go to God and experience confidence that is unshakable or developed in spiritual maturity. I would've continued to place my value in a humanistic belief system with a high need to find my worth through others' encouragement and opinions about me, struggling to trust what God says. I would be limited by my own evaluation, with a need for outside accolades, rather than a confident trust that in Him and through Him I am of high value and worth.

One morning, during my devotional time, the Holy Spirit highlighted a scripture:

> *"He will make your righteous reward shine like the dawn, your vindication like the noonday sun."* — Psalm 37:6 (NIV)

This scripture came attached with hope and promise! I realized that not only does God know the full story and I can find rest in His arms, but He wants my name cleared too. I had to choose to trust Him at His Word rather than taking matters into my own hands to vindicate myself.

Here's the thing, though, I became so anchored, confidently trusting the Lord, that I didn't care if I saw my vindication. I was saturated in God's comfort, trusting the plan He had for me and my kids, and I was able to move forward regardless of what others believed.

It's a win-win even if you don't see the vindication here on earth; we know in the end everything gets revealed.

> *"The time is coming when everything that is covered up will be revealed, and all that is secret will be made known to all."* — Luke 12:2 (NLT)

This confidence is what we all have access to through Jesus and breaks the need to get our value in what other people think of us. When our beliefs are established through God's value system with our worth and confidence secured in Him, we don't have an insecure need to vindicate ourselves. We are confident that in His perfect timing, He will bring justice in the most unjust situations.

Again, we either believe God at His Word or we don't.

This is the confidence we get to live with when our security is in Him, not in people.

We don't need to worry about the misunderstandings of others or validate ourselves; we just walk forward.

The truth of the matter is, people have egos and hurt that get in the way of seeing others as valuable. It doesn't matter how clean our track record becomes, there will still be a critic that will pop up in our lives who will oppose us.

Am I right?!

Realize you're not alone in these experiences. Trust me, I've experienced so much unfair criticism, rejection, hate-filled actions, misunderstandings, and false judgments, and I know I will continue to be judged unfairly on this side of Heaven. (Insert eye roll here)

I actually find comfort when I read my Bible and see constant opposition wherever the disciples and apostles went. I noticed that God didn't make everything cushy for them.

Instead, He empowered them!

We need to learn how to use these moments in our favor, bringing them to the secret place with Jesus, using them as a gauge in our own life. Often, these hurtful moments bring to the surface an area where we need to anchor ourselves deeper in what God says so that no outside voice or situation has the power to shape us.

We just go directly to God, hear what He has to say and stand firm in Him.

When our confidence is secure in Him, we no longer have an unhealthy, or codependent need in us that requires validation from anyone else.

I've learned that when I feel

When our beliefs are established through God's value system with our worth and confidence secured in Him, we don't have an insecure need to vindicate ourselves.

the painful crushing of opposition, I can go to God with my hurt and insecurities. And when I do, He takes me deeper in a confident trust as I learn to stand firm in what He says about me versus the critics. From there, He fills me with His power and gives me a greater strength to persevere.

How can I have the boldness to go and do what He wants me to do, and say what He wants me to say, and go where He wants me to go if there is any need in me that needs approval from others and an outside audience cheering me on?

This inner need would reveal that I still have layers of insecurity that will hinder me from running my race with confidence.

> *Am I now trying to win the approval of human beings, or of God? Or am I trying to please people? If I were still trying to please people, I would not be a servant of Christ.* — Galatians 1:10 (NIV)

It was during those painful moments when I realized God was using these hard and lonely seasons to remove any need for outside support and get all I need from Him, and Him alone.

This is His heart for each of us.

He wants us to become so confident in how He sees and feels about us, we are willing to go anywhere and do anything for His glory because we are no longer in need of anything outside of Him. This is where boldness and confidence rise up inside of us and others take notice. We become so sure that God is for us . . .

> *What, then, shall we say in response to these things? If God is for us, who can be against us?* — Romans 8:31 (NIV)

These are commonly quoted scriptures—we need to start believing them to be truer than what we are feeling and what others might be saying.

I hear it from people all the time: you're so bold.

You're so confident.

You are natural when you speak and share . . . You're such an extrovert.

I just laugh!

Honestly, I'm a behind-the-scenes kind of girl.

I'm tellin' ya, I have been shaped by the Holy Spirit into this confidence. I'm still being challenged and stretched daily as God continues to cut away the debris. I'm learning to go deeper, trusting in who God says I am, forming who you see today. This is not my natural wiring; this is 100% the training journey that I have been on where the Holy Spirit continually strips me of any insecurities as I surrender my will to His; until all I have left is a confidence that radiates for Him.

How did I get here?

Well, I'm glad you asked!

I simply yield to Him when I feel something surface in my heart. I don't run to anyone or anything else to make me feel better. I just turn confidently and directly to Him, and He meets me.

What people see now is not a secret need in me that has to live an outward life.

> He wants us TO BECOME SO CONFIDENT IN HOW HE SEES AND FEELS ABOUT US, WE ARE WILLING TO GO ANYWHERE AND DO ANYTHING FOR HIS GLORY BECAUSE WE ARE NO LONGER IN NEED OF ANYTHING OUTSIDE OF HIM.

I thrive in my alone time. Introverts unite (separately)! *fist bump*

I relate more to David who was trained in the field alone with God or the disciples who were just ordinary men who walked with Jesus. God has shown up in my life in such powerful ways, I am bursting inside, and I have to tell everyone! I suppose it's the way those we read about in the Bible felt when Jesus touched their lives.

You guys (and gals), this Spirit-filled life is our freedom!

I've been (and will continue to be) chiseled, held to the fire, and it's incredibly uncomfortable (to my flesh). But as I learned the power of surrender to God's refining process, He revealed what He desired to accomplish in me. The Holy Spirit began to teach me what it means to live as a New Creation in Christ. I have to get rid of all the old—old ways of thinking, believing, and understanding in order to experience life in the Spirit.

What people see in me is living proof that all it takes is a willing heart that turns to the Lord, allowing Him to build us according to His perfect plans in ways we cannot manufacture.

What we are met with is an incredible, unexplainable freedom and confidence that is beyond anything we can manufacture apart from Him! An unshakable freedom and confidence is available for all who spend time with Jesus and walk with Him.

> *The council members were astonished as they witnessed the bold courage of Peter and John, especially when they discovered that they were just ordinary men who had never had religious training. Then they began to understand the effect Jesus had on them simply by spending time with Him.* — Acts 4:13 (TPT)

This ripple effect that started over 2,000 years ago is still going. When an act of bold courage comes out of us, others will take notice. It becomes undeniable and obvious that we spend time with Jesus. This confidence is not reserved for the select few, the highly educated, or the "naturally" extroverted personalities. This is why those personality tests should not be our gauge. They limit us to our flesh, born from Adam, old nature, instead of our new nature, which is to be like Christ, empowered by the Holy Spirit.

There is a huge difference between gaining more information about ourselves and others versus true transformation. We have gained so much knowledge through our human understanding, but that has not changed us from the inside out to the point that who we once were can no longer be found. Our old self should become so far removed from our lives, we literally cannot find that old person!

We've also made a mistake in trying to transform our old nature instead of putting on the new garments that were already paid for. We've spent so much time trying to develop our "flesh," versus learning what it means to live by the Spirit. Many of my brothers and sisters are putting an emphasis on more resources that give us information about our human nature, missing the powerful transaction that takes place when we simply yield to the Holy Spirit, allowing Him to define and refine us as

He takes us from glory to glory.

In reality, we are struggling to trust that God and His power in us are truly all we need.

This faith and trust walk is missing in many of our lives.

God desires for us to simply believe Him at His Word, and allow the Holy Spirit to rewrite who we are according to His design.

If I had relied on a personality test to tell me my strengths and weaknesses, I would have put parameters around my capabilities instead of tapping into His power within me. You see, I am completely okay with my weaknesses, and I know I fall short . . . BUT GOD! Putting myself in a box through my personality would have caused me to see myself through a test and not through the righteousness of Christ. I would have created a vision for myself that made sense instead of letting God show me who I am through His eyes and allowing Him to breathe His vision into my life, which is nothing I would have envisioned for myself.

On the flip side, if you are naturally extroverted, those personality tests will tell you that you belong front and center because that's where you'll thrive and flourish the most. Oftentimes these tests lead us to believe we need to be *doing* something in order to be satisfied, so the goal is to set out to achieve that result. And maybe that "something" is God's will, but often that need becomes the driving force, and we forget that God is the one who satisfies us when we humble ourselves and stay intricately connected to Him. This is where we become Christlike in our wiring and our roots grow deep in Him. Our true satisfaction will not come from what we do, but from who we are in Him.

> *An unshakable* FREEDOM AND CONFIDENCE IS AVAILABLE FOR ALL WHO SPEND TIME WITH JESUS AND WALK WITH HIM.

Whether introverted or extroverted, we all need to humble ourselves before God and learn to get our complete fulfillment through Him. We need to recognize that our true value and worth cannot be based on what we are doing, or upon our successes, but on what God says to be true. His Truth establishes unwavering confidence within us. From there, we become unafraid of the refining process that God needs to take us on

> **If I had relied on a personality test to tell me my strengths and weaknesses, I would have put parameters around my capabilities instead of tapping into His power within me.**

to make us more like Him. What was once believed to be decreasing our value because circumstances made us feel less than, switches to a powerful transaction of purification as we are made into the glorious image of God. We learn what it looks like and feels like to be unwavering in our thoughts, overwhelmed with God's love, peace, and joy that is no longer determined by our outward situations because inwardly we are radically free, experiencing life in the Spirit.

> *Consider it a sheer gift, friends, when tests and challenges come at you from all sides. You know that under pressure, your faith-life is forced into the open and shows its true colors. So don't try to get out of anything prematurely. Let it do its work so you become mature and well-developed, not deficient in any way.* —James 1:2-4 (MSG)

With our value intact, we move to spiritual maturity, as we continually yield to the cutting process. This cutting away, pressing, and crushing feels incredibly uncomfortable to our flesh, but it is necessary to bring forth that shine that's within.

Do you realize that you can find a way "out" and bypass the refining process altogether?

Most are continually looking for a way out of the purification process, and they don't even realize it. When we are experiencing something incredibly uncomfortable, it's the beginning of the vital "crucifying of the flesh" that unlocks something incredibly supernatural, and life in the Spirit is established. We cannot live by the Spirit without crucifying the flesh, and we cannot crucify the flesh until we are pressed on all sides, forcing it out of us. Most feel the sting of their flesh being crushed and retreat or "find a way out."

Finding a way out is actually easy.

We can leave our job, ditch relationships, harbor unforgiveness, numb out, binge eat, busy ourselves, develop bad (or seemingly good) habits to avoid what we are feeling . . . anything that we can grab hold of that brings comfort to our flesh *is* a way out.

Avoiding the process and looking for ways to keep our flesh comfortable is costing us our spiritual maturity. James clearly says that when we yield to this process of tests and challenges, the end result is that we are not lacking in any area; we become spiritually mature.

Many of us do not understand why life here on earth seems so hard. It's because so many of us have a value system that is not lined up with God's. We've spent too much time and effort creating kingdoms for our old nature to be comfortable, leading us to false comfort, spiritual burnout, and frustrations with life. God clearly shows us through His Word that life here will be filled with hard times, but there are promises attached to this reality . . . He will be our comfort; He will fill us with His strength and His peace, and His joy will be our strength as He hides us in the shadows of His wings.

We will not walk through hard things without Him!

Through my journey of listening and observing I went to the Lord with what I had been seeing in the body of Christ. I couldn't understand why so many pure-hearted Jesus followers who truly love Him are struggling daily in their hearts, as well as with others. I wanted to know why so many are trying so hard to get to a place of confidence, but it feels like human strength and not the power of God.

Why are so many churches growing, but so many individuals still struggling with insecurity?

He said, "Many churches look like I built them from the outside, but behind the scenes, they are operating no differently than a strategic, worldly business model."

Ouch.

> What was once BELIEVED TO BE DECREASING OUR VALUE BECAUSE CIRCUMSTANCES MADE US FEEL LESS THAN, SWITCHES TO A POWERFUL TRANSACTION OF PURIFICATION AS WE ARE MADE INTO THE GLORIOUS IMAGE OF GOD.

How did this happen?!?

I pressed in.

He showed me a reality of what happens when the body of Christ, as a whole, does not have their worth and value secured in who they are to God. This has set us up to cling to things that lessen the power and presence of God in our own personal lives, as well as the church at large. Here's the negative cycle that the Holy Spirit was showing me as He took me deeper in this revelation:

> We cannot live BY THE SPIRIT WITHOUT CRUCIFYING THE FLESH, AND WE CANNOT CRUCIFY THE FLESH UNTIL WE ARE PRESSED ON ALL SIDES, FORCING IT OUT OF US.

I've heard many church and ministry leaders say that when they go to leadership meetings, where several pastors and various ministry leaders gather, the first question is, "how many members do you have at your church?" Or they will look at other means to measure platform size to see how "well" the ministry is doing. If a church or ministry leader has put their value in what they are doing instead of who they are to God, they will subconsciously measure their success against the success of others' church or ministry growth. If this act of comparison in their heart goes unchecked and they don't take it to the Lord to hear what He has to say and allow Him to direct their steps, they can feel inadequate when they compare. From there they begin to seek church growth models, sometimes even hiring advisors to implement marketing strategies that look just like a worldly business model. Sometimes it "works" and sometimes it doesn't.

I've even heard of some churches who will have people positioned within the congregation, ready to respond to the "spontaneous" water baptism in order to create the feel of the Holy Spirit moving through hearts.

You guys . . . this is not good! We really need to check our hearts, especially those who are called to lead.

I do understand the heart to reach the lost.

I'm not saying this is all wrong or bad (well, some of these methods are just straight up wrong), but what the Lord was showing me was that sometimes good intentions can cause us to lose sight of *Who* we should ultimately be relying on, and all of a sudden, we are putting all our efforts in building our own kingdoms from a need in us, instead of building His Kingdom purely for Him.

When one has been called to lead, should the church size (and ministry platforms) successes (or failures) be the gauge we measure by?

> We've spent TOO MUCH TIME AND EFFORT CREATING KINGDOMS FOR OUR OLD NATURE TO BE COMFORTABLE, LEADING US TO FALSE COMFORT, SPIRITUAL BURNOUT, AND FRUSTRATIONS WITH LIFE.

Are we more concerned about growing in numbers, not paying attention to whether or not individuals are growing spiritually?

Has our focus gone from teaching what it means to remain connected to the Vine at all times and living this out in our own lives first, to creating a well-orchestrated event?

In all honesty, church and ministry meetings should be seeking the presence of the Lord and allowing Him to determine the steps in the proper season. Rather than relying on how another church or platform ministry "did it" and then formulating a strategy or replica model. Ministry meetings should focus on confidently trusting God with the purpose and plans that He has for His house and those He's called to lead. It's imperative the leader's confidence and value is in line with what God says, and it's not attached to the outward appearance of success with their ministry. When men and women in leadership are struggling with their value, forming their worth around what they are doing, rather than who God says they are, they are left to measure themselves through their accomplishments.

When our leaders are struggling with their worth, not remaining connected to the Vine, and, instead, are following a man-made strategy, it affects the Body as a whole and those who are under their leadership. Subconsciously the leadership develops a need to have constant ministry growth.

Numbers matter.

What we end up with are ministry leaders who are not raising up disciples of Christ or training them to hear God's voice and follow His lead with bold faith. Rather than releasing them to follow Jesus, they are keeping them in to build their ministries and expand the house. While they may teach the importance of following Jesus, there is still an underlying message that says, stay, help me build, and feel guilty if you're not involved. As the Body, we are not being taught to truly follow Jesus; we are taught to follow man, believing that's how we remain connected to the Vine.

This negative ripple effect is happening in so many churches, and it's not God's heart for us.

This method is also the way we operate in the corporate world, and many are struggling to differentiate between working hard and finding value in our efforts and successes. This silent insecurity has left too many to measure their worth through human understanding and personal evaluations rather than trusting God, and it's affecting the body as a whole, polluting the power and purity of simply following Jesus.

We need to get back on course and it begins when each of us seeks the Kingdom of God first, building our value system around His, and walking confidently in what He says.

I am not writing this because I want to slam you, or anyone, if you are in leadership applying these strategies to build the church or ministries. We live in a culture that has given the body of Christ access into realms of possibility through media and various online platforms to get the message of Christ out, and I think it's awesome!

Shoot, you can even find me on a few media platforms. Ha!

However, if we have placed our value through self-evaluation or outward works and not through God, and God alone, it's quite easy for our focus to be off, stuck in a trap of comparison, checking to see where we measure up through outward success. From there we either believe we are "making it" based on what others can see, or we feel inadequate because we aren't measuring up to our idea of success.

> *Humble yourselves before the Lord, and He will lift you up in honor.*
> —*James 4:10 (NLT)*

Humbling ourselves before the Lord means to choose His will over our own and trust the outcome to Him. This takes a re-wiring of our human nature and requires that our value system becomes built through a Kingdom perspective, not an earthly one. From there, we are no longer swayed by what others may think or build our confidence around our own personal successes apart from God.

The verb meaning to humble, according to Dictionary.com, is powerful. It says: "to destroy the independence, power or will of."

When we humble ourselves before the Lord, we are saying "Your will God, not mine."

This means, we are destroying our strong, independent, and powerful pull to live for ourselves and, instead, wholeheartedly choosing to live for Him. This unlocks a deeper level of faith and trust as He gives us an incredible strategy for our lives. He is the Master Strategist and His ways are far above anything we can fathom! In order to be in this place of confidence with Him, we have to believe what He says about us and live from that place of security. If we have any need in us that we are not learning to get from God, we will set out to try to make our own mark apart from Him.

We will still have a void.

It doesn't matter how successful one becomes, if it's apart from God, we will still feel empty. Our successes in life will never be enough.

When it comes to developing step-plans for our lives, the Holy Spirit will give us strategies for our homes, families, careers, and even ministry. These are the divine strategies that require God's guidance and His grace to live it out. As we take each step in the proper season we will feel peace, freedom, a supernatural strength, and our confidence will not be attached to the success or the outcome but intact with who we already are to God. We will also notice that our family, relationships, and God-ordained priorities will not be placed on the back burner.

The other areas in our life will not start falling apart while another area grows and makes us feel good about who we are.

We will not worry about the outcome of what God has entrusted to us because we are already secure in His Truth that we are fully loved and accepted by Him.

No outward success can compare to this kind of confidence.

No ladder of accomplishment is going to determine what is already ours through Jesus.

> When we humble ourselves before the Lord, we are saying "Your will God, not mine."

We will have all we need to live confidently no matter what position we have in life. One can be a stay-at-home parent all the way to a president of a corporation, or the largest, globally known ministry to the one who rocks babies at church; the confidence will look and feel the same. All of a sudden, life is built on God's Kingdom perspective versus world perspective, and we are securely executing the assignment that God has for our lives no matter what our title is.

When it comes to the church experience, I know so many who are enamored by the flashing lights and big platforms, but then begin to struggle with their personal faith walk when a pastor or church leader falls into a snare of sin, or when they find out that the worship leader they've been following denounces God. If other people's experiences shake our faith and negatively affect our walk with God, it reveals to us that we started to follow man over Jesus, or fame over the presence of God. Our confidence has been placed in a person to lead us versus Jesus, Himself, as the lead of our lives. God is not impressed with what we humans are impressed with.

I've also been a part of churches where the pastor is truly preaching the Word from a place of genuine humility, and you can see the spiritual growth in the individuals in that house. When the leaders of the church's identities are intact, it ripples out to the rest of the body. From that place of confidence, our pastors and leaders see their position in the body of Christ as a high honor that gives them continual fulfillment because they know God chose them. They serve Him with their whole heart, trusting Him with the outcome of His flock. And this has nothing, I repeat, NOTHING to do with the size of the House. Their concern is the spiritual maturity and growth of the individuals as each one is pointed to remain connected to the Vine, Jesus. This leads us to the real and lasting fruit that God is desiring to produce in His children. This correct value system, coming from the leaders out, becomes the positive ripple effect of God's heart for the church as a whole.

If we continue to mix in this idea of works, measuring our success from an outside scope, with our faith, then what we end up preaching is a checklist of "how-tos."

Remember our Christian checklist?

Yes, we are still encouraged to spend time with God, and of course, our faith should produce an action, but there is still a subliminal message that says, "must do this, this, and this so I'm enough." All of a sudden, we feel pressure to carve out time with God and perform, feeling guilty when we don't, versus longing to sit at His feet because of what we have with Him and through Him, and from there serving is from Spirit-led desire, not a man-made pressure.

If you are feeling pressure or guilt in your walk with God, know that's not coming from His Spirit.

Many of my brothers and sisters are resorting to the Christian checklist to measure where they are with Jesus. Following the Christian list, we mistakenly believe we are living out of our "new nature" in Christ. We have learned what it looks like to be a Christian outwardly, but we are not learning how to draw close to God, which is where our true value becomes secure, and our new natures in Christ take form. Well-meaning church activities are performed out of a duty as a Christian rather than a Spirit-led response. When we read how people in the Bible who had a supernatural encounter responded, we try to replicate their response, but secretly feel burned out and won't admit it because our worth is wrapped around our performance, and what someone might say if we aren't doing all the things a Christian does. This list helps us know of God but will leave us feeling like we can never measure up as we struggle to become "better Christians." God doesn't want us to know *of Him*, He wants us to *know Him* intimately and personally.

I went through a deep depression many years ago. I tried to read my Bible, but the pages were blank to my eyes. I couldn't get more than "dear God help" out in my prayer life, and when I went to my church family for help, I was condemned and told I needed to read my Bible, pray more, serve more.

I was.

Truthfully, I was hurting inside and needed the real Jesus, not checklist Christianity.

All I had in me was to sit at His feet daily. One day the dark cloud lifted and I was filled with a joy I had never known before. Even though I had been all in with Him for several years at this point, I still didn't know what it felt like to experience a supernatural joy in the midst of hard times. Since that day His joy in me and through me has been a constant well that never runs dry even during my hard seasons.

His joy is truly my strength!

Nothing I did outside of learning to still myself at His feet could accomplish this.

It was by faith that I sat in His presence, believing He would meet me. It wasn't instantaneous, but I didn't give up, and He showed up!

This cycle of finding our worth and value in "doing" is breaking our Father's heart. He does not want to see His children trying so hard to find their worth outside of Him, "worn out by religion," trying to "carry their cross" in their own strength, believing that life in Christ is supposed to feel heavy and hard.

It's not supposed to be so complicated.

As a Church Body, we have complicated what Jesus paid for.

The more we seek Him, and know Him, the more we know ourselves in the purest form. Our worth is no longer tangled with anything outside of what God says, and when the pressure of man comes along, we recognize it, ask God what He says, and follow Him boldly and unashamedly.

My family and I were attending a local church, and the pastors told me (yes, told me) where I needed to start serving because "God has big plans for me"; if I obeyed this pastor (yes, they said to obey the pastor) and humble myself by serving where he thought I should be, God will open doors for me. They said if I don't humble myself, God will close doors.

This conversation was coming into my spirit sharp with warnings attached to it.

The Bible clearly tells us that we are to humble ourselves before God and He will lift us up in honor.

Not man.

God will open doors that no man can shut.

He was mixing parts of God's Word with his own motives.

The pastor went on to tell me that I have to go through a process before God will use me (he had no idea the stripping process of dying to myself began over twenty years prior), and as long as I do what he tells me to, he will call any of his "connections" all over the world and tell them I should go speak at their next event and they would invite me.

Truth: God absolutely has a process for all of us. But that process is through a personal walk with Jesus. We do not need to jump through hoops to get lifted up in honor. Interestingly enough, what the pastor described was in agreement with the vision God had given me for my life, only the pastor's version was through man and not through God. I'm not sure what his motivation was, maybe it's the way he was taught, and he was just following in step with that. I'm not sure. But when we resort to twisting scripture, that is called manipulation. Their process was also through following their step-plan, not yielding the step-plan that God had already given to me. The platform the pastor promised was through a counterfeit method and a man-made strategy. It was from a "do this for me, and I will do this for you." While I admit part of me was tempted because it seemed like it could be a God opportunity, the Holy Spirit whispered to my heart a clear no. He also confirmed that I was sensing manipulation and this was not an opportunity from Him.

Would this method have expanded my speaking "platform?"

Probably.

I had to know my worth was not in a platform size or in a measurable success outside of what God says. I had to go before the Lord and yield to His lead despite the pressure and promise I was getting from leadership.

Truthfully, I WAS HURTING INSIDE AND NEEDED THE REAL JESUS, NOT CHECKLIST CHRISTIANITY.

> *If you bow low in God's awesome presence, He will eventually exalt you as you leave the timing in His hands.* — 1 Peter 5:6 (TPT)

I'm so thankful for the refining process I have been on. I don't feel as if I'm missing out on something bigger or better for my life. I genuinely trust the purpose and plans that God has for me. This incident was several years ago, and I am still not living in the full vision that God has given me, yet I feel completely filled.

When our identities are secure, our arrival to the end result or vision is not our measuring stick. Also, we need to be checking in with God regularly and know His Word for ourselves so that we are not easily misled by anyone, including those in leadership who are there to show us how to connect with God. It's okay to say no to those in leadership if God has said something different to you.

Now, I am not talking about having godly and healthy accountability.

That's a must for all of us!

Just keep in mind that in unhealthy situations, God's voice should always override man's.

> *Peter and the apostles replied, "We must listen to and obey God more than pleasing religious leaders."* — Acts 5:29 (TPT)

This passage is referring to the religious leaders who were trying to stop the gospel message, but it's still valuable regardless of what kind of situation we find ourselves in. We have to choose to hear what God is saying to us personally and obey Him over anyone else. In order to live in this kind of bold faith, we have to have to know our worth and value tied to God. If we are insecure, we will struggle to follow God and obey His lead for our lives.

The shepherd of the house is one whom I have high respect for, teaching us God's Word and equipping the saints to be disciples. I honor their time and how they pour into our lives by following Jesus and living it out. But somewhere along the line, there is confusion in the body of Christ to follow our pastors' lead on what we do, how we serve, and what they can do for us. All of a sudden, we are being trained to follow man's lead and not God's. If we are relying on the pastors or elders to affirm our walks, getting our value from how we serve in the church, subconsciously forming our worth around what we do and they say rather than going to Jesus, diving into His Word, becoming rooted in what He says, we aren't actually connected to the Vine. This pattern will not lead us to deep confidence that is built upon the true foundation Jesus laid for us.

> When our IDENTITIES ARE SECURE, OUR ARRIVAL TO THE END RESULT OR VISION IS NOT OUR MEASURING STICK.

At that same church that wanted to give me my "step-plan to success" was a young gal who was receiving her award for all her acts of service.

There's nothing wrong with giving public recognition and awards.

The Bible does say to let others praise you and not to praise yourself (Proverbs 27:2), but in her case, the plate of responsibilities made my heart ache as they went down the list of the many ministries she was serving in.

She was a young single mom who was working full time and going to school full time; I had an uncomfortable feeling in the pit of my stomach. The unsettled feelings were two-fold. I was discerning a pressure from man, that is not God's heart, but I am also ultra-sensitive to the burden of being a single mom. I have been a single mom, and I know the load we carry being both mom and dad. I know the toll that it takes on a family.

I wondered, when did she have time to sit at the feet of Jesus, or just bond and lead her little ones?

Has this fairly new believer in Jesus been taught that her first and most valuable ministry is to her children?

The way she was praised for all she was doing and was brought up on stage as an example to follow made me sad. She wasn't radiating; she looked tired. Brothers and sisters in these situations are the precious ones the body of Christ should be caring for, not leading them to burn out. Not only was I a single mom, but I also coached single moms, and they are usually more concerned about their load of responsibilities and the exhaustion they feel.

During my season of being a single mom, I was serving with my whole heart. I hit a place of burnout and ended up going through a pretty overwhelming time of grief. I felt guilty for struggling to get to church early each week, along with getting four kids up, ready, and out the door, and found myself just going through the motions. I went to the Lord, and I was shocked that He told me to take a step back and stop serving ... what?!?

But serving is vital!

God called me out, and into a season of rest as He ministered to my broken heart. My heart that was so shattered by my previous marriage and all I thought it would be, had ended. I needed to grieve that loss and give God space to heal me completely. I had to let go of my concerns about what people would think at church if I wasn't actively involved. Some thought I was struggling spiritually, and I was definitely put in a "category" based on what they saw on the outside, but what was going on inside was powerful. I stopped caring about what other people thought of me. My value was secure in Jesus, and He was healing my heart. I was getting pieced back together in wholeness. I was going on dates (literally, not hypothetically) with Jesus as He restored what the enemy tried to steal from me: My value through Him, and not what my ex-husband's actions showed me.

The Holy Spirit began stirring up parts of me and forgotten passions that had been dormant in my life through survival. He began to put a burden on my heart to write books that I had never thought to write before. He started giving me visions for my future, and I saw myself the way He saw me: fearfully and wonderfully made, born for such a time as this.

That season of rest is what launched me forward into the purpose and the plans that God had for me, but in wholeness. I wasn't trying to manufacture anything or ignore that I was broken inside. God led me to His well, and it was the opposite of "doing" church or following a step-plan of what it looks like to be a Christian, convincing myself that God heals, but remaining broken.

Did you catch that?

How many are saying that they believe God heals, but they haven't slowed down, sat in His presence, and allowed Him to actually heal, and are still severely wounded inside, carrying around their broken hearts?

God's presence met me in powerful, life-changing ways as He filled me with His all-encompassing love, touching and piecing back together every piece of my broken heart. This is available to us when we don't care what others will think, stop the busyness, and run unabandoned into the arms of Jesus.

Healing happens when timelines and step-plans to success are not weighing in our decisions because our identities are not in what we've accomplished, but what God wants to accomplish in us. As He does this, we show the masses what it means to run to Jesus with it all. This faith walk is where we are living in "unforced rhythms of grace," and life is not heavy or burdensome.

God called me out, and into a season of rest as He ministered to my broken heart.

Truthfully, I didn't need a ministry to plug into for healing; I needed Jesus.

I still do.

We all do.

Do you see how the culture of our world, checklists, and how-tos is intermixed with our church culture, serving according to man's vision, not God's, has created the wrong ripple effect through the body of Christ, leading us to a life that is filled with broken hearts and insecurities?

God wants to undo all of this so we can fully live out the mandate of Christ. These methods are blocking our transformation that can only come through the Holy Spirit, and instead, many are experiencing spiritual burnout. I know this to be true. I've had so many private conversations with people in leadership, those who serve regularly, and even those who are just Sunday attendees . . . more than I can count!

We need to get this!

In today's times, we need to get a clear understanding of the Father's

God lead me TO HIS WELL, AND IT WAS THE OPPOSITE OF "DOING" CHURCH OR FOLLOWING A STEP-PLAN OF WHAT IT LOOKS LIKE TO BE A CHRISTIAN, CONVINCING MYSELF THAT GOD HEALS, BUT REMAINING BROKEN.

heart and see ourselves the way He does. We have to break some cycles and experience a life-changing encounter with Jesus, cultivating a lifestyle of intimacy with Him in the secret place. This is where we become firmly secure in Him. From there ministries and serving in church is no longer about performance or who can "bring it." Service is literally an overflow from our time with Jesus, and that kind of overflow releases the power and presence of God that becomes a ripple effect, leading the masses to true transformation until every place of serving within the body of Christ is from mature, spirit-filled believers.

When we are not owning our spiritual walks, doing church, projecting our godly images, struggling internally with our value, we end up crawling our way to church each week for another feel-good message only for us to get knocked right back down by life on Monday.

And the cycle continues.

We are not supposed to be projecting an image; we are to become the image of God.

What we read about the beginning of the church in Acts was a spontaneous, Spirit-empowered response to the true gospel and the life-changing power of Jesus. God filled them with the Holy Spirit, they preached boldly, men and women were healed from sicknesses and diseases, they were delivered from tormenting spirits . . . this was meant to be ongoing.

Healing HAPPENS WHEN TIMELINES AND STEP-PLANS TO SUCCESS ARE NOT WEIGHING IN OUR DECISIONS BECAUSE OUR IDENTITIES ARE NOT IN WHAT WE'VE ACCOMPLISHED, BUT WHAT GOD WANTS TO ACCOMPLISH IN US.

Because of Jesus, we have complete access to God's presence. When we sit in His presence, allowing Him to meet us, what comes out of us looks more and more like Him. This process is not faked, forced, or manufactured. We are becoming transformed through His presence and the refining fires of life, going from glory to glory to radiate His glory.

We are not SUPPOSED TO BE PROJECTING AN IMAGE; WE ARE TO BECOME THE IMAGE OF GOD.

> *We can all draw close to him with the veil removed from our faces. And with no veil, we all become like mirrors who brightly reflect the glory of the Lord Jesus. We are being transfigured into His very image as we move from one brighter level of glory to another. And this glorious transfiguration comes from the Lord, who is the Spirit.*
> *— 2 Corinthians 3:18 (TPT)*

When we turn to Him, we discover that we are already a highly valued treasure to Him. This confidence will lead us to trust Him with everything as He takes each of us on a personal and transformational journey. This refining process will naturally take place in our lives when our focus is not on ourselves, but fully on Him . . . when we no longer measure ourselves through human understanding, people-pleasing, or religious performance, but allow God to show us who we are to Him.

> *The mature children of God are those who are moved by the impulses of the Holy Spirit. And you did not receive the "spirit of religious duty," leading you back into the fear of never being good enough. But you have received the "Spirit of full acceptance," enfolding you into the family of God. And you will never feel orphaned, for as He rises up within us, our spirits join Him in saying the words of tender affection, "Beloved Father!" — Romans 8:14-15 (TPT)*

It's beautiful, powerful, and uncomplicated.

We are no longer doing church; we are the Church, the bride of Christ, confidently radiating His glory in the purest form.

Chapter Three
Responding as a Child

The idea of childlikeness and receiving the Kingdom of Heaven is a bigger challenge than we are recognizing. Mostly because we have become so accustomed to understanding these concepts through head knowledge and self-awareness, we have not developed the childlike ability to just receive what God says—who we are to Him, who He is to us, and all that's available through Him as children of God and carriers of His presence.

When we were little, we simply believed what our parents told us.

A child believes what they are taught.

Our parents also provided all our needs, food, shelter, clothing, protection (although I am aware that some people have come from heartbreaking situations where they weren't provided for). Typically, we didn't have to beg or plead; what we needed was readily given to us. As we grew up, we came to a realization that not everything they told us was consistent or believable, and, simultaneously, it became our responsibility to take care of ourselves and provide for our own needs. So, we moved away from trusting everything they said and their provision. As we did this we became more aware of the world around us. The more we became aware of the world around us, the more we subconsciously developed a belief system based on our independent human understanding and decided what our truth would be, implementing the work it requires to become self-sufficient.

Now, after all these years of learning, thinking for ourselves, and providing, let's go back and be that child who just believes and receives from our Heavenly Father without overthinking, justifying, or rationalizing.

Just hear like a child, believe, and form our world perspective around His.

Simple, right?

Not so much.

When we were young, we simply believed that our family life was the way it was supposed to be. As we got older, we learned there are many other beliefs in this world, and discovered that some of the ways we were raised had a negative effect on us. So we began to search for "truth." Through our searching, we begin to break away from a childlike response to life, relying on our own understanding and newfound knowledge. This development is called maturing and becoming independent from our parents. This independent wiring is inside of each one of us, and while we are called to mature spiritually, the method to maturity through independence is through our human understanding and not our spirit coming into full maturity. Unless we understand the difference, these concepts will mess with our walks with God, blocking us from experiencing all that is ours through Jesus.

> *"Learn this well: Unless you dramatically change your way of thinking and become teachable like a little child, you will never be able to enter in." — Matthew 18:3 (TPT)*

There it is!

We have to dramatically change our thinking and become teachable.

We have to become like that pure, innocent child that just believes what God says without hesitation or our interjected arguments (verbal or non-verbal—ahem our thought-life) that conflicts with God's heart.

We have to undo the thought patterns that have formed through life's painful and hard experiences and learn about the Kingdom of Heaven, and it won't be through our human reasoning.

Humanistic thought patterns will not allow us to become teachable.

Basically, we need to get our big smart brains out of the way so we can truly receive all that Jesus paid for. We might be able to quote scripture, explain the history of what was going on when the Bible was written, or even break down the scriptures and explain in depth what they mean, but all that skill can easily remain as just head knowledge, not realizing the faith it takes to live and experience Jesus and His power through childlike faith.

A disconnect forms between what we have memorized and what we are actually applying with a childlike willingness to live out God's Word in practical ways.

We can go to church each week, attend Bible studies, serve regularly, and still not experience the fullness of what we have through Jesus here on earth. We begin to believe that on this side of Heaven, we just have to accept this heavy and hard life, but our freedom and healing, (whether it be emotional, spiritual, or physical) is actually available now. Not realizing what's available and living in contradiction to what the Word says, we accept what the world throws at us. We live with brokenness in our hearts, anxiety, depression, stress, and knots in our stomachs, convincing ourselves this is just the world we live in.

Then what exactly did Jesus pay for?

We reason ourselves into believing that salvation and eternal life are all we have because of Jesus, dismissing the passages that invite us into something beyond our human comprehension on this side of Heaven. Accepting "this is just the world we live in," is human reasoning. It's having more of an awareness of self and the world around us than of God and His Kingdom.

> *Basically,* WE NEED TO GET OUR BIG SMART BRAINS OUT OF THE WAY SO WE CAN TRULY RECEIVE ALL THAT JESUS PAID FOR.

This reasoning leaves out the entire ministry that Jesus launched when He walked the earth; we decide that was for then and not for now. We have become so accustomed to building our belief system around rational thinking (sometimes wrong theology) and our limited experiences, we won't even consider the faith it takes to believe that what Jesus started was meant to be ongoing.

> *"Don't you believe that I am in the Father, and that the Father is in Me? The words I say to you I do not speak on my own authority.*

> *Rather, it is the Father, living in Me, who is doing His work. Believe Me when I say that I am in the Father and the Father is in Me; or at least believe in the evidence of the works themselves. Very truly I tell you, whoever believes in Me will do the works I have been doing, and they will do even greater things than these, because I am going to the Father. And I will do whatever you ask in My name, so that the Father may be glorified in the Son. You may ask Me for anything in My name, and I will do it." — John 14:10-14 (NIV)*

Notice the keyword here is "believe."

Most of us live with a belief system based on our experiences or what we've been taught through human reasoning. The Bible reveals the power of God, His nature, His love, His character, and all we have access to because of Jesus. This should stir a hunger in each of us for the real God to show up in our lives, today!

Oftentimes we are reading our Bibles just for memorization, going down our checklist of "time with Him." We can defend our "faith" to others and explain Christianity, but we are not totally experiencing Jesus. Then without realizing it, we set out to create the appearance of godliness through our Christian checklist of dos and don'ts like we've discussed so much about.

Or maybe we don't read our Bibles at all and feel guilty about it.

If we are struggling to open our Bible, we can ask God to give us the desire to dive into His Word and know Him better. This idea is a perfect example and a practical way to apply God's Word into our lives in a childlike manner. If we don't have a desire for something that we know is valuable, we turn to God for His help. When we ask for things that are in accordance with His will, they become our desires. This is not by force; it's through His Spirit.

> *This is the confidence we have in approaching God: that if we ask anything according to His will, He hears us. And if we know that He hears us—whatever we ask—we know that we have what we asked of Him. — 1 John 5:14-15 (NIV)*

There was a season I realized I didn't really have a desire to read my Bible. Knowing it was important and the way to the wisdom of God, I simply asked Him to give me a hunger for His Word, and He did. A deep thirst for His Word developed inside of me that could not be quenched otherwise. I picked up my Bible over twenty years ago and haven't put it down since!

> *Take delight in the Lord, and He will give you your heart's desires.*
> *— Psalm 37:4 (NLT)*

From there, I became saturated in the bigness of my God. Story after story began to impact me. A deep longing for the God of the Bible to be my God today began to stir in my heart. I was no longer satisfied with reading *about* Him; I wanted to *know* Him in tangible ways. I quickly realized that in order to fully experience all of who He says He is, I had to get me and my small thinking out of the way. I am finite; God is infinite. My human understanding and limitations had to be shattered!

The Bible REVEALS THE POWER OF GOD, HIS NATURE, HIS LOVE, HIS CHARACTER, AND ALL WE HAVE ACCESS TO BECAUSE OF JESUS.

Our thoughts, in comparison to God's, are so small . . . His ways are higher!

I asked Him to show me through His Word who He is, and who I am to Him; because I really didn't like myself all that much. I learned I had a self-hatred inside of me that was developed through negative life experiences. I would hear scriptures and go through studies on who God says I am. My brain could memorize the scriptures. I knew them well, but in my heart, I had deep-rooted insecurities. What I was experiencing and feeling led me to a belief about myself that was in opposition to what I read in my Bible. Rather than explaining it away, I boldly went to the Lord and asked Him to take His Truth from my head to my heart until I was living from His Truth, not my human understanding.

If I noticed that I was not experiencing what the Bible says is available, I would simply ask the Holy Spirit to move in me and through me in powerful ways. I had to choose (and still do) not to allow my limited life experiences, man's theology, or my inner wrestle of doubt and disbelief, to put parameters around the bigness of my God or how He moves.

This rhythm of going to God with a childlike, teachable spirit *is* living life in the Spirit. Living in the Spirit develops spiritual maturity as I lay aside my natural human response to "figure it all out," and run to God with everything.

Having a childlike approach with God means believing that when we go to Him for what the Word says is ours, and what life with Him should feel like, we will experience a greater facet of His nature, unlocking the Spirit-empowered life we have been given access to through Jesus.

We have been invited into a rhythmic life of childlike wonder where the Holy Spirit moves in and through us. Accepting the invitation syncs our heart with God's, and what began between us and Him becomes the ripple effect of the Kingdom of Heaven. This ripple effect begins with a willingness to be teachable, shattering our humanistic belief systems until our thinking is wrapped around the fullness of what we have in Him.

We need to surrender our hearts to God, giving Him full permission to move in our lives. When we give Him our whole hearts, inviting Him to increase our understanding of Him, He will.

As our understanding increases, trust deepens, and our ability to live by faith expands. It's through believing and receiving by faith, not by sight or by what "makes sense," that we gain access to the bigness of God. Through this transaction, we become transformed and, in turn, become change agents to the world around us.

If we build our belief system around human understanding and not through the Word of God by going to Him for the answers to our questions, we can easily miss a facet of God's nature that He wants to pour into our lives.

In my early twenties, my family and I moved across the U.S. to join with others to start a church plant. One night a group of us were all hanging out and somehow the conversation went to a subject I was not accustomed to. I was introduced to a controversial concept that, prior to this, I didn't know was a thing. The argument was that speaking in tongues, prophecy, the laying on of hands for healing, and things of that nature of God were "null and void" and not for today. I sat in silence listening to their confident belief about the God of yesterday and this particular theological stance.

An inner struggle and question started to develop in me.

I was raised to believe that everything they were saying doesn't exist anymore is still in effect.

The thought that plagued my mind more than anything was the fact that we both read the same Bible, worshiped the same God, but had a completely split belief about this facet of God. It stirred up a longing for truth in my heart.

His Truth.

I wanted to hear God.

While I had been a witness of divine healing through the laying on of hands and believed that prophecy was a gift from the Holy Spirit, experiencing this way of life for many years, I did not speak in tongues at the time. I was under a belief system that says to desire this gift and ask. At that point in my life, I didn't understand the value of speaking in tongues, so I never thought to ask God for that gift.

> We have been invited into a rhythmic life of childlike wonder where the Holy Spirit moves in and through us.

Silly, simple me just assumed that's why I didn't speak in tongues.

I didn't know of the split in theological stances.

I was genuinely shocked at this new (to me) idea that the gifts of the Holy Spirit were limited to a specific time in the past. I just believed that my lack of experience was a barrier on my end, not God's. This stirred confusion in me that I needed to settle in my heart.

At first, I didn't know where to turn. So, I started with some trusted people, only to end up feeling more frustrated and confused. The more I shared my question and the struggle I was having with my belief system, the more they would strongly give me their theological opinion.

Wow, did they know their 'why,' and their strong opinion certainly did not bring the peace and clarity that my heart needed.

What I discovered through this experience is that we can pick apart any opinion and create an entire argument that supports our own belief system no matter which stance one takes. We can even take out portions of scriptures to support our beliefs. Without knowing the context of when or why the scripture was written, we can so easily misunderstand what's being said and form a whole theology out of a few passages instead of looking at the whole picture. We need to make sure the theology lines up with the context of what was going on; the entirety of God's Word, and His character.

I was exhausted from the information overload that never solidified in my heart what's true and right about my God.

We have a culture with access to an influx of information, but what we truly need is the wisdom of God activated in our lives. The Bible says if we need wisdom, ask Him.

> *If any of you lacks wisdom, you should ask God, who gives generously to all without finding fault, and it will be given to you.*
> *— James 1:5 (NIV)*

So, I did!

I simply ran to Jesus with my questions, dove headfirst into the Word, invited the Holy Spirit to open my eyes and ears to His Truth so that I could stand firmly in what He says no matter what!

It was through my unhindered childlike approach that gave the Holy Spirit room to move through His Word, giving me understanding to my question. This posture became yet another major turning point in my walk with Him. This is what I do with every controversial situation and opinion that gets brought to my attention from world situations, personal situations, Christian beliefs that get presented to me, and all my questions that arise.

HIS WORD *is* the lamp unto my feet and what lights up my path, so I know which way to go in all things, at all times!

We have A CULTURE WITH ACCESS TO AN INFLUX OF INFORMATION, BUT WHAT WE TRULY NEED IS THE WISDOM OF GOD ACTIVATED IN OUR LIVES.

> *I gain understanding from Your precepts; therefore I hate every wrong path. Your Word is a lamp for my feet, a light on my path. — Psalm 119:104-105 (NIV)*

Do you see the childlike nature in letting God's Word be the pathway to our understanding and how it requires a childlike approach, believing that He will guide us in all things at all times?

Running directly to God is the key to receiving wisdom and understanding that smashes the borders of our humanistic thinking, unlocking the Kingdom of Heaven in our lives here and now.

Jesus paid for us to have this personal and direct relationship with the Father, the Son, and the Holy Spirit. Call me crazy, but Jesus did not die on the Cross for you and me to go through others to gain an understanding of Him. Jesus wants us to have direct access to God's presence, His wisdom, and His Power through our personal relationship with Him.

I can't say that I was consciously aware of my decisions to run directly to God in this way, but looking back I can clearly see what was happening, and now I can lead others to experience the same. My head was truly out of the way. My hunger for God came from a place of total surrender and unlocked a simple yet powerful desire to just go to Him. I didn't even give myself time to talk myself out of believing that I could run to Him with my questions.

Did you catch that?

Do you ever talk yourself out of believing you can run to Him with everything?

It's easy to allow emotions and thoughts, like fear, disbelief, doubt, our feelings of trusting our own abilities over yielding to God, or theological arguments that justify or rationalize our way out of going to Him for everything. There are endless reasons that we think and believe that are blocking us from even considering going to God.

Insert the thought that comes to mind that prevents you from wholeheartedly going to Him with everything, or maybe you don't even consider Him because you believe you can figure it all out.

We are subconsciously arguing with God's Word all the time. Our human understanding kicks in, we overthink everything, and the childlike nature of just believing God at

Running directly TO GOD IS THE KEY TO RECEIVING WISDOM AND UNDERSTANDING THAT SMASHES THE BORDERS OF OUR HUMANISTIC THINKING, UNLOCKING THE KINGDOM OF HEAVEN IN OUR LIVES HERE AND NOW.

His Word continues to be our internal struggle. When our understanding of God through human resources, and our own experiences (or lack thereof), has put parameters on the Holy Spirit in our lives, our belief system is formed around what we can explain rather than faith, which goes beyond the borders of human reasoning.

God wants us to grab His hand in every aspect of life and believe He's got us!

A child doesn't think twice about going to his or her parents for whatever they need.

When a child falls, they know their parents will pick them up.

When a child is hungry, they go to their parents to be fed.

When a child has a question, they ask, believing their parents have the answer.

This is the simplistic way that God desires us to approach Him.

Transformation happens when our relationship with God goes from our head to our heart. We can ask the Holy Spirit to give us eyes to see and ears to hear as we read the Bible, giving Him permission to shatter any belief systems that are in contradiction to His Truth. God wants us to approach His Word with the desire to get to know Him as if we are reading personal letters from His heart to ours, allowing the Holy Spirit to speak directly to us.

Most often we resort to finding an understanding of Him through our head, but that method puts the bigness of God in a box. Head knowledge limits Him from moving powerfully in our lives.

How does head knowledge limit Him?

Isn't He God?

Can't He do whatever He wants?

Well, yes to all of that and also no.

He is God, and He can move as He wills, but as far as experiencing the many facets of God and activating the supernatural in our lives, our belief system has to be built around an infinite God, which requires activation of faith in a childlike manner, believing Him at His Word. Remember faith is not in seeing, but in hearing and believing the hope we have in Him.

> *Now faith is confidence in what we hope for and assurance about what we do not see.* — *Hebrews 11:1 (NIV)*

Then, as we read God's Word, it reveals the barriers we put up in our hearts and minds so we can begin to undo belief systems that are inferior to God's Kingdom. From there, we have to get "self" out (human understanding) in order to receive all that Jesus paid for, and what we have access to through His Spirit.

If we are reading our Bibles regularly and nothing comes in that creates a severing of our flesh and spirit, then are we really reading through God's Spirit to the point where it unlocks something inside of us, launching us into a greater freedom?

Or are we just reading to read, without going to God to dialogue with Him about what we are reading, or without inviting the Holy Spirit to help us activate the life that we have been offered?

God wants us TO APPROACH HIS WORD WITH THE DESIRE TO GET TO KNOW HIM AS IF WE ARE READING PERSONAL LETTERS FROM HIS HEART TO OURS, ALLOWING THE HOLY SPIRIT TO SPEAK DIRECTLY TO US.

> *For the Word of God is alive and active. Sharper than any double-edged sword, it penetrates even to dividing soul and spirit, joints and marrow; it judges the thoughts and attitudes of the heart.* — *Hebrews 4:12 (NIV)*

As we read the Word of God, there should be a tangible exchange going on inside of us that causes us to let go of our feelings, fleshly desires, and beliefs until our human reasoning is shattered. Then we invite God to do the impossible in us and through us, opening us up to a whole new realm of possibilities of life in the Spirit. This life in the Spirit is the key to living in total freedom and victory in every aspect of our life and it's meant to be activated daily.

A Spirit-led lifestyle reveals the glory of God in us, and through us, becoming living testimonies to the world around us!

When we have ears to hear and eyes to see, scripture after scripture will begin to unlock in us as we spend time in the Word of God. If we do not renew our minds through God's Word and become teachable, our humanistic belief system puts parameters on God, limiting His ability to move in our lives.

Here are the passages that jumped out at me several years ago during one of my quiet times in the Word:

> He returned to Nazareth, His hometown. When He taught there in the synagogue, everyone was amazed and said, "Where does He get this wisdom and the power to do miracles?" Then they scoffed, "He's just the carpenter's son, and we know Mary, His mother, and His brothers—James, Joseph, Simon, and Judas. All His sisters live right here among us. Where did He learn all these things?" And they were deeply offended and refused to believe in Him. Then Jesus told them, "A prophet is honored everywhere except in His own hometown and among His own family." And so He did only a few miracles there because of their unbelief. — Matthew 13:54-58 (NLT)

We can read these passages and picture the time and the push back Jesus received based on His earthly family, or emphasize the part about a prophet not being received in their own hometown.

Totally fine, but let's take a look from another perspective.

At first, they were amazed by His wisdom and the miracles they witnessed, and then human reasoning took over. From there, doubt and disbelief set in, blocking the fullness of Jesus' ministry in that particular region. The Bible literally says He could only do a few miracles *because* of their unbelief. It's not Jesus who is limited; it's our human reasoning that talks us out of just believing.

Unbelief blocks God from moving powerfully in our lives, today. These passages should send alarms of warning to our system! We can

> If we do not RENEW OUR MINDS THROUGH GOD'S WORD AND BECOME TEACHABLE, OUR HUMANISTIC BELIEF SYSTEM PUTS PARAMETERS ON GOD, LIMITING HIS ABILITY TO MOVE IN OUR LIVES.

literally block the power and presence of the Holy Spirit from being tangibly effective in our lives every single day with human reasoning and unbelief. The barrier is never on God's end. It's on ours. Human reasoning can feel intellectual, but consider becoming "foolish" for a moment.

> *Stop deceiving yourselves. If you think you are wise by this world's standards, you need to become a fool to be truly wise. For the wisdom of this world is foolishness to God. As the Scriptures say, "He traps the wise in the snare of their own cleverness." And again, "The Lord knows the thoughts of the wise; He knows they are worthless."*
> *— 1 Corinthians 3:18-20 (NLT)*

When my husband and I were dating, he secretly believed he was the educated one, and I was the one who, well, just didn't have the same type of edumacation as he.

I won't go as far in saying that he thought I was dumb because I wasn't degreed up like him, but I will say that I had to remind him that I was a different kind of smart, HA!

After we got married, more of his secret thoughts about himself, and how he thought he knew more than me based on his memorization and training would leak out.

Now, let me clarify a few things so you know how I genuinely feel about my God-given partner:

> IT'S NOT JESUS WHO IS LIMITED; IT'S OUR HUMAN REASONING THAT TALKS US OUT OF JUST BELIEVING.

a. He is very smart! He has a degree in chemistry, and if there is anyone who can figure out any technical issues I may be having, he is my go-to guy. If my kids need help in anything math or science, he's the man! I actually prayed for a husband who could help in those areas in hopes of bringing balance to my home with my kids.

b. His education and degree are because God gave him an incredible mind that retains information, and through God's design, my husband provides for our family, which enables me to stay home with our kids and serve in full-time ministry. Which was exactly my heart's deepest desire!

c. If I need the address of a scripture (because my brain can be forgetful in this department), and if I don't want to Google search (refer back to "b" with his mind that retains information), I ask him. God's Word is rooted in my heart, and I can quote scriptures like nobody's business (it's literally ingrained in me), but recounting the actual address in the Bible is definitely not my strong suit. Again, he's my go-to guy!

I could keep going but I'll stop there. I just wanted to make it clear he is very smart, and I rely on his brain quite often!

Now back to some stories about how I wrecked his brain with my "foolishness." I'm like the little wrecking ball to his hard-wired thinking he didn't know he needed, ha ha! I say little because although I am five-foot-seven and he is slightly over six-foot-six, his height next to mine makes me look like a tiny person.

Oh, the theological debates that would stir.

For the record, I do not like to debate. I would have failed debate in college big time!

If I had gone to college.

My husband on the other hand ... well, let's just say debating comes fairly naturally to him.

I'll never forget one of our drives to his company Christmas party. Although I did forget the actual passages this conversation was referring to, I will never forget the way the Holy Spirit helped me navigate this conversation that quite honestly was putting knots in my stomach!

Side note: when conversations give me knots in my stomach, it's typically because I am feeling a spirit of pride operating through a person. I've learned this over time. Identifying what I'm feeling and recognizing the spiritual battle, helps me know to take a quiet spiritual stance in order to have a Holy Spirit-guided conversation. When we take our God-given authority in the spirit realm, we pave the way for the Holy Spirit to move powerfully through hard conversations.

We had gotten away for the night and were on our drive to join some Christmas festivities. Somehow, I got looped into a "conversation" (insert eye roll here) about a particular passage in the Bible. He quoted the passage, the address and went on to firmly explain to me what it means.

I gently disagreed.

Oh boy . . . what "can" did I just open?!

He went on, much firmer with his stance. Rather than countering his noticeably confident belief, I prayed quietly and invited the Holy Spirit to join in this conversation and silenced the religious spirit and spirit of pride that was at work in his life.

I replied, "Well, I would have to read it again and see what was actually going on to remind myself of this. Let me look it up."

He quickly let me know he didn't need to hear it again because he already knew what it said.

Geesh! He's a tough cookie!

I said, "I know, but could I read it out loud anyway?"

The Holy Spirit had already revealed to me that he was believing through a religious mindset and wrong belief system. I didn't wait for his reply. I had already looked the scripture up in my Bible app and began to read. While I was reading, I was simultaneously asking the Holy Spirit to open his spiritual eyes and ears to hear and receive Truth. I read the familiar passages, and what followed was a moment of silence. I waited and then gently explained what I felt the particular passages were revealing.

Peace filled the car, and our conversation went from heated debate (on his end) to revelation through the power and presence of the Holy Spirit. My husband was in awe of the treasure he heard through God's Word that he had never understood before. The familiar passage that he had memorized and was taught by man to mean one thing, was taking on a truer meaning in his heart.

The Holy Spirit was moving, setting him free from the chains of a religious belief system that was blocking him from experiencing the presence of God and producing fruit in his life. His "works" mentality caused him to read the Bible through that lens, and his interpretation of how he would read put blocks and barriers in his relationship with God.

> *Rather than* COUNTERING HIS NOTICEABLY CONFIDENT BELIEF, I PRAYED QUIETLY AND INVITED THE HOLY SPIRIT TO JOIN IN THIS CONVERSATION AND SILENCED THE RELIGIOUS SPIRIT AND SPIRIT OF PRIDE THAT WAS AT WORK IN HIS LIFE.

We talked about memorizing the scriptures versus reading the Bible through the Holy Spirit and allowing Him to be our Teacher. My husband admitted that he had never understood these passages in the way I had explained, and felt he had been blinded this whole time. This is the work of a religious spirit. It blinds us from hearing God's Word through the Holy Spirit and then pride sets in, convincing us that we know more because of our works and memorization, which leads us to pride in what we know. This is a common belief system that affects the body of Christ more often than we realize.

This one conversation led to many more and became the key to removing the barriers of his religious mindset, meeting a deep longing in his heart to experience the power and presence of the Holy Spirit.

My childlike approach to Jesus and walking this life with Him hand in hand appealed to my husband, but he didn't have words for what he felt. He slowly began to share with me that when he met me he thought I was crazy (true story), yet there was something different about me. I was filled with joy and an excitement for life, and he didn't understand how I was so happy. I was a single mom with four kids from a painful marriage and divorce. My children's father moved out of state before our divorce was final, started a new life apart from his kids, and I was left to rebuild from nothing.

I mean, I was sleeping on a couch because I did not have a bedroom, raising four kids completely on my own, had an old suburban with broken AC, and an average of thirty-five cents (on a good day) in my bank account.

How can I possibly be okay?!

My husband knew this part of my story as we got to know each other. He didn't understand how I was so strong, confident . . . and full of JOY!

Aside from desiring a husband and feeling challenged at times, I was excited about life. I was dreaming with God daily and walking in step with Him. He had given me incredible visions that I believed were coming, and my childlike zeal for life radiated out of me.

Basically, I confused the heck out of him! It still makes me "LOL" (laugh out loud) to think about it. I genuinely love the shock factor.

This is life in the Spirit!

This is the ripple effect of what naturally exudes from us when we are living in step with the power and presence of God. We don't have to try to be anything or pound Bibles down anyone's throat because what we carry is infectious to those around us.

My husband's church background was legalistic. The work of the Holy Spirit was not something that was talked about; actually, it was basically taught against in many ways. His relationship with God was all about "doing" the right thing and then getting publicly shamed if anyone fell short. His church experience was the definition of checklist Christianity to the extreme! My husband secretly carried a heavy pressure to perform. He had never understood the peace and joy that we have access to through Jesus. It was all about obtaining it somehow through accomplishments, yet no matter what, he had never experienced true peace and joy. He loves God, accomplished quite a bit in his life, but he had never experienced this life the Bible describes.

Then, I enter the scene.

Single mom.

Sleeps on a couch.

Struggling financially and barely breaking even.

I was totally filled with a sense of peace and joy that could not be explained through my life circumstances. My life and words lined up with the Word of God without even trying. I was living in a freedom and joy that he could not explain. He scratched his head often and just couldn't figure me out, yet he was secretly attracted to something he knew was missing in his life. The Holy Spirit was at work from day one, undoing complicated Christianity, drawing him to desire something he didn't know was available but hungered for. I was living in the rhythm of life with Jesus, and what was naturally flowing out of me was drawing him in.

As we did life together, the difference between how we navigate through life became very clear. I'm the "faith girl" and my husband is the "spreadsheets-and-facts guy." As my track record in faith proved more accurate than his spreadsheets and facts, he slowly began to realize he was not really living by faith. It required faith to come to Jesus, but a faith walk was not activated in his life. He was missing this facet of God. He knew *of* Him through memorization and head knowledge, but he didn't *know* Him on an intimate and personal level.

My husband witnessed a simplicity of faith where God had room to speak to me. I was fully aware of God's voice and presence in my life because of my alone time with Him and diving into His Word daily.

Getting into God's presence and learning His voice was a practice that was taught against in his church, yet he was witnessing firsthand something powerfully real between me and the Holy Spirit that he couldn't argue away. The power of my testimony and what he was witnessing began to unlock his spiritual blindness.

One morning I woke up from a prophetic dream (a dream from God) where there was a for sale sign in our yard. We had rented this home for a few years, and we were finally in a position to buy. This just so happened to be the same morning we were supposed to be signing contracts to buy another home a few streets over from the one we were renting. One that I was not excited about at all. It was a safe move and priced right. With human wisdom, it just made sense.

Quick back story on the rental we lived in: God led us to this home. Prior to that last move, all doors were closing for us, and our lease was coming to an end. We were scrambling to find a house for our family of seven to move into. My concern was knowing we would be moving one more time when we were ready to buy, and I wanted to keep my kids in the same area. They had moved so many times and never experienced living in one spot for more than a year. They were constantly uprooted. My desire was to give them a stable place to finish out their childhood. I surrendered it to God, knowing He cared more than I did. It wasn't so much about clinging to worldly things as it was more a concern that my kids had really gone through more than their fair share of instability because of my previous marriage. I asked God to guide us, and while I was nervous with every door closing, I had peace that God had a house prepared for us.

One day, I got a call from my husband, who was out of town on business, telling me to call and schedule an appointment to see this particular house that was up for rent. So, I did, but I wasn't excited about it.

Okay, the truth?

I was grumbling to myself the whole drive thinking this would be a stupid move!

> As my track record in faith proved more accurate than his spreadsheets and facts, he slowly began to realize he was not really living by faith.

I turned on a road that led up a long hill toward the housing community. I looked around and was pleasantly surprised by the area. My interest piqued and I gave myself a quick attitude adjustment!

The community was really pretty.

I turned onto the street toward the rental house and saw the realtor outside waiting for me. We walked into the house and took the downstairs tour. There was nothing spectacular inside . . . your normal carpet, tiled kitchen with white tile and grout countertops, but wait! There's a room down here that the description didn't mention! I asked the realtor if this was a fourth bedroom, but after seeing that there was no closet, she said it was a den or office. I was starting to feel giddy inside but wanted to keep that "chill vibe," you know?

Then, we made our way up the stairs to find five more bedrooms! This listing said four bedrooms, but it actually had five plus an office. I walked into the master bedroom to find a sliding glass door and a deck that overlooked the city and beyond. I had to hide my tears from the realtor.

The view overwhelmed me.

I couldn't believe this gem!

Once we moved in, there was more to be discovered. Hot air balloons would fill the sky every weekend, taking me back to my childhood memories of balloons launching from vacant land near my home. My children's school was within walking distance and right next to a park. Only God knew these were the secret seemingly small desires of my heart. This was home, and I knew God had led us there.

Back to the morning of my dream.

Now that you know the backstory of this rental property, you can understand why leaving to buy a home wasn't the easiest. We grew to love our neighbors, our community, and obviously, this home holds a special place to me personally because God met the secret desires of my heart. Being in a position to buy and finding a home for sale made sense. It was the next common-sense decision to make for our family. My dream caused me to ask my husband to put the contract signing on hold.

I called my husband, who was away, and told him about my dream. I told him we couldn't buy this other home until we contacted the owner of our rental and asked him if we could buy it.

Facts guy: "WHAAAAAAT?!? Are you kidding me right now? We are scheduled to sign on the house this morning! You can't just ask to buy a house that's not for sale!"

Faith girl: "Why not?"

Clearly, my husband was not too thrilled with my potential course change. Ha! Spreadsheets-and-facts guy was getting challenged.

At this point, he still wasn't totally used to me and my inner-hippie (seemingly childish) ways and wasn't so quick to jump on my faith adventure.

Shoot . . . he doesn't do well if I say I'm making one thing for dinner and then last-minute change to something else.

For me, I was so used to course changes that led to experiencing the bigness of God, AND I have had YEARS of dreams that have given me strategy in life as well as warned me of things to come to prepare me. So, to me, this was just another day in rhythm with the Holy Spirit. And I wanted to find out if this dream was telling me if there is a possibility to buy this house!

I pushed and told him my desire to stay and that I couldn't move without knowing. If it's a no, okay. I can live with knowing that we at least asked.

My husband reluctantly called the owner, and it was a quick no. After my husband relayed the message to me, I remembered a conversation I had with the owner's wife that gave me a bit more insight into their current living situation (us ladies, we talk!), and I knew we might have an opportunity to at least have them think about it a bit more before they so quickly rejected our proposal to buy from them.

My husband called back with the added thoughts and information which caused the owner to pause and invite his wife into the conversation.

Smart man. Wink-wink.

They came back to us with a firm number based on what they felt the home was worth and right away another conversation that I had with a local realtor came back to the forefront of my mind along with crazy peace that this was the right decision for us, and we should go for it!

No appraisal at this point, just the peace that was beyond human understanding that God was opening a door for us to stay in our home. We started with a verbal agreement and then proceeded through the proper steps to purchase our new home. God had done a miracle in my husband's heart simultaneously because he does not agree to these faith things at all, EVER!

Not at this point anyway. We've (he's) grown over the years.

At this point. HE STILL WASN'T TOTALLY USED TO ME AND MY INNER-HIPPIE (SEEMINGLY CHILDISH) WAYS AND WASN'T SO QUICK TO JUMP ON MY FAITH ADVENTURE.

We moved forward with our home purchase, and, in the process, the appraisal came back that this house was worth $15,000 higher than what we agreed to buy it for.

You better believe I broke out the Kid 'n Play (dance)!

Takin' it back to the old school, cuz imma old fool ... Okay. I'll stop now.

This is where my faith took my husband's need for the numbers to check out first (human understanding) beyond what he had ever experienced before. He was worried about the numbers. God gave me a dream (supernatural), and with prayer and God's guidance, we chose to act on it.

Now, please, this is not a formula to follow to buy your dream home.

Sometimes God has us sell our belongings to follow Him, and other times He provides something else with a different vision in mind.

We strongly believe that God has planted us in this neighborhood to be a light, and God provided a way for us to stay. We have a deep love for the families in this neighborhood, and it just continues to deepen as we do life with them and all the kids we have the honor to watch grow up and love on. This isn't just a house. It's our family ministry.

It's by faith that we surrender our ways for His as He supernaturally guides each one of us.

How many of us are not paying attention to course changes because we trust ourselves, our limited wisdom and understanding rather than believing that God is guiding us from a much larger vantage point? This life that we have been invited into is incredible if we would just lean in and trust Him.

Our united faith move with our home was also a game-changer for our marriage in the long run; however, it took some work to undo the residual effect on this next decision I'm about to share.

My husband had invested in timeshare property before he met me, which enables us to take family vacations each year with all of the kids. We stay local because flying with our family size would break the bank real quick, but we have our two faves that are just hop-in-the-car-and-get-there kind of places we look forward to each year.

My husband and I were attending a breakfast meeting where the timeshare company gave us all the updated info and new properties all over the world when they started talking about a system we would need to upgrade to. Now, we have been to meetings for years, and despite what you may have heard about timeshares, they actually never try to sell us something that's a lie. They are always very kind and usually tell us we don't need anything because of my husband's prior status, and they move us out of the meeting quickly with our info and gift card for listening to their spiel. Score!

It's by faith THAT WE SURRENDER OUR WAYS FOR HIS AS HE SUPERNATURALLY GUIDES EACH ONE OF US.

However, this particular meeting was hugely different! As the woman continued to talk about the upgrade we needed and the cost, my stomach was in knots and I almost felt this push in the atmosphere that made me feel cloudy and dizzy. I have connected to this "feeling" and oftentimes it's revealing a spirit of manipulation at work.

These are the nudges we need to learn to discern so we can understand what the Holy Spirit is trying to show us, and what spirit is operating in each situation that arises. The Holy Spirit gives us prompts and nudges, checks in our spirit when something is off if we are paying attention, and from there we can make decisions by faith and not by sight.

It was also already way past the allotted time for this breakfast, and I was getting antsy!

I wanted to get back to our kids.

This was a family vacation.

Not a sit down, hang with a stranger who's telling us we need more than we already have.

I looked at my husband and told him I didn't think it was necessary. I'm happy with what we have. I was trying to be kind, meanwhile, alarms were going off in my spirit. She continued explaining why we needed this upgrade.

My husband and I ended up having a private moment where I shared with him this offer was a no for me. I didn't have peace. After that, my husband and I both agreed that we would not move forward with what this woman was saying. I excused myself to go back to the kids while my husband stayed to finish the meeting.

A long time passed and I thought it was odd my husband was still gone. I got a call from him, and he very firmly said he was filling out the paperwork and moving forward with the upgrade.

My stomach turned.

I reminded him that we agreed it would be a no. He interrupted and told me that I didn't understand what it is, we need it, and he's moving forward with the upgrade. The knots in my stomach intensified. I had absolutely no peace at all. I told him I didn't need to fully understand, my stomach is in knots, and I have no peace with this decision.

He didn't care.

The Holy Spirit GIVES US PROMPTS AND NUDGES, CHECKS IN OUR SPIRIT WHEN SOMETHING IS OFF IF WE ARE PAYING ATTENTION, AND FROM THERE WE CAN MAKE DECISIONS BY FAITH AND NOT BY SIGHT.

He was convinced I didn't know what I was talking about.

I'll give him that. I had no idea what this woman was trying to tell us. What she was saying didn't make sense to me at all, but the knots in my stomach were telling me something wasn't right. The only thing I had confidence in was that I know the difference between having peace with a decision and not.

This was a big fat, NOT!

I did feel a release to let him make the decision and not hold it against him. I didn't change my stance. I just wasn't going to argue or get mad at him for not listening to me. I knew God would take care of it. I've learned that I truly can trust God over man's humanness. He always works things together for our good.

Seriously you guys, trusting God in all situations is next-level peace!

This situation turned out to be the biggest blessing to our marriage because the no peace on my end turned out to be the indicator that this was truly a bad decision. It hurt us financially and later we found out the saleswoman lied about everything. After this situation occurred and we had to face the consequences of it, my husband no longer leaves me out of major family decisions. It was a huge turning point for both of us. He began to value me in a way that he hadn't before. The faith and discernment that I had developed through my childlike belief that I get to invite an all-knowing God into life's decisions while paying attention to the promptings of the Holy Spirit was the missing key in my husband's life. God used little me with big faith to come in and defy humanistic reasoning.

> *Remember, dear brothers and sisters, that few of you were wise in the world's eyes or powerful or wealthy when God called you. Instead, God chose things the world considers foolish in order to shame those who think they are wise. And He chose things that are powerless to shame those who are powerful.* — 1 Corinthians 1:26-27 (NLT)

This is not a slam against my husband.

This is a reality that many of my fellow brothers and sisters are living.

I get it . . . living by faith in every facet of life can be scary. Many struggle to invite God into all areas of their life and they miss out on life in the Spirit. Most have a stronger need to feel in control. This just reveals that the true struggle is that we don't fully trust God.

It's common to believe in the power and presence of the Holy Spirit but still have Him in a box that's left for a church or worship service, and never activate the reality that we get to do life with Him. God's presence and power are not just reserved for a Sunday church service—we wake up with Him; He is in us. Once I grasped this way of living, and this rhythm became my normal, I started making fewer wrong turns. In fact, I rarely make a turn without hearing His guidance. The times I do, I can feel the burden of life weigh over me, and I know I stepped out of His grace covering where life should be light and free.

Have you ever stopped and checked in with your own heart to see what's going on in your mind and the pit of your belly to see if you are living out of what Jesus says is yours through Him?

Are you filled with supernatural peace and joy without end?

Or are you living in turmoil with knots in your stomach and pressure on your chest?

Tell me, where in the Bible does it say that kind of living should be expected?

The Bible says that we will face trials but peace is ours through Jesus.

Do you have peace?

If not, why not?

> *God's presence* AND POWER ARE NOT JUST RESERVED FOR A SUNDAY CHURCH SERVICE—WE WAKE UP WITH HIM; HE IS IN US.

Maybe you've been trusting yourself through life, and not God. Maybe you've even convinced yourself that because you're a Christian and the Bible says God will never leave you nor forsake you, seeking His guidance in life is just not something you think about. Maybe you are gauging your comfort and successes outwardly instead of checking in with Him, living with a constant inner peace.

It's easy to convince ourselves that once we arrive at our ideal destination is when we'll be happy, so we don't even bother learning to walk in the joy that is available through Jesus before we hit our goal . . . or the vacation that we believe will give us a break so we can finally have some "peace." If that's wired into our belief system, then what happens when something in life blocks our forward motion? Most likely we become defeated and hopeless. We are running our race, leaving God in the dust instead of grabbing His hand and learning what it means to live in unforced rhythms of grace.

Remember what Jesus said?

> *"Are you tired? Worn out? Burned out on religion? Come to Me. Get away with Me and you'll recover your life. I'll show you how to take a real rest. Walk with Me and work with Me—watch how I do it. Learn the unforced rhythms of grace. I won't lay anything heavy or ill-fitting on you. Keep company with Me and you'll learn to live freely and lightly."* — Matthew 11:28-30 (MSG)

Our humanistic belief systems are hardwired in us, and it is up to us to shatter the strongholds in our minds and get our thinking lined up with a Kingdom mindset. We have to get into the Word and read it with fresh eyes and an open heart that is willing to receive and believe that we have full access to the abundant life that Jesus paid for here and now! We have to stop *deciding* what we have through Jesus and *learn* what we have through Him. We have to start taking God's Word in as if our life depended on it . . . which in reality, it does.

If God is the Creator of all things, and His Word unlocks all that we have in Him and through Him, including the most infallible life manual (the *only* infallible one) you will ever read, then we have to start believing God at His Word with childlike wonder.

The truth of the matter is, learning to receive like a child means we have to surrender and relinquish control in order for the Holy Spirit to move in us freely. Control is a false freedom that leads us straight to stress and constant anxiety, the complete opposite of what Jesus paid for us to live out of. Control leads to pride in our hearts that not only limits the work of the Holy Spirit in our lives, but also blocks the Word of God from penetrating our hearts.

You might be thinking, wait!

Aren't we supposed to be "self-controlled?"

Isn't that a fruit of the Spirit?

Yes, but it's something that is produced in us by the Holy Spirit, and it feels like peace even in the middle of the most overwhelming situations. Manufactured self-control that is not from the Spirit does not feel like peace in us and doesn't look like peace when our internal chaos that we are "controlling" accidentally leaks out.

Jus' sayin'.

Manufactured "self-control" does not set anyone free. It puts us in bondage to a life that is heavy, keeping us in the chains that Jesus freed us from. Self-control through the Holy Spirit does not have a need to control self, others, or our environment, but a manufactured one needs control over most areas of our lives

We have to STOP DECIDING WHAT WE HAVE THROUGH JESUS AND LEARN WHAT WE HAVE THROUGH HIM.

in order to feel at "peace." Mostly because what we feel on the inside is so chaotic that outside situations can easily send us over the edge. That kind of control is not the true and lasting peace from Jesus.

I have been assumed to be a "type-A" personality because of the self-control people have observed in me as well as the way my home is usually in order.

This is a false assumption.

I am a color-outside-of-the-lines, messy, emotional, record playing, candle lighting, dancing in an open field "hippy" who loves off-roading and getting lost in a daydream watching the clouds make animal shapes and absolutely hates structure of any kind.

Phew.

That was a mouth full!

Ask my mom what I was like growing up. She will vouch for this truth . . . so would all the stuff I could shove underneath my bed, the mountain I could pile in my closet, and the fifty plus candles and incense that would be burning in my room all at once as I jumped on my bed with my guitar listening to my thrift store record finds!

Over the years, what people have witnessed is not my need for control, but a childlike willingness to allow the Holy Spirit to reshape me, producing the tangible and obvious fruit that others can see. What has become an outward order is inner peace and freedom that is unbelievable! I still have many creative outlets that keep my God-woven free spirit alive, but the self-control and the orderly home is a genuine reflection of the inward work that the Holy Spirit has accomplished in me from spending time with Jesus in the secret place.

If we have to shove down what we are feeling inside in order to remain in control, painting a perfect picture of "righteousness" over an internal mess, then we are missing out on the chain-breaking freedom Jesus died for! Trying to have control over our emotions, or even trying to control others believing it will create an inner peace is a false freedom and a façade that keeps us in bondage, creating another negative ripple effect that will hinder our purification process, blocking true transformation.

If we buy into any kind of labels like: type-A, perfectionist, OCD, control freak, or on the flip-side—a procrastinator and gen-u-ine-messy-jessie (sorry if your name is Jessie, it rhymed)...whether good or bad, we subconsciously limit ourselves.

I am not a structured person by nature. My free spirit that likes to color outside the lines hated any type of order. I felt as if I was being crammed into a cage of human expectation. If I would've decided that my personality type—free-spirit who hated structure of all kinds and refused to be put in someone else's orderly box of "how-to"—is who I am, instead of growing in an area, I would limit myself from learning how to become more structured and orderly. This means I couldn't handle everything that God has put on my plate that I am responsible for today. I would be way too stressed out and all over the map! My outward order has nothing to do with a need for control and everything to do with learning how to manage the "little" in my small beginnings so that God could trust me with His more for my life.

Luke 16:10 was fused into me:

If you are faithful in little things, you will be faithful in large ones. But if you are dishonest in little things, you won't be honest with greater responsibilities. (NLT)

My inner-hippie ways that could cause me to not care about the things that God has placed in my life to care for, could've interrupted this newfound rhythm in a childlike response to learn and grow in all areas. I desired to be faithful in the little with integrity and honesty, believing that God would entrust me with more. Not that I had any crazy big vision for my life at the time when this scripture took root. The Holy Spirit would whisper these words to my heart while I was cleaning my house or taking care of my littles. This birthed a deeper desire to honor God with every area of my life. I genuinely put so much care and heart in my little apartment days, be-

If we have to SHOVE DOWN WHAT WE ARE FEELING INSIDE IN ORDER TO REMAIN IN CONTROL, PAINTING A PERFECT PICTURE OF "RIGHTEOUSNESS" OVER AN INTERNAL MESS, THEN WE ARE MISSING OUT ON THE CHAIN-BREAKING FREEDOM JESUS DIED FOR!

lieving God at His Word, that as I was faithful in the little, He could trust me with more responsibilities. Including the hidden places in my life that no one would ever see.

I got really good at closet cleaning and under-bed order!

I know this was a result of the cleaning that God was doing inside of me in all those hidden places of my heart. The inward work of the Holy Spirit began to show up in various places in my life.

I'm not saying this is the way it will look for all of us, so please don't use my story and create a checklist to measure yourself by.

Remember this is what we are undoing.

This is just my journey and what God was doing inside of me.

We have to stop trying to find "how-to" methods to get the result someone else got in their life and just learn to walk with Jesus in our own individual lives, trusting His plan for each of us. And He will transform us as He takes us from glory to glory, becoming more like Him in every area of our lives!

On the flip side, if your natural wiring is in order and structure, you will need to learn to be teachable and childlike in other ways in order to experience the inner freedom and peace that Jesus has for you, even in the midst of all your responsibilities. Oftentimes this natural wiring that has a structured and intentional flow through the day can't handle the life interruptions that can knock your itinerary off course, leading you to believe your day is now bad, and you are no longer experiencing peace. You are in turmoil because of the things that were out of your control. If your peace is determined by how smooth your day goes, you are not living with a teachable, childlike ability to receive the peace that transcends all understanding that you have access to all day every day. The need for order and control will keep you in chains to a life in opposition to what Jesus paid for. This will be one of your areas that requires growth in order to develop spiritual maturity, setting you free in greater ways.

It was 2010.

My divorce was final. My children's father had caused so much pain in my children's hearts, and I was left to undo the damage. My oldest, just barely ten, developed a hatred and bitterness, refusing to talk about her pain. She shut down but would have outbursts of anger and rebellion toward me that I knew was from her shoved-down insecurity and hurt.

I was exhausted.

I was responsible for four kids under ten, with very little income, and overwhelming emotions of my own. This was the season just before God called me into a season of rest with Him. One day I

> *We have to* STOP TRYING TO FIND "HOW-TO" METHODS TO GET THE RESULT SOMEONE ELSE GOT IN THEIR LIFE AND JUST LEARN TO WALK WITH JESUS IN OUR OWN INDIVIDUAL LIVES, TRUSTING HIS PLAN FOR EACH OF US.

felt like I was going to snap. I didn't have anything left to give. I was truly at the end of myself. I told my kids that mommy needed a time-out and begged them not to knock on my door. (Ok, I threatened that if they came in, I would have to apologize for some potentially bad behavior that I felt creeping up from inside of me!)

I shut myself in my room, face down on my floor, and told God I wasn't getting up from this place until He did something inside of me!

I know what I am supposed to have running through me as a child of God and a carrier of His Spirit, and I was not feeling any of that!

I don't know how long I laid there. I thought I felt a shift in me and believed I was in a good place because I prayed. I peeled myself off of the floor and slowly opened my door to see that one of my kids was standing there, waiting for me to re-enter life.

Nope.

The pressure of their demands came over me and I felt instant stress! This was my indicator that I did not have the Holy Spirit working through me. I was still in my flesh. The knots in my belly and the way I felt inside revealed this to me. I did not shove it down or convince myself that I prayed, "so I'm good" and press on.

I didn't feel good inside.

I shut the door once again and planted myself back in that face-down posture and began declaring what I have in Him. My prayer shifted from begging to declaring:

> *God, You are for me, You are in me, You are my ever-present help in times of need. Your Spirit is alive in me. In my weaknesses, Lord, You are strong! You are love, mercy, grace, peace, and in You, I have access to an overwhelming flood of joy without end. This is what is in me, and this is what will flow out of me! Lord, when my children see me, let them see You in me in ways I cannot manufacture. I am yielding fully to You, Holy Spirit, fill me with Your love and power! I am Yours, Your vessel. Have Your way in me.*

I wasn't trying to get myself "there." I was clothing myself in Truth until the peace that transcends all understanding enveloped me. Something broke over me. The heaviness of life that was pushing me down was lifted off of me and I got up with a lightness. I slowly opened my door and the voices of my children that I heard from the other room went from pressure to peace.

My circumstances didn't change.

My God changed me, and He used my circumstances to teach me how to climb into His lap and run to Him like a child who needs their Daddy!

One who will never leave me nor forsake me.

This is what we all have access to.

He is waiting there for each of us with open arms, bringing us His comfort that is beyond anything in this world (even better than ice cream, french fries, and chips, fill in the blank with your pleasures!) as He ministers to our weary soul. It's supernatural!

The supernatural access to God is the chain-breaking freedom that we have from our Heavenly Father and the abundant life that Jesus came to bring us. Anything that is in opposition to what the Bible says we have access to is the work of the enemy trying to steal us away from all we have in Him. Jesus came to pour out everything that our Heavenly Father has until we are overflowing with His peace, His presence, His power, His strength, His joy, and all the fruit of the Holy Spirit until all of Him is running freely in us and through us.

> *"A thief has only one thing in mind—he wants to steal, slaughter, and destroy. But I have come to give you everything in abundance, more than you expect—life in its fullness until you overflow!"*
> *—John 10:10 (TPT)*

As we relinquish our need to manufacture self-control, fully surrender to Him like a child to their Daddy, believing Him at His Word, removing the barriers and independent belief systems that we have built in our hearts and minds, nothing we will ever face in this life will have the ability to take us down. Because when we read His Word, something in us unlocks and we are not just reading to read, but rather reading from a teachable, childlike place to know what is rightfully ours from our Father in Heaven.

My God changed me, and He used my circumstances to teach me how to climb into His lap and run to Him like a child who needs their Daddy!

Much of our Christian culture is under the impression that we need to be taught in full accuracy about the Bible and encourages us to spend more time learning under people or reading books and devotionals instead of sitting at the feet of Jesus, opening our own Bible. There's a belief that reading others' work and written books is "devotional" time with Him, but if we are truly honest with ourselves, inside, we are still hungry.

Don't get me wrong.

Books and devotionals are great!

I'm an avid reader and clearly I write books, too . . . one of which just so happens to be in your hands. But as you read testimonies, books, and devotionals because of someone elses time with Jesus, it should stir a hunger in you to experience God in your own personal way by going directly to Him. Don't settle for the crumbs of my time or anyone else's time with Jesus. You will starve and never be fully satisfied. You will never experience what it means to have your cup running over from the Living Water Himself who satisfies and quenches the thirst of our souls.

> *"All you thirsty ones, come to Me! Come to Me and drink! Believe in Me so that rivers of living water will burst out from within you,*

> *flowing from your innermost being, just like the Scripture says!"*
> *— John 7:37 [b]-38 (TPT)*

We have access to a well of life-giving water without end when we run unabandoned into the arms of our Heavenly Father.

Books and devotionals should never be a replacement for diving into the Word of God for ourselves, spending time with Jesus, inviting His Spirit to teach us, breaking us free of any strongholds in our minds that are hindering our life with Him. The Holy Spirit is the ultimate Teacher. Like a child, we can trust Him to show us Truth.

> *But you have received the Holy Spirit, and He lives within you, so you don't need anyone to teach you what is true. For the Spirit teaches you everything you need to know, and what He teaches is true—it is not a lie. So just as He has taught you, remain in fellowship with Christ. — 1 John 2:27 (NLT)*

This is what it looks like to become teachable and childlike in order to receive the Kingdom of Heaven here and now.

There is a cry in all of our hearts that needs to know God in this way. It's by design that we have a need for Him as Father.

> *The Spirit you received does not make you slaves, so that you live in fear again; rather, the Spirit you received brought about your adoption to sonship. And by Him we cry, "Abba, Father."*
> *— Romans 8:15 (NIV)*

Jesus was fully aware of what would prevent us from receiving the Kingdom of Heaven . . . He called out the religious, the prideful, unbelief, and those who thought they had it all figured out and told them it would require a childlike heart.

We have ACCESS TO A WELL OF LIFE-GIVING WATER WITHOUT END WHEN WE RUN UNABANDONED INTO THE ARMS OF OUR HEAVENLY FATHER.

If we're honest with ourselves, we may find pride and an independent spirit has prevented us from running to Him unabandoned and without restraint. It's up to us to ask the Holy Spirit to help us identify what the block is so that we can remove all the barriers in our heart and mind, and learn what it means to humble ourselves and receive like a child.

> *So anyone who becomes as humble as this little child is the greatest in the Kingdom of Heaven.* — Matthew 18:4 (NLT)

Run to Him with a childlike wonder and learn the rhythm of His heart.

Chapter Four
Restored Mind

The first three chapters were foundational in taking us deeper into our faith walk and relationship with Jesus. We talked a lot about self-awareness, human understanding, and how those perspectives hinder us from the childlike simplicity of just believing and receiving all Jesus has invited us into.

In this chapter, we will identify what may be blocking you from receiving some of the things written. After reading this chapter, you may want to go back to some of those places where you became defensive, confused, and/or questioned what I was relaying. Journal through them and allow the Holy Spirit to bring you revelation and breakthrough!

While it's easier to shut down when a disagreement stirs in your mind, instead take the time to pause and reflect. You may find that God wants to bring breakthrough to you in a specific area, undoing any and all forms of complicated Christianity. Remember, God wants to shatter our humanistic thinking, setting us free in greater measures! He wants to take us beyond the borders of our human understanding. Let's be open to receiving more of what He has for each one of us.

Now that we are totally aware of our awareness (HA HA! That made me laugh typing that), I want to throw a curveball and point out an area where awareness is almost completely non-existent and has blocked us from recognizing the driving force that determines everything we believe and how we respond in life. As a result, we are not experiencing the fullness of what Jesus paid for.

It's our mind and thought-life.

Before we dive into this topic of conversation, I would like to remind you, just like I already have, but it's worth repeating: All of us are on a personal journey with Jesus. Each one with varying life experiences, traumas, and hurts. I've had my fair share of heartbreaking experiences and life continues to rock me. I am no stranger to overwhelming pain. I'm also a living testimony of the healing nature of our big and mighty God. This includes the healing work He has done in my mind and miraculously in others whom I know personally. With that being said, God cares deeply for the brokenness in our minds just as much as He cares for the hurt in our hearts and our spiritual growth. He wants to minister and heal each of our hurts brought on by life.

This chapter is not meant to feel like a "do more in order to receive," which so often becomes the translation when we are broken and hurting, conditioned to live by the checklist. That belief will only lead to crazy frustration.

I know.

I've experienced this push from my church family in my most vulnerable seasons.

The "here's what you should do" doesn't always help; it can deepen the hurt. This entire book is about breaking the negative cycles and the wrong ripple effects that checklist-Christianity has created, showing us how we've been blocked from experiencing the love, power, and healing nature of Jesus by simply going to Him with everything, including our mental health.

Now, keep in mind, there is a "His part" and "our part" but when we do our part, we are met with His supernatural strength and healing touch as we remain connected to Him.

Please know the heart I am coming from as we discuss some of the major mind-barriers. I'm not saying you need to do more. I'm encouraging you to *believe for more*, and out of this believing mindset, you will receive more healing and greater breakthroughs.

Our minds need the healing touch of Jesus, and when we turn to Him, He meets us.

While I acknowledge that there are therapists, and various communities of support that can help us identify what's going on in our minds, and how life-hurts and traumas can have a hugely negative impact on our lives, we are going to learn to take our faith walk deeper, by accessing the power and presence of the Holy Spirit. Our communities of support are good, but they cannot heal us, and we cannot heal ourselves. Only Jesus has the power to heal and restore minds.

> I'm encouraging YOU TO BELIEVE FOR MORE, AND OUT OF THIS BELIEVING MINDSET, YOU WILL RECEIVE MORE HEALING AND GREATER BREAKTHROUGHS.

Do you ever experience flashes of past scenarios that interrupt your daily life, instantly taking you back to a painful or negative memory? Jesus can heal that part of your brain that has stored the traumatic moment and take that jarring sting away.

Do you have flashes of past sexual relationships, or did you struggle with porn, opening yourself up to images that you can't blink away? Jesus can remove them from your mind.

Have you been diagnosed with a mental illness that is causing you to struggle in your daily life from past hurts and traumas? Jesus can meet you in the brokenness of your mind and take you on a journey to restoration.

What's going on in your mind that is leaving you in a head-war, confusion, frustration, bound with worry and fear? You have access to a sound mind that will lead you to the peace that transcends human understanding.

Trauma, life stressors, and wounds from our experiences can trigger the most intense panic attacks that require divine intervention from our Healer. Jesus wants to come into every broken place in our hearts and minds, including all the residual effects of life's overwhelming experiences. We don't have to do this in our own strength, but it will require partnering with Him in ways that may feel impossible. Especially when flashes of past scenarios are running through our minds and they are coming in sharp, fast, even creating physical pain. We can bring these painful moments to Jesus and ask for His help. With Him, all things are possible.

My ex-husband would pin me against the bed or wall with both of his hands around my neck.

He dragged me down the stairs one night by my arm and hair, and on another occasion, he pinned me on the stairs with his bare hands, crushing several of my ribs. I still have pain in my chest from that particular night.

When I was going through the divorce, I would get nightmares of him coming back, and life scenarios would trigger flashes that would send me into an intense panic. I struggled going out on my daily runs, in fear I would see him driving down the road, or felt instant panic when my phone would ring, wondering if it was him calling to cuss me out for some unknown reason.

I felt tormented when random scenes of his raging fits came flooding to the forefront of my mind, interrupting the newfound peace in our home. I even felt panicked if one of my kids came up behind me and wrapped their little arms around my neck for a hug, sending me back to those scary nights where he would put his hands around my neck and pin me to the wall.

I didn't just go through a grieving process after my divorce.

I needed Jesus to heal my mind from the trauma.

Every time I would experience these triggers and flashes, I would bring that memory before Jesus, inviting Him into those painful moments, and He healed them. One by one, layer by layer, those scary flashes from my past no longer carry the power to interrupt my current daily life.

They are gone.

So are all of my other past triggers that created panic or an anxious feeling. Jesus has restored my mind, and He continues to every time I experience something painfully overwhelming in my life.

When our minds need the healing touch of Jesus, not only do we feel the pain of the current situation, but if there are past situations that have traumatized us, those incidents can take us all the way back to that initial bad experience in our current pain, intensifying it. Sometimes the memory is so intense, we completely shut down.

When past traumas surface, we can use these opportunities to go to Jesus, invite Him into that memory, and ask Him to heal our mind until those past flashes no longer invade our present life. Sometimes the healing happens all at once and sometimes the healing is a process of becoming consciously aware, inviting Jesus into the memory, or feeling, each time something surfaces until those triggers are gone.

Oftentimes what launches complete healing is forgiving and releasing a particular person who harmed us. I'm not going to dive into the topic of forgiveness, but just note, forgiving and releasing someone into God's hands does not mean the person who wronged us is safe to be reconciled to.

> *Every Time* I WOULD EXPERIENCE THESE TRIGGERS AND FLASHES, I WOULD BRING THAT MEMORY BEFORE JESUS, INVITING HIM INTO THOSE PAINFUL MOMENTS AND HE HEALED THEM.

Forgiveness and reconciliation are two different processes, so know when I say forgive and release, I am not saying to throw your pearls to a pig—

> *"Don't throw your pearls to pigs! They will trample the pearls, then turn and attack you."* — Matthew 7:6 [b] (NLT)

I'll just leave that there.

I strongly encourage you to visit every single painful memory as the Holy Spirit highlights them and bring each to our Divine Healer. Here's the beauty of bringing each one to Him: you don't have to do the digging. Life will bring to the surface a hurt that still carries the sting, and through this process, it's an invitation to bring it to Jesus.

That's our part; we have to bring our pain to Him. We don't have to shove our pain back down, try to cope, self-talk our way out of it, or manage through it. We just bring it to Jesus and invite Him to do His healing work inside those broken places. This process frees us up so that our minds are clearer, as we learn to replace all the old thought patterns with our new ones according to God's Word and begin to live with a renewed mind. Until we understand that God wants to fully restore

> Life will bring to the surface a hurt that still carries the sting, and through this process, it's an invitation to bring it to Jesus.

our mind, we live bound with triggers, strongholds, and belief systems that are in opposition to God's Word.

If a stronghold is in place, we struggle to believe God at His Word. We stay bound by old or wrong beliefs, feelings and thought patterns because that stronghold in our mind won't let God's Truth penetrate. This could be a wide range of thoughts and belief systems from what we think, feel, and believe about ourselves, others, God, or circumstances. We can ask the Holy Spirit to give us eyes to see and ears to hear where we have a gap between God's Truth and our belief system that is costing us the ability to live from a place of total healing and victory.

Have you ever wondered why you have areas in your life that conflict with what God says is available?

Maybe you don't even realize it.

Most of the people that I have come alongside through ministry and coaching, even casual conversations, do not connect with this reality. Not only that, if I point them to a scripture, many will have a rebuttal to explain why they cannot have what's available to them. This reveals a stronghold in their mind. If we do not identify the stronghold that is blocking us from simply receiving and believing God at His Word, His Truth and what we have access to will not root in our hearts. We remain internally unchanged, forcing ourselves to manufacture what being a Christian looks like, just like we have discussed so much about.

Strongholds are the barriers and belief patterns built into our mind from life circumstances that oppose God's Word. When strongholds remain unidentified and unchecked, they create a thought process that is out of agreement with God's Word. If our belief system is out of agreement with God's Word, we will not turn to Him for help in the areas we need Him the most. Even a subconscious belief that God cannot heal our minds (trauma, PTSD, mental health, etc.) can block us from the healing that is available to each of us. That stronghold has convinced us God can't, so we don't go to Him.

Oftentimes we need someone to come alongside us who has the wisdom and discernment to help us identify our thought patterns and bring us back to Truth. After identifying and removing strongholds, we often find that there is some deep-rooted pain that was behind each belief. Pain that you may be aware of, but didn't know what to do with, or you didn't think was an issue because the situation happened so long ago. We believe the hurt was in the past, so we remove it from our conscious mind, but that unhealed pain is still subconsciously messing with our current lives. These strongholds need to be identified and removed for us to experience a greater depth of healing for our minds.

> If we do NOT IDENTIFY THE STRONGHOLD THAT IS BLOCKING US FROM SIMPLY RECEIVING AND BELIEVING GOD AT HIS WORD, HIS TRUTH AND WHAT WE HAVE ACCESS TO WILL NOT ROOT IN OUR HEARTS.

Strongholds can range from struggling to believe we are loved and valued because of how we feel about ourselves or what others have said about us; living under shame and condemnation; struggling to trust God; confusing our identities with worldly concepts; living with anxiety, depression and believing that God can't do something. The list is endless where our minds can be in conflict with God's Word. Leaving any thought unaddressed will block us from living by the Spirit, keeping us from that steady and sound mind that is ours as new creations in Christ.

We cannot live by the Spirit and by the flesh simultaneously. If we have been given the mind of Christ, we have to learn what that looks like, practically. Meaning, we have to get our belief system lined up properly. From there, it becomes a positive ripple effect as we live out of our new natures, which is to be like Christ.

When we address strongholds in our minds, we can easily feel like we're being pressed hard and become overwhelmed. Feeling overwhelmed can cause us to pull back in fear, doubt, and disbelief. Our thoughts form neural pathways in our mind and send signals to our body. These signals are what determine our reactionary responses to life. If these pathways are sending fear through our body, our reactions will be

> **If our belief system is out of agreement with God's Word, we will not turn to Him for help in the areas we need Him the most.**

from a place of urgency. The automatic human response is to either retreat or react.

Both responses are from a need to control based on the out-of-control feeling along with a strong need to protect and find comfort.

This is our natural response when we feel afraid.

God promises to bring us comfort beyond anything we have ever known as we learn to trust Him. If we reach for other things (or people) to bring us comfort while struggling to believe that God is our true Source of Comfort, this will reveal to us where we have a stronghold in our mind that is causing us to doubt that God can truly comfort us the way we need it. Instead, we reach for other coping mechanisms, missing out on a powerful experience of lasting comfort straight from the Comforter Himself.

I have experienced several seasons in my life where I was in so much emotional pain, I wanted out. I wanted something that would come in and help me forget or give me relief. The pain was intense. I was lonely and broken. There were so many times I tried to call someone from my church or a friend, and more often than not, they weren't available. I cried myself to sleep most nights and felt like I was going through my days as an out-of-body experience.

I was barely surviving.

To be completely honest, I really wanted a man's arms around me.

I wanted to feel that strong protection and comfort because being a single mom with four kids was scary at times, and painful. I knew I needed to fight past that fleshly desire and not seek out temporary comfort; I turned and reached out to God. And there I was, lying on the hardwood floor in my own puddle of tears, when a comfort beyond anything I had ever known before began to envelop me. In that moment, I didn't give myself a way out or fill my need with anything or anyone else; I turned to Him, and right there in my living room was Jesus. He held me in His arms as I cried. My tears went from excruciating pain and loneliness to relief with His embrace.

> *The Lord is close to the brokenhearted; He rescues those whose spirits are crushed.* — *Psalm 34:18 (NLT)*

This is a powerful testimony of a very big, real, and powerful God that is who He says He is. Too many false comforts come between us and God, causing us to miss out on His comfort and healing power. In order to experience this incredible facet of God, we need to believe and turn to Him in our painful moments with our WHOLE heart and not allow anything else to come into His place.

> *"You will seek Me and find Me when you seek Me with all your heart."* — *Jeremiah 29:13 (NIV)*

When we pray and ask for God's help, we need to seek Him with our whole heart and believe that He will meet us. If there are any parts of our mind that doubt God can fulfill the need we have or help us in these painful moments, we will not be seeking Him with all our heart . . . we naturally withhold parts of ourselves. If our whole hearts aren't seeking Him, we will struggle to find Him for comfort in the hard moments of life.

Oftentimes our belief system says God can't bring us the comfort we think we need and we don't turn to Him. This is because we've fixated our idea for comfort from another source only to find we continually get tossed by life.

> *If you don't know what you're doing, pray to the Father. He loves to help. You'll get His help, and won't be condescended to when you ask for it. Ask boldly, believingly, without a second thought. People who "worry their prayers" are like wind-whipped waves. Don't think you're going to get anything from the Master that way, adrift at sea, keeping all your options open.* — *James 1:5-8 (MSG)*

These passages rocked me when the Holy Spirit highlighted them to me years ago. God's Word shows us that we can literally be the cause of being tossed around by life when our belief systems are doubting

TOO MANY FALSE COMFORTS COME BETWEEN US AND GOD, CAUSING US TO MISS OUT ON HIS COMFORT AND HEALING POWER.

God at His Word. Even after we pray and go to Him, if we struggle to believe and have other options that we run to, then we are not met by God and drift. These are some hard truths to swallow, aren't they?

We can say we trust God, and we may very well trust Him in some areas; but our lifestyle, coping choices, and our thought-life reveal to us where our trust is actually rooted. This is the cycle of a stronghold that is set up against the knowledge of God so that we don't fully, wholeheartedly, trust Him and run to Him with everything. If we don't trust Him with our whole heart because of strongholds (belief systems) that contradict what's available through Jesus, we don't go to Him first and seek His Kingdom so that He can give us all we need in all situations at all times.

Many of us are not realizing our thought-life is arguing with the Word of God regularly and a direct contradiction to His Truth. It is easy to justify our distorted and broken beliefs instead of connecting with a greater reality: if our thought-life is not lined up with what God says, it's a wrong thought that leads to rebellion against the knowledge of God, and it needs to get evicted!

> WE CAN SAY WE TRUST GOD, AND WE MAY VERY WELL TRUST HIM IN SOME AREAS; BUT OUR LIFESTYLE, COPING CHOICES, AND OUR THOUGHT-LIFE REVEAL TO US WHERE OUR TRUST IS ACTUALLY ROOTED.

When we are caught in the tension between living in the Spirit and our thought-life from our old nature (the flesh), we remain stuck, living a life that is inferior to the Word of God. The tension creates turmoil on the regular, making it impossible for us to live as a new creation in Christ.

Realize that we cannot live as a New Creation in Christ Jesus if our thought-life is unchanged. As long as our thought-life remains unchanged, and it's not a reflection of God's Word, we continue to live from our old nature which causes us to constantly be in conflict with patterns and behaviors of this world versus the righteousness of Christ.

Do not conform to the pattern of this world, but be transformed by the

renewing of your mind. Then you will be able to test and approve what God's will is—His good, pleasing and perfect will.
— *Romans 12:2 (NIV)*

God-fearing, lovers of Jesus still struggle with trusting and believing God at His Word and are often bound by a belief system through deception, trauma, and pain from life with an unhealed mind, forming who they are today.

Many of us ARE NOT REALIZING OUR THOUGHT-LIFE IS ARGUING WITH THE WORD OF GOD REGULARLY AND A DIRECT CONTRADICTION TO HIS TRUTH.

If you were to take the time to trace back and see clearly where strongholds have rooted in your mind and where your belief system contradicts the Word of God, you will see behind every opposing thought is doubt or fear ... doubt that God can, and/or fears that most likely came from a wound or past trauma that has not been fully met by our Healer, Jesus.

If you look deeper, behind every fear we can have an idol that we've made our automatic go-to for comfort. An idol is anything we have placed in our lives that we turn to for comfort rather than seeking God as our Comforter.

This can be anything from:

- spending money

- mindlessly scrolling through social media

- TV and various entertainment outlets to avoid facing real life

- obsession with fitness or careers

- a codependent relationship with a high need for comfort from a person, food, drugs, alcohol ...

Realize that WE CANNOT LIVE AS A NEW CREATION IN CHRIST JESUS IF OUR THOUGHT-LIFE IS UNCHANGED.

Anything can become an idol from an obviously bad thing or a subtle, seemingly good thing. An idol is anything that we turn to as a coping mechanism that makes us feel good in the moment.

But it's not the real deal.

God is our true Comforter and Healer.

On the note of idols . . . I want to mention some major ones that I have witnessed that we don't consider.

Did you know that people, including spouses, our children, church communities, therapists, and BFFS can become idols?

We can be completely connected with our communities of support, but totally disconnected from God and without realizing it, we've replaced Him with people. This includes a high need for comfort from our children or spouse to fill a need in us that we should be getting from God.

Through Jesus, we have received the Holy Spirit who is our true Comfort, and with Him, it is lasting and complete. But if He is not the One we run to, we will not experience Him this way. Oftentimes we run to our spouse, our pastor, our small group leader, our Christian community group, our best friend, our mentor, etc., which are all good people, but if they are our only go-to and we do not go to God, we are still going to struggle and not get the comfort directly from the true Source of Comfort. A counselor, therapist, best friend, spouse, and all the temporary comforts on this earth cannot heal us, but our great and mighty God can.

While someone can help us identify strongholds that have built barriers in our minds, the next and most vital step is to bring them to Jesus. Relying on a person the whole journey through and not pursuing the next step with God can develop a cycle of codependency and false comfort.

It feels good to express what we are experiencing and connect with what may be going on in our hearts and minds, but that does not bring lasting breakthroughs and healing. It keeps us locked

An idol is ANYTHING THAT WE TURN TO AS A COPING MECHANISM THAT MAKES US FEEL GOOD IN THE MOMENT.

into a cycle of reaching toward a temporary comfort from a person instead of getting a total victory in an area.

We can check in with ourselves to see if we are actually trusting God like we say we do; if we are trusting Him with everything, including the brokenness in our minds, seeking Him for true and lasting Comfort. He is our safe place. He is trustworthy and will not shame any one of His children. He is just pleased when we are willing to trust Him with everything, including our doubts, greatest fears, and deepest hurts.

> *Through Jesus,* WE HAVE RECEIVED THE HOLY SPIRIT WHO IS OUR TRUE COMFORT, AND WITH HIM, IT IS LASTING AND COMPLETE.

Living with idols in God's place creates a negative ripple effect that leads to anxiety, stress, depression, sin, and overindulgences causing us to be a slave to our flesh rather than a life in rhythm with the Spirit. Anything that our flesh craves versus what our new life in Christ should look like knocks us out of the abundant and empowered Holy Spirit life that we have access to.

Through Jesus, empowered by the Holy Spirit, we are no longer slaves to anything our old natures once craved!

This is why the Bible tells us to crucify the flesh and live by the Spirit.

> *Those who belong to Christ Jesus have crucified the flesh with its passions and desires. Since we live by the Spirit, let us keep in step with the Spirit.* — Galatians 5:24-25 (NIV)

The key highlight is this: "they have crucified." Not, God crucified, or it just went away when the Holy Spirit came over us. We crucify the fleshly desires.

Crucify sounds pretty intense and aggressive, don't ya think?

Not only is this passage revealing that we do the crucifying, but we can't be passive about it either. If we choose to allow our flesh and wrong thoughts rule, we cannot live by the Spirit. When the flesh is allowed to rule in any situation, we are then forced to try to do the right thing or shove down what we are really feeling, which is exhausting and limited through our human nature. Our human nature is the flesh, that regular old born-from-Adam sinful nature and thinking that desires the cravings of this world to bring us comfort and peace.

Truth bomb: Nothing the world has to offer is lasting, so even the brief relief that you may get from your decided source of comfort outside of God will go away, and you will be back to square one.

This cycle is frustrating and discouraging!

This bondage blocks us from God's unforced rhythm, which can leave us crawling our way through our days, getting caught up in circumstances and feelings, leading us on a downward spiral of heaviness and weariness. Oftentimes this is when a secret battle of defeat and hopelessness begins to set in, and we struggle to believe that God is for us. This is exactly what the enemy looks for in God's children. He is looking for those who are struggling to believe God at His Word with strongholds that are the opposite of His Truth.

What we believe reveals whether we are in rhythm with God and in sync with His Spirit or stuck in our old nature, struggling in our mind, and living by our flesh. You may believe in God, love Jesus, go to church, and read your Bible, but still, on some level, live captive to the enemy. Satan is behind many hardwired, anti-God belief systems.

When we entertain a lie from the enemy, allowing the lie to root into our belief system, it becomes a stronghold and within that stronghold, satan has access into our lives. Basically, our thought-life is a segue for the enemy as he forms weapons against us. If this silent war in our minds goes unchecked, and the thoughts that oppose God's Word remain, these keep strongholds in place. If the stronghold remains unnoticed, it roots into our hearts, becoming the belief system we live from.

These strongholds are where the enemy camps and hides, so he can lead us away from the rich and satisfying life Jesus came to bring us.

> *"The thief's purpose is to steal and kill and destroy. My purpose is to give them a rich and satisfying life."* — John 10:10 (NLT)

This passage reveals the reality of what happens in our spiritual walks when we are bound by the flesh with an unrenewed mind giving the enemy open access to mess with us. If we are living or experiencing less than what the Bible says belongs to us through the blood and power of Jesus, we are being robbed of the life that Jesus paid for.

I'm not sure if you already know, but until Jesus returns and sets His Kingdom here on earth, satan roams freely. Basically, we reside on enemy territory. He knows his days are numbered, and seeks to lure as many people as he can away from a trust-relationship with God, causing them to believe anything opposite of what the Bible says so he can mess with them. God not only sent His Son to die for us so that we can have eternal life with Him, but He also desired for us to have the power to stand against the enemy in the name of Jesus. The devil has absolutely no power over us—unless we believe his lies over God's Truth.

What we believe REVEALS WHETHER WE ARE IN RHYTHM WITH GOD AND IN SYNC WITH HIS SPIRIT OR STUCK IN OUR OLD NATURE, STRUGGLING IN OUR MIND, AND LIVING BY OUR FLESH.

> *Then Jesus was led by the Spirit into the wilderness to be tempted by the devil. After fasting forty days and forty nights, He was hungry. The tempter came to Him and said, "If you are the Son of God, tell these stones to become bread." Jesus answered, "It is written: 'Man shall not live on bread alone, but on every word that comes from the mouth of God.'" Then the devil took Him to the holy city and had Him stand on the highest point of the temple. "If you are the Son of God," he said, "throw yourself down. For it is written: 'He will command his angels concerning you, and they will lift you up in their hands, so that you will not strike your foot against a stone.'" Jesus answered him, "It is also written: 'Do not put the Lord your God to the test.'" Again, the devil took Him to a very high mountain and showed Him all the kingdoms of the world and their splendor. "All this I will give you," he said, "if you will bow down and worship me." Jesus said to him, "Away from me, Satan! For it is written: 'Worship the Lord your God, and serve Him only.'" Then the devil left Him, and angels came and attended Him. — Matthew 4:1-11 (NIV)*

The devil tried to tempt Jesus in His vulnerable state, hoping to lure Him away from the will of The Father, and he does the same with us. Especially when we are vulnerable, hurting, and feeling weary from life.

Jesus fought back with the Word of God; we have to know the Word and stand firm! Recognizing where the enemy has been messing with one's life is biblical. The enemy knows that if he can get us to believe things that are in opposition to God's Truth, then our minds will be blocked from healing, unable to live out the fullness that Jesus paid for.

Jesus' death and resurrection paid the price and restored what the first Adam gave up in the Garden of Eden. The enemy, who gained access into our lives and authority here on earth, because Adam gave it to him when he obeyed the serpent over God, is no longer in effect. We have access to a rhythmic life with God Almighty because of Jesus, empowered through His Spirit, with full authority over satan. We need to walk out our authority!

The Holy Spirit will show us what this looks like in our daily walks. He is our Teacher, and He wants to give us revelations of what the scriptures reveal so we can undo all belief systems that come against the knowledge of God. We have access to the knowledge of God through His Word and the Holy Spirit who dwells within us.

> *I am writing these things to warn you about those who want to lead you astray. But you have received the Holy Spirit, and He lives within you, so you don't need anyone to teach you what is true. For the Spirit teaches you everything you need to know, and what He teaches is true—it is not a lie. So just as He has taught you, remain in fellowship with Christ.* — 1 John 2:26-27 (NLT)

Remaining in Christ is the key that unlocks everything that Jesus paid for to be activated in our lives. Diving into the Word and asking the Holy Spirit to teach us until His Truth is the belief system that we live from ensures our total victory over ALL of the devil's schemes. This is what empowers us to live in our new nature, which is to be like Christ with a clear (sound and sobor), healed mind.

As children of God, the enemy knows he has no power over us, so he lies and manipulates his way through our thoughts and circumstances to get us out of agreement with God and into agreement with his lies so that we ultimately destroy ourselves—either through a life of devastation and turmoil, or destructive sin.

That is how he fulfills his plan.

The areas that the enemy has held us captive in our minds through demonic forces cannot be dismantled through humanistic tools. We do not wage war against these battles in the flesh; we use our weapons of warfare to cast down all the arguments that are set up against the knowledge of God!

> *The weapons we fight with are not the weapons of the world. On the contrary, they have divine power to demolish strongholds. We demolish arguments and every pretension that sets itself up against the knowledge of God, and we take captive every thought to make it obedient to Christ.* — 2 Corinthians 10:4-5 (NIV)

Jesus Christ is the Word made flesh so when we are taking our thoughts captive and getting them to obey Christ, we are renewing our mind with the Word. We have to demolish the strongholds that are convincing us to live with things the Bible says to get rid of and bring those contradictory thoughts to Him.

We have access TO A RHYTHMIC LIFE WITH GOD ALMIGHTY BECAUSE OF JESUS, EMPOWERED THROUGH HIS SPIRIT, WITH FULL AUTHORITY OVER SATAN.

These passages that direct us to "crucify" (Galatians 5:24-25) and to "cast out" are powerful and intentional; there is nothing casual in nature with what we are directed to do. Our response to wrong belief systems that have held us captive for too many years should be the same. We have to be intentional and aggressive, removing all thoughts from our mind that want to argue with God's Word!

Do you see how when we continue to live with a mind that is at war with God's Word, we are vulnerable, making us susceptible to satan's traps?

Our vulnerability is what the enemy hopes for as he roams the earth "looking for someone to devour."

> *Cast all your anxiety on Him because He cares for you. Be alert and of sober mind. Your enemy the devil prowls around like a roaring lion looking for someone to devour.* — 1 Peter 5:7-8 (NIV)

Anxiety stems from an unsettled mind and deep-rooted strongholds that can date back all the way to childhood and is the breeding ground to destruction by the devil himself. Casting away anxiety means to throw off by force. It is our responsibility as believers in Jesus to keep our thought-life in check, but many of us are allowing thoughts that are the opposite of faith and God's Truth to rule, not aware that we are far from being "sober-minded."

I am not talking about alcohol here and what it does to the mind.

I am talking about a mind that is filled with anxiety-driven thoughts, fear, and worry.

A mind that is far from calm and steady.

This passage is referring to a sober-minded person, meaning to have a sound, calm, and clear mind. One who is "sober-minded" is on high alert, fully present in all situations, and can easily hear God's voice. They are not caught up with anxious-driven thoughts that make them a target to the enemy.

Bottom line, we need to pay attention to our thought-life because if our mind is not steady, we are not steady, and the devil knows he's got an advantage over us!

If we don't begin to catch these things, and our belief system remains in contradiction to the Word of God, our wrong thoughts have permission to rule us, and we become paralyzed in so many areas of our life through insecurity, worry, and fear. This is exactly what the enemy wants. He wants to keep us prisoners to the things of this world, to a wounded and insecure heart, including hurt from our past, so we can't even imagine what it looks like to live Heaven-minded.

The enemy knows that if he can keep us bound through an unrenewed mind, we will struggle to live out the mandate of Christ, unable to live out the purposes and plans that God has for us. This negative cycle limits the ripple effect we could be having, impacting the world around us.

As a Church, we got a lot right.

Go, teach, make disciples, and baptize, but acknowledging the work of the enemy and driving out demons is so far removed from the church at large. For freedom's sake, we need to acknowledge the reality that people in the body of Christ are struggling with the demonic forces that are working against them.

Jesus' time on earth was training for all of us to be a continuum of what He taught the disciples to do. As I've put these things into practice in my own life, recognizing where the enemy was at work, and as I come alongside others, this is 100% a vitally important reality that needs to be embraced by the church. I have watched people become free from major struggles that have robbed them for so many years in areas that they never thought they would escape, simply by identifying the operating spirit and teaching them their God-given authority over their struggle.

Our God-given authority is available even in the more extreme cases of mental struggles which we identify as mental illnesses. Let's take a look at an example of how the enemy is behind mental illnesses and the reality that deliverance is necessary.

> *When they came to Jesus, they saw the man who had been possessed by the legion of demons, sitting there, dressed and in his right mind;*
> *— Mark 5:15 [a] (NIV)*

"In his right mind" is the highlight here. If you are not familiar with this testimony of how Jesus healed the demon-possessed man, I encourage you to read the full story recorded in Mark 5.

While I realize this is an extreme example, this is still a reality of what we have access to through Jesus.

The complete healing of our minds!

Could you imagine if we, the Church, embraced this facet of our amazing God?!

On the other hand, we can spend a lifetime going to deliverance ministries, still finding ourselves in the same old patterns, leading us to believe we need more deliverance, ending up in a cycle of frustration, not understanding why we are still not "free." This frustrating cycle can lead us to deceive others and ourselves, by putting on a front that we "have it all together" leaving a possible open door to the enemy.

One who is "SOBER-MINDED" IS ON HIGH ALERT, FULLY PRESENT IN ALL SITUATIONS, AND CAN EASILY HEAR GOD'S VOICE.

Let me explain . . . The enemy has access to us when we operate on his playing field. We have to recognize the subtle ways that we are giving the enemy access in our lives. We do not have authority over the devil if we are partnering with him in even the smallest ways.

When deception is in the mix, we are convinced that our human reasoning is right, even when it's wrong. The problem with deception is we don't know we're being deceived. If we did, it wouldn't be called deception; it would be called denial.

Deception blocks us from seeing the truth and denial is just the refusal to admit the truth. This is why it is so important to have a few people we trust more than we trust ourselves to speak into our lives and hold us accountable.

We were not made to do life alone.

God designed us to live within a community.

Isolating and walking through life alone, not connected to the Body, will slow down our breakthroughs in life. We can convince ourselves that everything is God's will and timing, and that can be true, but if pride is in there at all, we won't receive from the source in front of us that could bring revelation toward our breakthrough. I cannot tell you how many times God has used the most casual conversations from the most random people that have brought breakthrough into my life with just one sentence of Truth. If pride was in my heart, I would reject what they were pointing out. Walking in humility keeps us open and willing for God to move us into a life of radical freedom and transformation, using whoever is willing to speak His Truth in love.

Back to deliverance from demonic forces, we still need to be cautious of where we put our emphasis. Deliverance is vitally important, but it is just one part of the whole picture for healing.

There is a next step.

We need to learn the practical and what our part is in order to walk out our freedom.

Let me show you what the Bible teaches us that I see happening all the time with men and women who put an emphasis on deliverance but seem to be in the same cycle of believing they need more deliverance while remaining broken inside and feeling worse over time. They live with a belief system that says they are on a journey, which I can agree with, but as I've mentioned before, in our humanness we have complicated this Christian life.

> *Walking in* HUMILITY KEEPS US OPEN AND WILLING FOR GOD TO MOVE US INTO A LIFE OF RADICAL FREEDOM AND TRANSFORMATION, USING WHOEVER IS WILLING TO SPEAK HIS TRUTH IN LOVE.

> *"When an evil spirit leaves a person, it goes into the desert, searching for rest. But when it finds none, it says, 'I will return to the person I came from.' So it returns and finds that its former home is all swept and in order. Then the spirit finds seven other spirits more evil than itself, and they all enter the person and live there. And so that person is worse off than before." As he was speaking, a woman in the crowd called out, "God bless your mother—the womb from which you came, and the breasts that nursed you!" Jesus replied, "But even more blessed are all who hear the Word of God and put it into practice."*
> — *Luke 11:24-28 (NLT)*

When I was reading these passages several years ago, what jumped out at me was the answer to the question, "if one has gone through deliverance, why aren't they living transformed?" It is found in the brief conversation Jesus had with the woman who shouted from the crowd, "even more blessed is the one who hears the Word of God and puts it into practice."

We can chase after all the ministries, read all the books written, have a powerful encounter with God at every conference, and go to class after class, but if we do not put into practice what the Word of God says and live it out for ourselves, we are that man whose house was swept clean but never put new things in the place of what was there before. The enemy sees the vacancy and knows he just needs to move right back in through thought patterns and circumstances that trigger us, and we go right back to that old way of thinking, and living.

I have observed this cycle in so many lives that I have mentored and coached. As we identify where the enemy is at work, I teach them their authority over the devil through Jesus, and then we talk about the practicals of putting God's Word into practice. They begin to access the power that comes from the Holy Spirit within them and yield to Him over their old nature and human responses until those old ways no longer carry power. New patterns and behaviors are now in place and the enemy knows there is no room for him to operate!

He got evicted FOR GOOD!

Now that we have come into the understanding that the enemy is behind the wrong belief systems that tempt us to agree with him over agreeing with God in many areas of our life, we need to take back the ground that the enemy has moved in on our life with force.

Honestly, this should make us so mad at the devil for messing with our life that we are willing to do whatever it takes to stand firm, fighting for God's Truth to prevail. No more letting the devil win by believing anything in opposition to the Word of God!

I mentioned an anxious mind earlier and I want to discuss this a bit deeper. Serving as a life coach in the Christian community for many years, I have found that this is one of the most common struggles in the body of Christ. Since anxiety has to do with the mind, and we read in scripture that God has given us a sound mind, the mind of Christ, I feel strongly to address this concept. I cannot find a scripture that says I should be living with the anxieties of this life.

Remember what I said about "toilet talk?"

This is another way we can use that concept.

When I have thoughts that are in opposition to God's Truths creeping in during vulnerable moments, I bring those thoughts to the Word of God and read His Word to see if my thoughts line up or if I need to renew my mind. From there I have to consciously choose to trust in what He says over what I'm feeling until I'm experiencing is His peace. If I am not feeling God's peace, then I have to face it, understanding that I am getting caught up in the things of this world rather than keeping my mind Heaven-focused, taking my rightful position in the Heavenly places with a larger vantage point.

Since, then, you have been raised with Christ, set your hearts on things above, where Christ is, seated at the right hand of God. Set your minds on things above, not on earthly things. For you died, and your life is now hidden with Christ in God. When Christ, who is your life, appears, then you also will appear with Him in glory.
— *Colossians 3:1-4 (NIV)*

Notice again the major connector is in the mind; "set your minds . . ." Our mind determines our perspective on life.

Are we Kingdom-minded, activating all that we have access to as citizens of Heaven, or are we earthly-focused, still living by our flesh?

Being Heaven-minded lets us see things from Heaven's perspective, which is far higher and far greater than what we can see in front of us when our focus is earthly. Being Heaven-minded opens us up to more of what Jesus accomplished during His time here on earth.

Setting our minds on the right track according to the Word of God is our job.

We are guided over and over again through the Bible to get our minds in agreement with Him. While we can ask the Holy Spirit to help us identify where our thought-life is leading us to anxiety, and we can lean into His help to redirect our focus, we still have to choose what we fixate on. If our thought-life is believing the opposite of what we read in God's Word, and we don't stop to connect with it, the battle between what we think and feel versus what God says to be true wages war in our minds. Until we have renewed our minds, and we are living out of God's Truth over the thoughts that attack our flesh, our minds will always wage war against the knowledge of God.

This is why the Bible says to take every thought that is in rebellion to God (the opposite of His Word) captive and get it into obedience with Christ.

This is what it means to renew our minds in Christ Jesus.

Do we believe God at His Word, or do our unsettled, anxious thoughts and feelings still have more power than His Truth in our lives?

Many (men and women alike) have expressed to me that they experience intense anxiety regularly yet Philippians 4:6-9 (NIV) says:

> Do not be anxious about anything, but in every situation, by prayer and petition, with thanksgiving, present your requests to God. And the peace of God, which transcends all understanding, will guard your hearts and your minds in Christ Jesus. Finally, brothers and sisters, whatever is true, whatever is noble, whatever is right, whatever is pure, whatever is lovely, whatever is admirable—if anything is excellent or praiseworthy—think about such things. Whatever you have learned or received or heard from me, or seen in me—put it into practice. And the God of peace will be with you.

The Bible shows us that anxiety is attached to experiences and situations that need to be brought to the Lord for healing and freedom. Thoughts that are the opposite of praise, His Truth, and our insecurities will also lead us to experience intense anxiety. Situations can arise daily that can create fear and worry leading us down a spiral of anxious-driven thoughts. These passages teach us what to do to have peace, to remain in Christ, to focus on what's good, lovely, noble, etc., to put into practice the things we read about in the Bible, and we will be filled with a peace that goes beyond our human understanding. His peace will guard our hearts and our minds—our thought-life—safely in Him.

Until we have RENEWED OUR MINDS, AND WE ARE LIVING OUT OF GOD'S TRUTH OVER THE THOUGHTS THAT ATTACK OUR FLESH, OUR MINDS WILL ALWAYS WAGE WAR AGAINST THE KNOWLEDGE OF GOD.

Do you know that as children of God and carriers of His Holy Spirit we have access to a supernatural peace that we should be living out of every day of our lives, no matter what is swirling around us (or in our heads)?!

> "I am leaving you with a gift—peace of mind and heart. And the peace I give is a gift the world cannot give. So don't be troubled or afraid." — John 14:27 (NLT)

Again, you can see that the Word points us back to our mind in order to experience His peace.

I think we know to a degree but struggle to get to a place of peace, get caught up in the turbulent, anxious moment, and succumb to our feelings. Those feelings, if you stop and check in with them, lead to a thought, and that thought is typically in opposition to what the Bible says. If we don't catch the thought that opposes God's Truth and we entertain it (fixate, believe it, or decide "it's just the way I am" or our circumstances fault), we get knocked out of peace.

Remember, not only do we not experience God's peace, our minds and hearts are left unguarded and susceptible to the attacks of the enemy. From there, we subconsciously settle, accepting what the world or our circumstances are saying and live out of a belief system that is in rebellion to God, rather than to a well of His constant peace.

From my observation, anxiety seems to be the most common mental battle in the body of Christ that is widely accepted as something we are stuck living with or ours to manage. Yet when we read the Word of God and start to connect with the mind of Christ that Jesus paid for us to have, we should submit that battle to the Lord and partner with Him for our freedom from anxiety.

Rather than recognizing where this might be an area for Jesus to come in and build a foundation of confidence, filling us with His everlasting peace and strength, we own the anxiety instead. We have a habit to live with statements like:

- "I have anxiety and panic attacks."

- "I have had anxiety my whole life, ever since I was a kid, I have just learned how to manage it."

- "I am anxious."

When we start our thought-life with, "I have," or "I am" statements, we are subconsciously owning something that is opposite of what God desires for us to partner with. I have found that when I am intentional with what I say about my feelings, I am less likely to allow them to grow in my life.

I will replace I have with I feel.

I keep the level of anxiety that I am feeling to just that, a feeling. I am

From my observation, anxiety seems to be the most common mental battle in the body of Christ that is widely accepted as something we are stuck living with or ours to manage. not owning it as if it's mine to manage. This might seem so ridiculous and insignificant, but I assure you, as I have applied this simple shift in my belief about anxiety as well as using this as a tool with my clients, anxiety loses power, enabling us to put it in a different category of our lives. One that says, "I am not going to live with anxiety because I do not live by my feelings," and we work through a process of renewing our minds, inviting Jesus into the root for healing.

Here's one of the many anxious feelings that I've identified in my life. It's not as heavy as some; it's more simplistic compared to other situations that bring on anxiety and panic, but it's a good connecting point. It is easy to ignore the tiny ways that anxiety can come in and potentially keep us out of the peace from Jesus.

I usually feel anxious when I have to pack for a trip.

What I connected with was an underlying reality that I was afraid I was going to forget something. So, my fear-driven thought left me feeling insecure and led to knots in my stomach and a panicky feeling. I had to go after those underlying thoughts.

Firstly, fear has to go. While this may be little and silly compared to some other fear-driven thoughts, I still had to recognize where fear was trying to override faith. Then I go to the Truth; I trust God with the smallest details of my life because He cares for me.

> *"Therefore I tell you, do not worry about your life, what you will eat or drink; or about your body, what you will wear. Is not life more than food, and the body more than clothes? Look at the birds of the air; they do not sow or reap or store away in barns, and yet your heavenly Father feeds them. Are you not much more valuable than they? Can any one of you by worrying add a single hour to your life? And why do you worry about clothes? See how the flowers of the field grow. They do not labor or spin. Yet I tell you that not even Solomon in all his*

splendor was dressed like one of these. If that is how God clothes the grass of the field, which is here today and tomorrow is thrown into the fire, will He not much more clothe you—you of little faith? So do not worry, saying, 'What shall we eat?' or 'What shall we drink?' or 'What shall we wear?' For the pagans run after all these things, and your heavenly Father knows that you need them. But seek first His Kingdom and His righteousness, and all these things will be given to you as well. Therefore do not worry about tomorrow, for tomorrow will worry about itself. Each day has enough trouble of its own."
— Matthew 6:25-34 (NIV)

See how easily worry and fear can creep into our lives?

Instead of telling the worry to go and get back to God's Truth, we tend to justify our why and give ourselves permission to live with anxiety, manage our anxiety, or worse, become paralyzed by it and avoid all situations that trigger it instead of renewing our mind in Christ Jesus and filling our mind with God's Word. I know many who have just decided not to travel because the anxiety is just too much to bear. In fact, I worked with a client who was bound by fear her entire life and missed out on family vacations because she could not get on a plane. After we worked together to identify the root of her fears, we talked about her authority through Jesus that she has as well as how to replace those panicked thoughts with the Word!

One day, I got a random call from her. She had packed up her bags and driven herself to the airport to surprise her family on their vacation all on her own.

And guess what?!

She was saturated in Heavenly peace!

Something she had never experienced before.

We both celebrated this incredible breakthrough and victory!

How amazing is our God?!

These are the victories He has for each of us from the smallest to the largest areas of our lives!

This is life in the Spirit, no longer bound by the human limitations that block us from experiencing everything that Jesus paid for. When we read scriptures like the one in Matthew, we can see the simple and practical method that crushes worry, and it always begins with what we are fixating on in our mind. If we are experiencing anxiety, we need to recognize the area where we are struggling to trust God. A lack of trust gives room for fear. When there is fear, thoughts come in that create knots in our stomach, tightness and heaviness in our chest, causing intense panic that can be so overwhelming we become paralyzed. We can learn to discern through the Holy Spirit that anxiety is attacking our flesh. We do not have to live under the feelings of our flesh anymore. We have access to the mind of Christ. We are born again by the Spirit, filled with a supernatural strength. From there, we make a conscious decision to not agree with our flesh.

As citizens of Heaven, we are not supposed to agree with our flesh (our feelings). We live by the Spirit, and with the conscious choice of turning to Truth, our mind begins to shift to what we have in Christ. Faith gets activated as we choose to live out what we believe even when what we are seeing and feeling may be the opposite. We choose to focus on what God says to be True and meditate on the promises from His Word. The Word of God has to become more powerful to us than what we are feeling. We have to value His Truth over our feelings so that we are actually living out what we believe.

I get really practical.

I tell myself things like, "you know, you can go to the store if you forget something. It's not the end of the world. You will survive and not die (drama much?!) if you have to wash something in the sink and hang it to dry, you can."

Go ahead and laugh at me.

I actually find myself quite funny with my ridiculousness, but it works.

I have all kinds of conversations with myself. I've learned to start a new dialogue in my mind so that I can come out of agreement with whatever is causing me to feel anxious. This new dialogue has been formed by renewing my mind through God's Word, learning what it looks like and means to take each thought captive, choosing to declare His Word over my feelings and then reminding myself of some practicals.

My new way of thinking was a layer-by-layer process that didn't magically happen overnight. It was a continual yielding to the Holy Spirit, asking for His help to identify where my thoughts were in contradiction to His Truth, and then a conscious choice to believe what He says over what I feel. I needed His supernatural strength to help me with this. In my humanness and brokenness, it is impossible to do on my own. There was also a fight in me that refused to give in to anxiety from the largest to the smallest scale. If I have knots in my stomach, and I am out of alignment with something that Jesus paid for, I will do what it takes to be living in the promises that I have in Him and through Him.

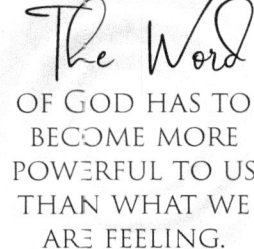
The Word OF GOD HAS TO BECOME MORE POWERFUL TO US THAN WHAT WE ARE FEELING.

I realize my example of packing for a trip can be insignificant compared to someone else's thought-life battles. With all the talk about anxiety that I hear daily from my brothers and sisters literally deciding they are stuck to live with and manage it, I encourage you to consider asking the Holy Spirit to help you receive what He's laid on my heart to share with you.

God does not want you to manage anxiety—He wants you to cast it upon Him.

He wants to carry the burden of the anxiety and lift it off of you.

This is where you learn to walk in His protective covering.

Culture has normalized anxiety so much and somehow we have embraced it rather than activating the power and presence of the Holy Spirit and learning what it means to renew our minds. The Church has outsourced to worldly tools leading us to believe these tools are how to manage our anxiety, leaving God out of the equation. In short, the body of Christ has adopted a worldly standard of normal. That acceptance puts parameters around the bigness of our God who still heals minds today, and this includes the pounding panic of anxiety.

Let's undo this negative ripple effect that has blocked our infinite God from moving powerfully in our lives and start believing for more with childlike faith, ready to receive the fullness of what Jesus paid for.

Let's stop boxing in the power and presence of God by believing we need to accept what the world says is normal. Our life with God should not look the same as someone's life without Him.

No more giving anxiety permission to stay in your life, okay?

Like I said from the beginning of this chapter, while we have a proactive role in renewing our minds, we are not left in our own strength to figure this all out. We have the Holy Spirit living inside of us and He wants us to partner with Him as we learn what it means to live with a renewed mind through Christ Jesus.

When our minds are not submitted to the Word of God, without realizing it, our prayer life can become a list of complaints that feed into our negative thoughts and feelings and yes, even anxiety! When we feed these things, they gain more power in our life than the power of the Word.

For example: "God, I am so overwhelmed with all that's going on and my anxiety is bad! Please take away my anxiety and stop this feeling. I can't get out of bed. I am worried about (fill in the blank). I can't (fill in the blank). Did You see what they (said to me, did to me, fill in the blank)? Please change my boss, my spouse, my (fill in the blank). I can't handle the people at work. I need a new job, Lord please open another door for me. I can't handle this anymore. Please change my circumstances. Please remove (fill in the blank) from my life…why aren't You showing up? Why did you let (fill in the blank) happen to me… why God, whyyyyy?!"

Can you relate to this type of prayer?

> *Our life* WITH GOD SHOULD NOT LOOK THE SAME AS SOMEONE'S LIFE WITHOUT HIM.

If our prayer life comes from a place of fixating on what we are believing to be the problem, begging God to please show up, we can feel heavier after we've prayed and not understand why. Many of my brothers and sisters are not connected with this reality because they went down their checklist of "time with God" magnifying the problems over seeking His Truth about what they have access to as a citizen of Heaven.

I realize the Word says to bring our petitions to Him. I also believe that God is big enough to handle everything we are feeling and thinking. Believe me, I've been so real before God, I'd be embarrassed if anyone overheard some of my conversations (protests, yelling, screaming, crying) with Him. But if our prayer life is only giving account to all that's wrong, never shifting to declarations of God's Word over our situations, or believing that God is going to fill us supernaturally, we remain the same. Instead, we believe that God is not showing up and our struggles are just what we have to accept and live with. And we remain broken and unchanged.

Can I give you a quick perspective shift?

Of course God is going to show up in your situation—He is in you!

We need to check in with our thought-life to see what we are believing and find out how often we are believing things that oppose Truth. Then we hold each thought up to God's Word to see if they are in agreement with what He says. If our thoughts don't line up, we have to capture them, remove them, and replace them with God's thoughts so that we are living from a belief system that lines up with our new natures in Christ. While it is our responsibility to become aware of our thought-life, it is also our responsibility to choose which direction we will allow our minds to go. We do not have to do this in our own strength. We do this in His Strength!

> *I can do all this through Him who gives me strength.*
> *— Philippians 4:13 (NIV)*

Not some things ... ALL!

Choosing to fight back with Truth over what we're thinking and feeling, and partnering with the Holy Spirit is vital. God needs us to partner with Him to experience a deeper level of healing. We have to believe that a healed and "sound mind" is available, and turn to Him.

We need to make a conscious decision to place a higher value on God's Word and recognize that His Word has the power to fully transform us. When our feelings have permission to rule over us, and our thought-life remains in contradiction to the Word of God, we lessen the

> **Of course GOD IS GOING TO SHOW UP IN YOUR SITUATION— HE IS IN YOU!**

power that His Word could have in our lives through doubt and disbelief.

Let's stop putting limits on our limitless God by giving our feelings more authority than His Word in our lives. Amen?

I love reading Psalms. David was so real before God, but you can also read a shift in His prayers from desperation to believing God is who He says He is. That is what we have to do too. Remember, the mind is the powerful driving force that determines what we believe and how we navigate our lives. Our thoughts will either take us to powerful prayers and declarations of God's Truth over everything we see and feel, activating faith, or the opposite. Interacting with God through prayer and getting into His presence should lead us to a tangible shift.

For example: "God, I am not okay. I have things going on in my heart that I am pretty overwhelmed with, but I know You are faithful! You are for me, You are good, You are rich in grace and mercy. I'm bringing it all to You. I know that You care for each and every detail of my life and that You want to help me in my greatest place of need. Lord, I am coming to You for help. Thank you so much for loving me. Thank you for Your promise to stand by me and never leave me no matter what I face in this life. Father, I am choosing to forgive those who have wronged me. I'm releasing them into Your hands. I believe that You are who You say You are and that when I am weak, Your strength becomes my strength. With You, I have nothing to fear. You are my Provider, my Fortress, my Shield, my Peace, my Comforter, and in You I have fullness of life and joy. Thank you for empowering me through Your Holy Spirit to face and overcome any and all situations that may arise. Thank You that You both go before me and beside me and that nothing that comes my way is a surprise to You. I may face seemingly impossible and painful life experiences, but in You and through You, nothing is impossible for those who believe. God, I believe! I am casting all my worries and fears to You; I know You care for me. Your grace for each day is sufficient. You guide me along the right path, and I am believing that You will show me which way to go as I continually yield to You. In Jesus' name, I pray, amen!"

When our thoughts are lined up with God's Word, our prayers go from petitions into declarations of praise, power, and His Truth. All of a sudden, we can taste and see the goodness of God woven into the details of our lives as we are simultaneously filled with a supernatural strength that was not activated before. From there, we are given insight and strategy as we partner with the Holy Spirit. He shows us things that we cannot see through our human, limited scope. He expands our capacity to manage the hard areas of our lives, giving us a clear vision to see what we could not see before. When we re-establish a new pattern of thinking, leaning into the power of the Holy Spirit, life in the Spirit becomes our new normal as we learn to walk in His strength and peace—all day, every day!

> *Let's stop* PUTTING LIMITS ON OUR LIMITLESS GOD BY GIVING OUR FEELINGS MORE AUTHORITY THAN HIS WORD IN OUR LIVES.

Here is what I've learned as I've lined my heart and my prayers up with the Word: He either changes my situation (which leads to peace) or He changes me (which also leads to peace).

It's a win either way.

Either outcome gives me a powerful testimony of God's goodness, and anxiety, fear, worry, and everything that is in opposition to God's Word gets evicted from the situation!

We have to stop praying flesh-led prayers that limit God from moving powerfully in our lives. We have to move our thought-life and prayers to a place of bold faith, believing that God is who He says He is. As we learn this new rhythm with Him, we are clear-minded in all situations so that we can know what God wants us to do. We are no longer consumed with swirling thoughts that keep us in a cloud, making it impossible to hear God's lead in our lives.

> *Don't act thoughtlessly, but understand what the Lord wants you to do.* — Ephesians 5:17 (NLT)

Did you catch that?

Don't act thoughtlessly.

Here we go again with another scripture that points us to the power

When we re-establish a new pattern of thinking, leaning into the power of the Holy Spirit, life in the Spirit becomes our new normal as we learn to walk in His strength and peace—all day, every day!

of our thoughts ... Our actions are ruled by a thought-life that can easily knock us off course.

Fear and pride are other barriers that will block the healing of our minds.

Believing God at His Word requires an activation of faith. When fear is operating, faith is smoldered, and pride comes into effect. Most people do not want anyone to be close to them let alone see their fears, so pride is the cover-up. It feels like a natural protective barrier but it's from the wrong spirit. Pride doesn't want anyone to see our shortcomings, sometimes even God, because fear binds us to a belief system that says God will shame us, people will judge us ... the pride barrier makes us feel a level of protection, but it's a false safety. Pride becomes a protective wall. Unfortunately, that protective wall also blocks healing. What started as a way of self-protection becomes the way to a hardened heart and a mind that justifies feelings. Usually, feelings that will lead them to a thought-life that is far from God's heart.

Realize, when I am talking about fear and pride, I also want you to recognize that spirits are operating with them. Remember, these battles are not against flesh and blood. These are the spirits who have been given permission (by us) to operate in our life through strongholds (the belief system in our minds). Pride gives access to the enemy, and pride is what satan himself developed, which is why God cast him out of Heaven. When we give in to pride, we are in agreement with the enemy.

The Bible also clearly shows us that we have not been given a spirit of fear, which indicates to us that fear is a spirit:

> *For God has not given us a spirit of fear and timidity, but of power, love, and self-discipline.* — 2 Timothy 1:7 (NLT)

We have full authority to tell fear to go, as we walk in God's love, power, and self-discipline!

Oftentimes fear and pride have rooted in one's life because they have experienced a lot of pain and disappointment from people (or maybe themselves). We can ask the Holy Spirit to show us where we are struggling with pride and even identify where fear is operating from being hurt. This is where we learn what it means to humble ourselves before God. God knows that pride will always be our block. Fear and pride create such blinding barriers, blocking us from seeing ourselves in truth.

When we are blinded from seeing ourselves in truth, we can't be honest with ourselves.

When we are blocked from being honest with ourselves, we are not going to be able to be honest before God.

If we aren't honest before God, we are not inviting Him into the places that need changing, and we remain unhealed. Living in a self-protective barrier of pride becomes our prison.

This prison of pride and fear can lead to isolation (hiding our inner struggles) because we just can't seem to get "free" and shame begins to set in. Shame's cover-up is also pride. Pride will always block us from receiving Truth from those closest to us, even when it's from a place of love. Shame causes us to feel condemned all the time instead of loved when someone has a concern or challenges us in a particular area, blocking us from identifying an area where we need a breakthrough.

In chapter one we discussed how shame started in the garden with Adam and Eve through sin. Jesus came and bore our sin and shame so we no longer have to hide. Wearing shame keeps us in bondage to our old nature. This is an anti-God, self-protective method that many are living from, making them want to hide from God and even others.

We have **FULL AUTHORITY TO TELL FEAR TO GO, AS WE WALK IN GOD'S LOVE, POWER, AND SELF-DISCIPLINE!**

Shame is nothing we should be wearing as new Creations in Christ! We need to come out of agreement with everything that blocks us from unashamedly running to our Heavenly Father!

Isolation is a whole other ball of wax that we want to avoid because when we are isolated (physically, spiritually, or emotionally), we put on a Christian front to those around us. When we hide behind a façade of how we feel we need to be seen, we keep people at a distance in fear of them getting too close and seeing our "mess" within. But what is perceived on the outside doesn't matter because God knows what's hidden. Perfectionism, control, and various other unhealthy methods of hiding begin to form in our lives, and they all stem from a broken thought-life instead of a renewed mind that leads us to our new life in the Spirit.

> *Shame* IS NOTHING WE SHOULD BE WEARING AS NEW CREATIONS IN CHRIST!

I have learned the value of finding safe people to hold me accountable, giving those I trust permission to speak into my life, and even call me out.

My husband is one of them.

No one knows me like he does.

We can honestly fool anyone, but we can't fool those we live with.

This willingness to let others challenge me has produced so much spiritual growth, healing, and breakthrough, it's worth the initial sting! I have to include the importance of making sure they are solid spiritually and safe. We don't have to give everyone permission into those vulnerable places.

On that note, while we don't have to trust unsafe people, and what they say, I'm still in awe of how God has used them in creative ways. There have been "unsafe people" who have said things that I struggled to receive. Instead of rejecting what they said altogether, I've learned that I can go quietly to God with what they brought to my attention. Sometimes He used them to point something out, and I asked God to come into that place and help me (I mean if God can use a donkey . . .), and other times He tells me to dump the thoughts because they are irrelevant and came from that person's own brokenness. Both have been huge in learning to take in each of my situations and go to God for wisdom and understanding in full humility. I never want to get myself to a point where I believe I'm always in the right. That prideful mindset will only block my personal growth and healing. Remember . . . we are uprooting pride so we can walk in our freedom!

These moments where we choose to remain humble no matter what and go to God are powerful, unblocking greater levels of healing, leading us to incredible spiritual breakthroughs! When we are willing to give God all of us, and not just parts of us, we are now walking in humility. When we are humble, pride is no longer active creating that negative ripple effect in our lives.

From there, we can clearly see where our thought-life has kept us bound from living out everything Jesus paid for and renewing our mind through the Word gets easier. We aren't blocked by all the coverups that have held us back from taking an honest evaluation of ourselves. We become proactive in removing the smaller strongholds that show us where our belief system is not formed around God's, but our own. When we uproot the strongholds that have blocked us from everything Jesus paid for, wrong and ungodly thoughts no longer carry power and the enemy is cut off from having access into our lives.

Let's break down stronghold removal in simple form:

Repent. Remove. Replace.

Repent: When you find wiring in your belief system to be in contradiction to the Word of God: Stop. Connect with that thought, go directly to God, and repent. Ask God to forgive you for this thought that had the power to drive you away from His Truth.

> *So then, since we have a great High Priest who has entered heaven, Jesus the Son of God, let us hold firmly to what we believe. This High Priest of ours understands our weaknesses, for He faced all of the same testings we do, yet He did not sin. So let us come boldly to the throne of our gracious God. There we will receive His mercy, and we will find grace to help us when we need it most.* — Hebrews 4:14-16 (NLT)

Remove: Turn from that belief pattern completely by removing it. If it helps, say this out loud (I do), "I am removing this idea, thought, and false belief from my wiring! It is not God's heart or His Truth, and I am no longer going to live out of a belief system that is inferior to what Jesus died to give to me!"

> *For the word of God is alive and powerful. It is sharper than the sharpest two-edged sword, cutting between soul and spirit, between joint and marrow. It exposes our innermost thoughts and desires. Nothing in all creation is hidden from God. Everything is naked*

and exposed before His eyes, and He is the One to whom we are accountable. — *Hebrews 4:12-13 (NLT)*

When we uproot the strongholds that have blocked us from everything Jesus paid for, wrong and ungodly thoughts no longer carry power and the enemy is cut off from having access into our lives.

Grab hold of the Word of God that has the power to cut through Truth and lies, exposing every wrong belief system, and boldly go to our gracious God for His mercy and strength as you come against every lying and deceptive spirit that has kept you from living whole and healed.

Replace: Grab your Sword, the Word of God, and declare a scripture of Truth. Learn to override what was once thought and believed, replacing those anti-God thoughts with His Word. Ask the Holy Spirit to bring His Word from your head to your heart until His Truth is the only belief system you live by. Your belief system will line up with God's in such a powerful way, everyday life (and thoughts) will no longer be your battle. You will experience what it looks and feels like to live with a renewed mind. And the whispered lies of the enemy will no longer have you bound as you continually learn to rise into your rightful place as a victor and the righteousness of Christ!

All of us have areas where our mind needs healing and restoration; a fully restored mind is available for each of us. With God, we have access to a completely healed and sound mind, through His Spirit, partnered with our obedience, and taking His Word seriously.

God wants to meet us, heal us, and do a powerful work in us, so He can move through us, impacting the world around us. We are called to be a light to this world, hope-bringers, offering to those around us what Jesus has done in us.

Our journeys toward a steady mind will vary, so don't compare your journey to another. Put your eyes on Jesus, the founder and perfecter of your faith.

When you invite Jesus into each area of brokenness, you can expect healing.

This includes the healing of your mind.

YOU have been given the mind of Christ!

> *What we have received is not the spirit of the world, but the Spirit who is from God, so that we may understand what God has freely given us. This is what we speak, not in words taught us by human wisdom but in words taught by the Spirit, explaining spiritual realities with Spirit-taught words The person without the Spirit does not accept the things that come from the Spirit of God but considers them foolishness, and cannot understand them because they are discerned only through the Spirit. The person with the Spirit makes judgments about all things, but such a person is not subject to merely human judgments, for, "Who has known the mind of the Lord so as to instruct him? But we have the mind of Christ."*
> *— 1 Corinthians 2:12-16 (NIV)*

Chapter Five
Rhythm of Grace

Most often we hear about God's grace from the perspective of His unearned love and favor toward us. Grace is what our Christian faith is wrapped around. The grace that God has shown us by sending His Son for you and me, to stand on our behalf and pay for crimes He didn't commit. By grace, we are alive. By grace, we have gifts and abilities that are woven into our design. By grace, we can live close to God and experience His presence. By grace, we are filled with His very own Spirit . . . His limitless power. None of which we earned or even deserve. We cannot earn our way to be in right standing with God and because of grace we are the righteousness of Christ—a spotless bride, and heirs to the throne of Heaven.

One of the components of grace that we often miss is the ability to live by God's power. This gift is what enables us to live a Spirit-empowered life that leads us to transformation, living beyond our human capabilities, unlocking our light and burden-free life.

Rather than experiencing life in the Spirit, we're living with heaviness and stress not even close to that light and free life Jesus describes.

> "*. . . Learn the unforced rhythms of grace. I won't lay anything heavy or ill-fitting on you. Keep company with Me and you'll learn to live freely and lightly.*" — Matthew 11:29-30 (MSG)

Learning to walk *with* Him unlocks a facet of grace that much of the body of Christ is not grasping. The checklist Christianity has developed a "how-to" step plan that we have been conditioned to believe *is* connecting us to Jesus. But these methods have set us up to do much of life in our own strength, living by our standard of measurement, oftentimes leading many to religious burnout. This kind of living is exhausting and the complete opposite of what Jesus says our life with Him should feel like.

We are going to talk about grace from a different perspective and how we can even live outside of God's jurisdiction, which blocks His power (given to us by grace) from being activated in our lives.

Yes.

You read that correctly.

If you take the time to read the ministry of Jesus and see the contrast between those He rebuked and those He received with open arms, you will find that the ones who seemingly "did it all right" were the furthest from Him.

They didn't recognize their need for Him.

They felt they were doing pretty all right themselves as experts in the law, and they had their puffed-up knowledge to prove it. They were the self-righteous Pharisees who had their checklist to righteousness and looked down on others who didn't measure up. This mindset yokes us back to the law. If we are going to create a how-to list, we will have to follow the entire law of Moses. We cannot create a checklist based on religious duties and live by His Spirit simultaneously; the checklist blocks the flow of the Holy Spirit completely.

This little truth bomb is found in Galatians when Paul is angry that "someone" is creating confusion with the Galatians about circumcision.

> *So Christ has truly set us free. Now make sure that you stay free, and don't get tied up again in slavery to the law. Listen! I, Paul, tell you this: If you are counting on circumcision to make you right with God, then Christ will be of no benefit to you. I'll say it again. If you are trying to find favor with God by being circumcised, you must obey every regulation in the whole law of Moses. For if you are trying to make yourselves right with God by keeping the law, you have been cut off from Christ! You have fallen away from God's grace. But we who live by the Spirit eagerly wait to receive by faith the righteousness God has promised to us. For when we place our faith*

> *in Christ Jesus, there is no benefit in being circumcised or being uncircumcised. What is important is faith expressing itself in love. You were running the race so well. Who has held you back from following the truth? It certainly isn't God, for He is the one who called you to freedom. This false teaching is like a little yeast that spreads through the whole batch of dough! I am trusting the Lord to keep you from believing false teachings. God will judge that person, whoever he is, who has been confusing you.* — Galatians 5:1-10 (NLT)

First and foremost, we read that Christ has truly set us free. This is an inward freedom that should have an outward effect on our lives. From there we see what the breakdown looks like when we decide that we have to acquire certain religious practices to gain favor with God. Paul challenges that belief system and points us back to a reality that if we are trying to work toward acceptance, then what in the world is the benefit of Jesus' suffering and what He paid for at the Cross? If you are working toward acceptance in your life, following the list of religious practices in your own strength, then the sacrifice of Jesus no longer carries the same power for you. You have been cut off from Christ.

WE CANNOT CREATE A CHECKLIST BASED ON RELIGIOUS DUTIES AND LIVE BY HIS SPIRIT SIMULTANEOUSLY; THE CHECKLIST BLOCKS THE FLOW OF THE HOLY SPIRIT COMPLETELY.

When we are walking in our own strength, working this life from whatever we can give it, we stop the flow of grace. The unearned gift of grace that empowers us to live through His strength, which gives us the ability to live a light and free life, is not activated. Grace is a benefit that we have from God and everything we have access to because of Jesus, through the power and presence of the Holy Spirit. God's sufficient grace is living with undeserved, unearned gifts and abilities with His power attached to them.

> *But He said to me, "My grace is sufficient for you, for My power is made perfect in weakness." Therefore I will boast all the more gladly about my weaknesses, so that Christ's power may rest on me. That is why, for Christ's sake, I delight in weaknesses, in insults, in hardships, in persecutions, in difficulties. For when I am weak, then I am strong.* — 2 Corinthians 12:9-10 (NIV)

When you understand the power and the Source of His grace, your scope will expand at what you have been invited into as a citizen of Heaven and child of God. Notice what Paul writes that was relayed to him directly from God: "My grace is sufficient, for My power is made perfect in weakness." Simply put, because of God's grace to us, we have access to His power. A power that actually works best when we are not trying to operate in our own strength.

You might be saying that doesn't make sense. Aren't we supposed to work our hardest in this life?

According to the culture of this world, yes.

According to the Kingdom of Heaven, no.

Let me explain the perspective I'm coming from. I am not talking about being a committed and faithful servant of Christ that has a good work ethic. That should be a no-brainer as a Jesus follower. We've been talking about checklist Christianity and a "works mentality" without the flow of the Spirit. This chapter is going to take us deeper and expand our understanding as to why so many of us feel heavy and stressed. This world says, work hard and be the best version of yourself. The Kingdom of Heaven says that God takes us beyond our human limitations through our weaknesses as we yield to Him, and walk with Him. In our weak moments, Christ's power rests on us. Too many of us fear weakness, shove down what we are feeling, and work harder.

That is not the expectation for God's children.

God chooses the weak to lead the strong.

Why?

Because they rely on Him and not themselves, which gives them an advantage over even the strongest most competent person you will ever meet.

Look at the testimony of David against Goliath. David knew who his God was and who He was to him. That's all it takes. God's grace and anointing on someone's life supersedes anything we can muster up on our own. This is why I spend more time with my clients identifying with them who God says they are versus who they think they are. This unlocks something in each of them when the Holy Spirit gets to breathe His power in them and through them; they rise and take their God-ordained, rightful place!

This is another reason why I think we need to flush those strengths finder tests that put parameters around us instead of recognizing what we have access to! When we live from a place of human understanding, trying to do better and be better (or just feel limited by our lack), we limit God from moving in us and through us. We live with hopelessness and defeat of never measuring up. When we are using our own strength, we are not yielding to His strength within us. We have access to a supernatural power through the gift of grace. We need to realize what we have, and grab hold of it!

Think of it this way.

We have tools in our cabinet.

On one shelf we have all the hand tools: screwdrivers, socket wrenches, and hammers. On another shelf in the same cabinet, we have power tools. The power tools have a source that multiplies our abilities and gets the job done faster with ease. Which one would you grab to build with?

> *God's grace* AND ANOINTING ON SOMEONE'S LIFE SUPERSEDES ANYTHING WE CAN MUSTER UP ON OUR OWN.

The one where you have to use your own strength or the one that has a source of power behind it?

Same cabinet.

Two different options.

Let's be real, we are going to choose the power tools!

Choosing the power tools is life in the Spirit, and because of undeserved grace, we have access to God's power, the Holy Spirit. We can live life in our own strength or we can access His.

Same body.

Two options.

We get to choose which one we live from.

Through His Spirit with unlimited grace or through our flesh with human limitations.

God calls us to live by the Spirit. Because of grace, we are now filled with the same power that released the Kingdom of Heaven here on earth and raised Jesus from the dead.

> *The Spirit of God, who raised Jesus from the dead, lives in you.*
> *— Romans 8:11[a] (NLT)*

This grace and power are not just reserved for ministry life. We are invited to live with God's grace and power every single day of our lives not only to be freed from sin and death but to accomplish abundantly more than we could on our own. The rhythmic life is filled with grace upon grace that lifts the heaviness off of us so we can live light and free.

Here's the problem though: not only are we not using the tools in our "cabinet" to live in the Spirit's power, but we also have a tendency to pile our life-plate too high with obligations and pressures (whether our own or from others). Consider, maybe, that you more often than not, have said yes to things outside of what God has designed for you to do. When God says that His grace is sufficient for the day, He means for what He has for each of us in season, according to His purposes. Anything we choose to do outside of His parameters will require us to live in our own strength. We don't have the grace to accomplish it all and trying to do so leads us to lift heavy loads that we were not made to carry.

Here's the simple way that I look at this concept: God's grace, the grace that empowers us to accomplish what we need to in a day, has a jurisdiction area. I am not talking about whether or not we are loved, accepted, forgiven; all of these are God's grace we cannot lose ... What I am referring to is this facet of grace that unlocks the light and free life that Jesus says is ours, empowered through the Holy Spirit. When we are living outside of God's jurisdiction, His plans for us and His grace (power) to get things done are not available to us. In our humanness, we are not realizing that the light and free life is available as we do life *with* Him.

> *We can* LIVE LIFE IN OUR OWN STRENGTH OR WE CAN ACCESS HIS.

His sufficient grace becomes enough for us when we remain in rhythm with Him.

There are ways we can live outside of this facet of grace, complicating our life here and now, through the open doors of sin; when we are going at life on our own; doing more than what God has asked us to; living in places He did not send us to; working jobs He did not design for us; carrying burdens that are not ours to carry; saying yes to others when God never told us to say yes; keeping relationships in our lives that are not God-honoring . . . are you catching what I am relaying to you? Whether it be sin (leaving an open door for the enemy) or responding to the demands of life and people (leaning on our own understanding and not following God's path), life remains heavy. We are living under the obligations of this life, doing things our own way, potentially trapped in some sin snares, not really following Jesus personally, or truly learning His ways.

If any of these areas are speaking to you and are revealing to you why you might be living heavy and burdened, don't worry! This is where grace calls us back to God's heart with no shame or condemnation. Just run back into the arms of your Father, He will accept you with wide open arms and teach you His unforced ways, empowering you with a strength you have longed for!

Again, this is why Jesus said:

> *"Get away with Me and you'll recover your life. I'll show you how to take a real rest. Walk with Me and work with Me—watch how I do it. Learn the unforced rhythms of grace. I won't lay anything heavy or ill-fitting on you. Keep company with Me and you'll learn to live freely and lightly."* — Matthew 11:29-30 (MSG)

Notice He says we need to work "with Him." The tendency is to work things in our own strength, asking Him for His help but running full speed ahead leaving Him in the dust. We have convinced ourselves that we are connected to the Vine because we believe in Jesus, we love God, we go to church, but we have compartmentalized what it means to actually get away with Him and learn His ways. In short, we are working without Him, not with Him.

God's grace is sufficient for what *He* wants us to do, not what *we* want to do, to accomplish all the obligations that come at us in a day. It's so important to check in with what's going on in the pit of our bellies and our chest.

Are we feeling heavy, burdened, stressed out, struggling to take a breath?

If I am overwhelmed with my responsibilities, or I have heaviness and dread over me, I check in with the things that I have piled on my plate.

Have I said yes to too many things?

Am I doing something in this season that I'm not meant to?

Most likely.

I have to sift through everything that I have piled on my plate, invite God to speak into each area of my life, and have the willingness to let go of some things in order to live in the lightness that Jesus promises is mine.

These are the same things you can connect with in your own life. I learned this way not just for me, but to teach others the same. These are great journal points for you to consider, so please take note.

If we don't evaluate what's going on in our minds and hearts, then we practically beg Jesus to help us, when in reality we have to do some letting go in practical ways. Sometimes life pressures can make us feel like we need to take on more than God is requiring of us, and we don't have His grace covering us to walk it out. This is where life becomes heavy and overwhelming.

Paying attention to what we are feeling is vital.

Are we light and free, or burdened and overwhelmed?

Get away with Jesus, and yield to what He has to say. Many of us would be surprised at how many things we've said yes to that God didn't give us the grace to accomplish, and that's why we're under pressure all the time, making commitments that are outside of what God has for us in season. Sometimes we've said yes to things we feel is right, leaning on our human understanding, but the heaviness and anxiety as the outcome could be God's way of getting our attention that it's not what He wants us to do.

Sometimes, without realizing it, people expect us to be "god" for them, we feel burdened and naturally respond to that role. This lifestyle can stretch us too thin. The expectations people may put on us to be there for them also costs us the ability to tend to what God has placed in our lives to take care of. Then, the things that God has given to us to care for ends up on the back burner (or total burn out), and we are left in our own strength to be all for everyone, instead of trusting that God will show up in the lives of those around us because He cares for them even more than we do.

Beyond that, what I've learned in these moments is responding to a role out of season doesn't just have a negative effect on me, it's also blocking that person from realizing who they really need is God, not the temporary relief of my presence and help. God's presence has the power to bring a lasting comfort that goes beyond the moment. My comfort, while it may seem valuable, is not lasting. This does not mean we ignore the needs of people altogether. It means checking in with God more often, making sure our priorities are in sync with His. If we can't be there for someone because of what God has asked us to do, then we have to trust that God will meet that person in another way.

We need to trust God to be God in our lives and in the lives of others.

We can't rescue everyone!

I know.

I have tried to be all for everyone and it just doesn't work out so well.

I have crashed and burned so hard I really wanted to put in my two weeks notice to life.

I'm not exaggerating. I actually found myself daydreaming this idea.

If we don't EVALUATE WHAT'S GOING ON IN OUR MINDS AND HEARTS, THEN WE PRACTICALLY BEG JESUS TO HELP US, WHEN IN REALITY WE HAVE TO DO SOME LETTING GO IN PRACTICAL WAYS.

Anyone else?

No? Just me?

I stretched myself so thin, I didn't have room to respond to the emergencies that happened in front of me, causing me to fall harder than I would've if I wasn't saying yes out of obligation to others' demands. When I say yes to more than I'm supposed to, outside of my already established responsibilities, I end up snapping.

For example, my marriage and my children are my first priority. If people outside of my immediate family need me, and I'm consuming myself with the needs of others, I will not have the physical or emotional capacity to care for my family like I would have if I learned healthy boundaries. Typically my family will get the worst of me, rather than the best of me. This does not honor God. The people I'm helping may feel relieved but at the cost of my family I'm called to care for. This is a reality that many of us find ourselves in and we don't stop to connect with how we've stretched ourselves beyond where God would have us.

These overwhelmed moments where I snapped at my family made me realize that God has boundaries for me to live within, and these boundaries are where His grace is sufficient. I learned to go to God first, hear what He would have me do, and be okay with saying no, potentially letting someone I genuinely love down. While I knew I was letting them down, and many times they ended up bitter toward me for doing so, I had to choose to rest in confident trust that I was not letting God down. I remained in His peace and grace that was empowering me in my everyday life to manage well what He called me to do.

One time, in particular, I was really wrestling with a phone call that I knew needed to be made; God was changing my course and I had to let some commitments go. I was so concerned that I was going to let down some very precious people in my life that counted on me to show up each week. I wrestled with my feelings for some time and finally decided to go to God with my concerns. His response humbled me. He said, "Do you trust me enough to be God to them in this season as I am to you? I love them more than you."

Whew . . . that was a loaded reply that put everything into perspective real quick!

This season of letting some people down outside of my immediate family positioned me for some storms up ahead that I didn't know were coming. I was able to act immediately, and God's grace during those overwhelming moments was evident.

This way of living has also helped me not have my feelings hurt when I reach out to someone and they are not there for me. Learning that I needed to be okay with saying no, was two-fold. I needed to be okay with hearing no as well.

Living in God's grace means we extend grace to those around us, trusting that God will meet us when we need it, even when people don't show up for us. This means we trust God and believe that the outcome during hard seasons was a part of His good plan with a purpose. God provides what we need. Not people.

Sometimes He uses people, sometimes He removes them to teach us that the One we really need is Him.

My most powerful encounters with God were when I had no one showing up in my life. When I thought what I needed was a person, He showed up; that's when I came to a greater depth of understanding that He truly is all I need! These powerful and tangible encounters with our ever-present God shifted my humanistic reaction from running to a person in my time of need to running directly to Him.

Have you ever thought of that?

Have you ever stopped and recognized where God might be teaching you more of what you have in Him and through Him by leading you into a time of aloneness?

While it may feel lonely at first, that season might just be the Father's way of calling you to cultivate intimacy with Him, in the secret place where His sufficient grace can saturate you, tend to you, revive you, heal you, strengthen you, empowering you to rise again!

When we turn to God in those moments of loneliness we will find that inner

> "Do you TRUST ME ENOUGH TO BE GOD TO THEM IN THIS SEASON AS I AM TO YOU? I LOVE THEM MORE THAN YOU."

need and the pains of isolation we once felt completely disappear. I've been there so many times in my life, including recently. He really is more than enough.

How often did we see Jesus pull away to be alone with the Father?

Remember, He is our example.

Let's remove people from the chopping block in our lives, and not be so quick to cut them with our thoughts, words, and actions when they don't give us what we think we need from them, and go to God. Okay?

We also need to recognize when we are putting an emotional burden on someone to be our all in all we will not become spiritually solid or emotionally healthy individuals. We stunt our own personal growth when we put people in God's place. Let's not just quote the scriptures that say God is enough—let's live this Truth out in our everyday lives!

We need to learn what it means to live within the parameters of God's grace, taking ownership in our lives, and releasing others to do the same.

It's time to trust and believe that God is who He says He is and that we can truly get all we need from Him in all seasons.

Trusting God with everything we need *is* living in the rhythm of God's unwavering grace that keeps us light and free as we extend grace toward others. We need to embrace whatever season we find ourselves in and trust that God is doing something.

We will experience many different seasons in life. Understanding what season we're in and what God wills for us in that time keeps us in rhythm with His sufficient grace.

> When we turn to God in those moments of loneliness we will find that inner need and the pains of isolation we once felt completely disappear.

I've been through overwhelming emotional seasons of devastation and loss, isolated and lonely journeys when I thought I needed others the most. I've experienced seasons of extreme simplicity, and seasons where I am wearing so many different hats my brain should be exploding daily, but it doesn't. God continually met me; His grace has been sufficient in all of them. I learned how to walk with Him, yielding to His ways over mine and accessing His supernatural strength. In fact, I fully understand when God says, "My power is made perfect in weakness" because I am living this reality. When Paul writes in response to what God says to Him, "I will boast all the more gladly about my weaknesses, so that Christ's power may rest on me." I actually get this!

The rhythm we've been invited into is a way of life with God where His power is made perfect in and through us in our weakest moments, and we become unshakable for the Kingdom of God. This is not made-up talk, but living with God's power just like the Bible says it should be.

> *For the Kingdom of God is not just a lot of talk; it is living by God's power. — 1 Corinthians 4:20 (NLT)*

The exchange between us and God is powerful.

There are different experiences of grace for each of us in our varying seasons. When I was struggling in an area that had not yet been fully surrendered, God would show up and meet me. I knew I did not deserve His grace because I was blatantly doing the wrong thing. His gift of grace caused me to fall on my knees before Him as I learned to choose His way over my fleshly, sinful nature. He continually poured His power in me, and I learned to flee from the sin traps the enemy had set up.

Grace is freely given, but it's not to take advantage of what Jesus paid for; it's to draw us to His heart and to learn to walk with Him, surrendering to His way over ours. Grace upon grace is available for each of us in each season and God knows exactly what we need; when we need it most.

To fully access this facet of God, living in His rhythm, we have to give up any need for control and fully surrender to Him.

I have learned the distinct difference between living in God's sufficient grace through a surrendered heart, versus trying to make my plans succeed while disconnected from the Vine, allowing my flesh to lead me down the

The exchange BETWEEN US AND GOD IS POWERFUL.

wrong path. One way is light and free, the other is heavy and sometimes painful. I may have moments of gratification in my own accomplishments, but the process is not met with a sense of endless freedom, joy, or peace as the Bible describes it should be.

I hear these phrases from my church fam all the time:

"Oh, the process is so painful, I am being stripped daily."

"Life on this side of Heaven is just so hard!"

> Grace is FREELY GIVEN, BUT IT'S NOT TO TAKE ADVANTAGE OF WHAT JESUS PAID FOR; IT'S TO DRAW US TO HIS HEART AND TO LEARN TO WALK WITH HIM, SURRENDERING TO HIS WAY OVER OURS.

Fighting with our emotions instead of yielding to God increases the weight of life. Now, I agree that there is pain in life. It is human to experience an influx of emotions, hardships, and loss, but the process that God wants to take us on is a trust-process. Trusting Him leads to supernatural peace, a peace that cannot be explained because our circumstances are saying otherwise.

Our willingness to pray brave prayers like, "Your way God, here I am," and actually mean it, requires a level of trusting God at His Word, believing that His grace is sufficient, and then following Him. Our peace, our freedom, and that overwhelming, indescribable joy that the Bible speaks about are real and available for each one of us! Like we discussed in the last chapter, we have to get our thought-life lined up with God's Truth and believe His Word over our ideologies; otherwise, we will find ourselves settling for an inferior life over the one Jesus paid for, living out of our own strength instead of through His power.

I have been faced with so many overwhelming situations in life, and the truth is, God really does give us the choice as to whether or not we are going to go out on our own to try to figure everything out or yield to Him. Trusting God over what we think, see, and feel is where we experience His sufficient grace. I broke down the concept of broken trust in my previous book, *Life is Muddy*:

"When Adam and Eve sinned, it wasn't just the sin factor that shifted everything; it was the fact that man was deceived into believing that God was holding out on them. This concept was a major 'aha' moment for me and I hope it brings a breakthrough in your life the way it did in mine. Let's look at the fall of man from a different angle.

> *The serpent was the shrewdest of all the wild animals the Lord God had made. One day he asked the woman, 'Did God really say you must not eat the fruit from any of the trees in the garden?' 'Of course, we may eat fruit from the trees in the garden,' the woman replied. 'It's only the fruit from the tree in the middle of the garden that we are not allowed to eat. God said, "You must not eat it or even touch it; if you do, you will die."' 'You won't die!' the serpent replied to the woman. 'God knows that your eyes will be opened as soon as you eat it, and you will be like God, knowing both good and evil.' The woman was convinced. She saw that the tree was beautiful and its fruit looked delicious, and she wanted the wisdom it would give her. So she took some of the fruit and ate it. Then she gave some to her husband, who was with her, and he ate it, too. — Genesis 3:1-6 NLT*

I think so often we look at the fall of man and focus on the sinful nature and the pain we now endure because of it. That was the outcome, yes. It was a sinful act to go against what God said, but have you looked at their why? The initial cause was a lack of trust. They were led by a lie that said God was holding them back from something good, and instead of trusting God at His Word, they took the bait and bit!

Can you relate to Adam and Eve?

I think if we were honest with ourselves, we could all say that there are areas in our lives where we have bitten the bait because we felt like God was holding out on us. It just shows how human we are, how badly we need to be anchored in a trusting relationship, AND what happens when we aren't trusting Him. We all have a sinful nature, and we all fall short. We so often go through life our own way rather than God's, and we are easily led astray by the tempter because at our core we are struggling to fully trust Him. Most of us do not connect to this silent inner-wrestle that struggles to

Fighting WITH OUR EMOTIONS INSTEAD OF YIELDING TO GOD INCREASES THE WEIGHT OF LIFE.

believe that God is who He says He is.

That our fulfillment in life is with Him.

That His love is enough.

That we are who He says we are and what Jesus made available to us is more than enough.

In turn . . . our faith can be pretty shallow.

We succumb to relying more on ourselves than Him in the good, the bad, and the messy mud pits of life, and then when life gets hard, we crumble." (pages 97-99)

Broken trust is the inner struggle that has to be recognized for us to live in the effortless rhythm of God's grace where life is light and free.

Broken trust puts us in chains, making us captives to the enemy!

If we don't trust God, then our doubt will show up in our decision-making processes. Remember, James refers to this as "a way out." Getting ourselves out of hard situations skips the entire process of what God is trying to do in us and through us. In short, we miss an opportunity to experience a supernatural grace that empowers, making us mature, spirit-filled believers that can make it through anything.

> *Consider it a sheer gift, friends, when tests and challenges come at you from all sides. You know that under pressure, your faith-life is forced into the open and shows its true colors. So don't try to get out of anything prematurely. Let it do its work so you become mature and well-developed, not deficient in any way.* — James 1:2-4 (MSG)

It's easy to assume that God will magically work everything out for us while we continue to live an un-yielded life. When we are exercising our free will without yielding to God first, we are living outside His parameters of grace and everything that comes along with living connected to the Vine.

And we wonder why we are so heavy and burdened by life.

It's because we are constantly finding a way out, making our own plans, versus relinquishing our need for control and surrendering to His perfect will and plans, living in unforced rhythms of grace.

I was out on a run a few years ago, praying and listening to worship music when the Holy Spirit gave me a vision that was so powerfully clear, it is etched in my mind's eye forever!

> If we don't TRUST GOD, THEN OUR DOUBT WILL SHOW UP IN OUR DECISION-MAKING PROCESSES.

It was of me in a childlike manner. I was on the feet of My Heavenly Father, my hands in His. The music that was playing was soft and slow as He led me quietly with this melody. Slowly, the scene got increasingly dark, and the music became intense. My feet stayed secure on His, my hands safe in His embrace, and every part of me remained in sync with Him. His peace and strength were evident as I remained connected.

I was unfazed by the intensity of what was swirling around us.

I was light and carefree, and His strength became my strength. His enveloping peace was upon me. My eyes locked into His, with no worry or care of what was going on around me, as He continued to lead me in a dance of unforced rhythms of His grace.

He said to me: "This is what it looks like when you stay in step with me. No matter what goes on around you, my grace, my strength, my peace will be yours. Dance with Me."

It was soon after that vision, my life hit another overwhelming storm that lasted a very long time. I had to keep going back to that picture and remind myself what God promised.

His grace continually met me as I learned to dance with Him through it.

This is His invitation to all of us.

We have access to a rhythmic life as we remain in step and dance with Him. When we yield to His lead, life's burdens cannot weigh us down, and His grace is sufficient. This type of freedom cannot be found through a religious checklist. Connecting with Him in this way is the key that unlocks a life in rhythm with Him that is light and free.

I've learned that to live in rhythm with God, I have to surrender any need for control, my need to make myself comfortable, my ideas, my plans and trust Him with everything. The more we fight with life, the heavier it becomes. The more we think things should look or be a certain way, the more we are living in a tension that was not our design to bear. Our freedom, our peace, and our joy are found when we live in step with Him, trusting that He will carry us through no matter what goes on around us.

An unyielded life is a heavy life.

If we have stress, anxiety, and heaviness over us, we most likely have an area in our life where we are not yielded to God. We have disconnected ourselves from the Vine, and are living by our human understanding, not going to God for clarity. The block is never on God's end. If we have an area that is in opposition to what God's Word says is ours, it is revealing an area that we are trusting ourselves, leaning on our own understanding, allowing our emotions to lead, rather than trusting Him, leaning to His understanding.

> "*This is what* IT LOOKS LIKE WHEN YOU STAY IN STEP WITH ME. NO MATTER WHAT GOES ON AROUND YOU, MY GRACE, MY STRENGTH, MY PEACE WILL BE YOURS. DANCE WITH ME."

Stress and anxiety reveal where we need to give control over to Him and trust that He is big enough to handle the things that we cannot control. If we do not pause and connect with what we are feeling and truly allow God to speak into it all, then we are settling for the world's standard of living that is completely inferior to God's. Not through His grace.

How can we possibly be a vessel of transformation and light to the world if we are caught up in the same things the world is burdened with?

We can't.

We are ineffective and have to resort to debates on belief and why people need Jesus instead of showing them the powerful difference of life with Him versus without Him.

I remember years ago, I mean we are talking back to the high school days of my life, where "surrender" to my strong will sounded more like "get in the cage little bird." This life of "rules and regulations" seemed impossible (and painfully boring). The "outside world" seemed to be having way more fun than I was. Interestingly enough, when I tasted what the world had to offer there was momentary fun, but I was never met with a true inner-freedom. I often felt lonely inside, heavy, insecure, and carried an inner shame.

After running with the world for a season, and then running back to Jesus, I learned something profound. I learned about the power and the peace that floods me from the inside out with a surrendered life to God.

A life that is light and free!

> How can we possibly be a vessel of transformation and light to the world if we are caught up in the same things the world is burdened with?

My faith journey has not been a perfect one. I had to learn to surrender my will for God's, crucify my flesh, strip off the sins that were weighing me down and tripping me up, so I could run my race well!

God's supernatural grace continually shows up in my life as I surrender it all to Him!

There is a powerful difference between *knowing of God*, which makes us feel like we can never measure up, and *knowing Him personally*, which unlocks the transformed life the Bible describes. The exchange of our total surrender to God and obedience to His way over our own, giving Him our whole heart for an inner freedom is unexplainable!

I have been on this incredible journey toward an overwhelming freedom that just continues to get richer over time, as God's grace abounds in my life. I've learned the peace my soul is longing for is truly in seeking His will in everything, allowing Him to show me which path to take.

> *Seek His will in all you do, and He will show you which path to take.*
> *— Proverbs 3:6 (NLT)*

Most of us have these popular and well-known scriptures memorized, but do we actually apply them?

That's the real question.

So often we hear the Word but may not apply these passages in our lives, recognizing that being doers of the Word is how we enter into the rhythmic life with God as He transforms us and brings us from glory to glory.

I am under this crazy belief system that says if it's in God's Word, and I believe that He is the Creator of all things, including me, then I think it's a really good idea to read His manual for this life.

You get me?

We have to stop putting our own understanding in place, thinking we can figure it all out. That mentality is why so many are living a heavy, burdened, stressed out, overwhelmed life!

Jesus said to follow Him, and He will show us how to live.

He promises that life with Him is light and easy.

Rich and abundant.

Where His Spirit is, there is freedom.

We will never experience these things apart from Him. When we are living in sync with God, we should feel differently on the inside, and others should see the difference from the outside. This is the power of a ripple effect that flows supernaturally, yet effortlessly, in us and through us, impacting the world around us!

There is a POWERFUL DIFFERENCE BETWEEN KNOWING OF GOD, WHICH MAKES IT FEEL LIKE WE CAN NEVER MEASURE UP, TO KNOWING HIM, EXPERIENCING A TRANSFORMED LIFE THE BIBLE DESCRIBES.

God has given each of us His sufficient grace. It is enough for every day as long as we remain in step with Him, yielding to Him continually. But we have to surrender our way to His. We have to invite the Holy Spirit to shatter our limited scope until we are seeing life from His vantage point. This can only be done in Him and through Him. If you do not believe this is your invitation, you will block yourself from experiencing this facet of living life in sync with Jesus.

Life with Jesus was never meant to be a one-and-done prayer of salvation, and then leave Jesus in our little church box, going down our Christian checklist of dos and don'ts.

Life is not supposed to be a strive-until-we-arrive, or fake-it-till-we-make-it lifestyle. We don't have to hold our breath until we're retired or wait to relax until the task list is taken care of . . . come on!

That kind of life is heavy and not what Jesus paid for.

If we are not experiencing peace, joy, and freedom in our everyday life, and yes, I am talking even while we are taking care of our responsibilities and when life is hard, then the truth is, something is not surrendered to Jesus, and we are not living by the Spirit. Period.

> When we are LIVING IN SYNC WITH GOD, WE SHOULD FEEL DIFFERENTLY ON THE INSIDE, AND OTHERS SHOULD SEE THE DIFFERENCE FROM THE OUTSIDE.

If Jesus came to give us new life, an abundant life, a rich and satisfying life right now, then where is it?

Stop and ask yourself these questions. Then turn to God's Word. You will find your answers.

There has never been one single season in this yielded life with Jesus that I have not found my answer to what I am facing already written about. It amazes me; His Word is our lifeline for all times!

We can bring our worries to Him and He'll meet us as long as we remain in step with Him, connected to the "Vine" at all times. His fruit will burst in our life and we will live light and free!

> *Remain in Me, and I [will remain] in you. Just as no branch can bear fruit by itself without remaining in the vine, neither can you [bear fruit, producing evidence of your faith] unless you remain in Me. I am the Vine; you are the branches. The one who remains in Me and I in him bears much fruit, for [otherwise] apart from*

Me [that is, cut off from vital union with Me] you can do nothing.
—John 15:4-5 (AMP)

The fruit of the Holy Spirit supernaturally flows out of us when we are in sync with Him. His supernatural peace is a fruit of the Holy Spirit. Anything outside of life with Him is false peace and temporary comfort, and we are left to manufacture everything in our own strength.

Here's the thing: we can easily come up with an excuse as to why we are not experiencing peace, and, instead, we are struggling, overwhelmed, depressed, anxious, etc.

Remember, I call this pattern of arguing with God's Truth the "yeah buts."

Jesus said peace is ours today, and instead of wondering what is out of agreement between us and Him, we come up with our list (human understanding) of the endless reasons why we can't have peace; why we can't be living with a supernatural joy; why we feel boxed in, overwhelmed and heavy laden. As soon as we say "yeah but" and give in to what our circumstances are telling us, or the feelings of our flesh, we are giving our thoughts and feelings more power than the presence of the Holy Spirit that is in us, not living life in rhythm with Him.

Then we give responses like, "Well, you don't know what I've been through" or "You have no idea what I am living with (or *who* I'm living with—careful on that one)," or "I have so many responsibilities in my life . . ."

The answer: You are correct.

Most don't know what it's like to live in your shoes, live your experience or feel what you are feeling. I know my journey. I know my losses. I know the pain in life that I have experienced, and I am not going to compare your pain to mine or your life responsibilities to mine. Pain is painful, and each one of us has our personal lives to tend to. Comparing our lives or our pain with each other automatically takes our eyes off of Jesus and onto others' lives. Taking our eyes off Jesus sets us up for automatic insecurity and heaviness. God cares about our painful experiences in life; He says to bring it all to Him, and He will heal our brokenness. But as soon as we start comparing our pain and our lives to those around us, we are subconsciously making ourselves the victim, giving ourselves permission to remain in the pain, burdened by life, making excuses as to why we can't be confident, joyful, and free. If we are holding onto what's happened to us in life versus what we have access to as children of God, we cannot walk in or toward our victory. We remain victims to life's circumstances versus living victoriously as a child of God.

This is just the truth.

God's grace will sustain you beyond what your human limitations can bear. This is His promise to each of us. His promises are failproof. He also never promised us a pain-free, perfect, or comfortable life for our flesh. He promised He would bring us peace and strengthen us through it all as we yield to Him and live by the Spirit.

I put myself through some checks and balances as I go through life.

If I am feeling anxious, I connect with what I'm thinking about, and I will typically find fear-driven and worrisome thoughts.

If I have fear or worry, then I know I am not trusting God with something. I am not living by faith.

Recognizing this reality and the mind war that's going on, becomes an opportunity to release (or cast) my worries upon Him, growing in both faith and trust. Faith and trust work hand in hand, leading me to His perfect peace, and His grace meets me.

When we are moved in faith (what we cannot see) and trusting Him (with what we know of Him), supernatural peace is released into our lives.

> *You will keep in perfect peace all who trust in You, all whose thoughts are fixed on You!* — Isaiah 26:3 (NLT)

Notice again, that our thought-life is the game-changer and proves where we are resting in trust (or not).

I often think about Paul and his time in prison during severe political oppression, major religious pushback, and still, he released the Kingdom and remained steadfast with a strength that overrode his weaknesses. He reminds

IF WE ARE HOLDING ONTO WHAT'S HAPPENED TO US IN LIFE VERSUS WHAT WE HAVE ACCESS TO AS CHILDREN OF GOD, WE CANNOT WALK IN OR TOWARD OUR VICTORY.

us to strip off the things that weigh us down and the sin that so easily entangles us, so we can run this race. Paul's life was a fully-surrendered, all-in, focused-on-the-goal life, and when we observe what this human being filled with a supernatural strength looks like, we begin to realize that this is the key component to unlocking the very same power to be activated in our lives too.

Paul inspires me!

The same Holy Spirit that empowered Paul, and every man and woman we read about in the Bible, including Jesus Himself, is in us too. This should translate to us, even in this hour, that God's grace is sufficient for whatever we are currently walking through, and whatever we may walk through in the future. We do not have to fear the future because of Who and what we have access to. God knows what we are facing and what we will face up ahead. He has designed us for this very hour and very moment and will pour out His supernatural grace as we remain in step with Him.

> *From one man, Adam, He made every man and woman and every race of humanity, and He spread us over all the earth. He sets the boundaries of people and nations, determining their appointed times in history.* — Acts 17:26 (TPT)

This scripture is so powerful when you really take the time to soak in the meaning.

You are here by a God-appointed time in history.

He made you for such a time as this.

He has a purpose and a plan for your life, and it's for here and now.

His favor is upon your life.

His grace is sufficient, more than enough, and you are not in this life alone.

At the end of ourselves is where our true life begins with Him, in His undeniable, overwhelming, all-encompassing, totally fulfilling rhythm of grace.

Surrender it all to Him.

Pray with me:

> *Father, I thank You for Your grace. Today, and every minute that follows, I am yielding to You. Holy Spirit, continue to highlight the areas of my life that I have not relinquished control and where I have been seeking my way over Yours. My need for comfort in the temporary things of this life, over finding my true comfort in You. Teach me your ways, Lord. I want to learn what it means to live in Your unforced rhythm of grace. I want to know what it looks like and what it feels like to live in Your promises. My life has been heavy and burdened, but when I read Your Word, I find that this life I have accepted is not the one You paid for. Forgive me for living out of sync with You. I feel Your nudge calling me into this rhythmic life with You, my Savior. Today I am responding to that call and saying yes, Lord, here I am. Show me where I am taking on more than You have graced me for in this season. Help me with all my areas of doubt and unbelief until Your ways are the ways I am living from, fully, freely without the cares of this life holding me down. Show me what it means to walk connected to You at all times. Help me undo this complicated religious checklist that has blocked me from the power and presence of Your Spirit being activated in my life. I'm surrendering it all to You. In Your name I pray, amen.*

Chapter Six

Respond To Him

As Jesus was walking beside the Sea of Galilee, He saw two brothers, Simon called Peter and his brother Andrew. They were casting a net into the lake, for they were fishermen. "Come, follow Me," Jesus said, "and I will send you out to fish for people." At once they left their nets and followed Him. Going on from there, He saw two other brothers, James son of Zebedee and his brother John. They were in a boat with their father Zebedee, preparing their nets. Jesus called them, and immediately they left the boat and their father and followed Him.
— Matthew 4:18-22 (NIV)

I was having my Jesus time one morning and these passages jumped out at me differently. They went from a familiar story that I had heard my whole life to deep ponders of what this actually looked like. My imagination played out the entire scene of what it would be like to stop, drop, and go with full surrender and full obedience when Jesus said, "come, follow Me."

The fishermen's response was immediate.

I imagine they must've had an encounter with Him in a way that drew them to want to abandon everything and go. I started to think about their families and what that may have looked like. Did they get support or criticism? This is not recorded in the Bible so we don't really know, but I can imagine it feeling drastic and shocking to onlookers. I mean, they left their families and their livelihood to follow Jesus, and, at this time, He was not yet known.

It was out of full surrender and obedience the men chose to follow

Jesus. This surrender was the beginning that unlocked a lifestyle with Him that set up everything we read about in the Bible.

A life that we've also been invited into.

Now, don't get me wrong, I am not saying we all need to drop our careers (unless that's what Jesus has said to you, then yes, do it. He did with me). I'm talking about dropping our nets symbolically. Nets being those things we cling to that stop us from responding and following Jesus in full obedience.

This will look different for each of us.

I can look back in my life and clearly see where the Holy Spirit was giving me a nudge, a warning, or a clear direction, and I struggled to listen. My human understanding was constantly overriding faith. Years ago, before I understood that following Him in full obedience and surrender *is* my freedom, I was afraid I would be missing out on something that I believed was fun or fully living. I was wrong. Living my own way was not only a wide-open door for the enemy to mess with me, but the thought that plagued my mind said something was missing.

There was.

It was a lifestyle of dropping the nets in my life, and walking in full obedience with Jesus that was missing!

I also didn't recognize the nudges from the Holy Spirit that were setting my path straight for my protection, and course changes were necessary. I justified and reasoned my way out of responding to that inner check in my spirit, and lived by what made sense.

I went to church.

Worshiped God.

Served.

Went to Bible studies.

Had my prayer time . . . you get the idea.

I was living what I thought to be the Christian way. I did not know the power and value of trust and faith that required activation in my life, or the devastation that could come from not seeking Him first and listening to His warning signs.

Again, Proverbs 3:5-6, which we know so well, fits in our daily life when we start to realize how many times we go at life with our own understanding instead of checking in with God.

> *Trust in the Lord with all your heart and lean not on your own understanding; in all your ways submit to Him, and He will make your paths straight. (NIV)*

Fully submitting everything to God can be a hard pill to swallow because it feels like submitting equates to control. In our human understanding, giving up control, and fully surrendering to God is a struggle. Our flesh's natural response is to fight or retreat. "What if" questions run through our heart and mind, taking us down a cycle of fear and doubt, away from peace and joy. This natural humanistic thinking causes us to react and reach for something we can control, or find comfort in, rather than releasing our fears, doubt, and worry, yielding to the Holy Spirit and learning to trust God with everything.

If our belief system is built around "human understanding" and feelings, we are missing what Jesus came to accomplish in us and through us. Dropping our nets and relinquishing control is where childlikeness becomes our launching pad to experience what the Bible says we have access to. We become so steady in our confident trust with God that we walk through life believing that He is for us; we have nothing to fear.

When we understand His love and protection, realizing the reality of who we are to Him and His divine design, something unlocks inside of us because now we know that His heart for us is not to control us but to protect us and give us everything He has in mind for each of us both corporately and individually.

We've been discussing through this whole book that leaning on our own understanding actually limits the bigness of God from being activated in our lives. Back in 2008, I was sitting in our family car with my ex-husband, married at the time, and I wanted to spark a conversation on dreams and goals. Our marriage was not in a solid place. I had moved the kids and myself out for safety reasons, but we were still both (at least I thought both) willing to get help and had reached out to pastors, family, and counselors.

My questions to him were: "Where do you see us in the next five or ten years? What do you dream about for our family, a home, a career, ministry?"

His pattern of quitting or getting fired from jobs left us in a constant state of instability; I was trying to get him to dream bigger for us. I believe without a vision for our life, we die inside. If we have no focal point, we run aimlessly. I shared with him one of my secret desires, to one day be in a position to buy "the ugly house" in a pretty neighborhood. I didn't want the home with all the upgrades; I wanted to have the home that needed the upgrades so I could make it my own. I desired a home for our family. A place to gather and build memories. I also wanted to be used by God in whatever plan He had for my life. I just wanted to live for Him.

> *Dropping* OUR NETS AND RELINQUISHING CONTROL IS WHERE CHILDLIKENESS BECOMES OUR LAUNCHING PAD TO EXPERIENCE WHAT THE BIBLE SAYS WE HAVE ACCESS TO.

My ex-husband's reply crushed me. I'd rather not share his exact words to protect people I care about, but it was more clear than ever—he didn't want to work hard for himself or for our family. He was perfectly fine with someone else doing the work and receiving the benefits.

I had no words.

I felt like my whole desire to build something with him for our family was not only crushed, but this conversation brought to the surface some things that were in his heart that left me even more concerned for our marriage. He didn't want to work hard or do the right thing in any area of his life. God was not his foundation, even though he spent years convincing me he loved God—his continual pattern of using people for what they could give him and what he got out of it was confirmed once again.

> *"A good man brings good things out of the good stored up in his heart, and an evil man brings evil things out of the evil stored up in his heart. For the mouth speaks what the heart is full of."*
> — Luke 6:45 (NIV)

After that conversation, life situations buried my dreams and I didn't think to visit those thoughts again. In 2009, my life went in a direction

I never wanted for myself and my children, but I was trusting God with every decision and every step forward from that point on as He led us out of our chaotic and abusive homelife and into safety. From that point on, I surrendered everything to God in greater measures and clung to Him like never before.

Fast forward to 2016, remarried for four years at this point, you already know the story of how God gave us our home, but He wasn't done.

While my husband was away on a business trip, we hired good friends to paint the interior of our house. One project at a time, we were ready to begin investing in the much-needed repairs. All of a sudden, I got this whole picture of tearing down a particular wall to open up the entire living space. My vision didn't stop there. I saw a window seat and a double-sided fireplace wrapping around the room with an extended sitting area for reading and intimate conversations. I had already moved our dining room table out of the "dark cave" that was the dining room, since we all hated eating in there, and changed what was once a living room off the kitchen to the family dining area. From there, I saw barn doors closing off what was once a hidden dining room, making it a cozy additional room for guests and what would eventually become my future office, where I'm currently sitting, typing this book.

I ran downstairs to share the whole idea with our friends. Josam, my visionary partner, reminded me that he had mentioned tearing down this particular wall. Larry joined in with us, brainstorming the plans, envisioning how removing this wall would open everything up and create the feel I was seeing in my mind.

Then, there was the call to my husband who was out of the state with a customer.

This phone call was another one of those God-moment calls, because while my husband and I had already had future plans to remodel the kitchen, there was absolutely no plan of tearing down any interior walls.

Remember how much my husband loves course changes?

I'm pretty sure calling him while he was away on a business trip telling him I wanted to knock down a wall and do some demo was not something that excited him. He thought he was going to come home to a nicely painted house. Not a construction zone. But this vision I had. . . I couldn't remove it from my mind. Like I said, this was a God-moment conversation because while my husband was not on board initially and really struggled to envision what I was trying to relay, he gave me the thumbs up to make plans with Josam and Larry and budget in the cost.

THAT right there was a miracle in itself!

Two years later, and a complete remodel of our downstairs, I was sitting near my new fireplace, looking around, and I was reminded of my lost dream: to own the ugly house in the pretty neighborhood and make it my own. I was reminded of my secret desire as a little girl to have a window seat to curl up on and get lost in a book. Today that book is my Bible, only I am not lost in it, I am found.

My dream was now a reality, my home.

The simple dreams and visions I had from childhood to the things that no one but God would know of, were right in front of me. And here's the most incredible thing about it all . . . I did not make a plan to get to that point!

Seriously.

Those ideas were not even in my mind when I got that picture or what unfolded from start to finish until God reminded me. My focal point was not in obtaining earthly treasure, it still isn't. My focus was yielding to the Holy Spirit in all my ways and leaning to God to direct my path in each season of my life. My life was not caught up in what I needed to get next or comparing my life to others. I was actually enjoying the journey I was on with Jesus, delighting in Him.

> *Take delight in the Lord, and He will give you your heart's desires.*
> *— Psalm 37:4 (NLT)*

I'm not giving you a step-plan to owning a home and remodeling it, just so you know. I'm just painting a picture for you to see that God wants us to trust Him with the desires of our hearts and not manufacture a way to get there. When we line our heart up with His, these desires don't really matter anyway, and they become gifts and added blessings to our already full life in Him.

Let me take you back to what started my rhythm of dropping my nets and living in trust.

I began to recognize where I had been making so many decisions out of my human understanding, insecurity, and fear, instead of pressing in and actually putting the Word of God into practice, you know, seeking the Kingdom of God first and then letting all these things be added ...

> *"No one can serve two masters. Either you will hate the one and love the other, or you will be devoted to the one and despise the other. You cannot serve both God and money. Therefore I tell you, do not worry about your life, what you will eat or drink; or about your body, what you will wear. Is not life more than food, and the body more than clothes? Look at the birds of the air; they do not sow or reap or store away in barns, and yet your heavenly Father feeds them. Are you not much more valuable than they? Can any one of you by worrying add a single hour to your life? And why do you worry about clothes? See how the flowers of the field grow. They do not labor or spin. Yet I tell you that not even Solomon in all his splendor was dressed like one of these. If that is how God clothes the grass of the field, which is here today and tomorrow is thrown into the fire, will He not much more clothe you—you of little faith? So do not worry, saying, 'What shall we eat?' or 'What shall we drink?' or 'What shall we wear?' For the pagans run after all these things, and your heavenly Father knows that you need them. But seek first His Kingdom and His righteousness, and all these things will be given to you as well."*
> — *Matthew 6:24-33 (NIV)*

These scriptures fused into my heart as I began to understand what this looked like on a practical level. The key highlights for us to apply are:

1. We cannot please God while also pleasing ourselves with the things of this world.

2. Do not worry about our basic needs; God will provide.

The major takeaway is clear: Devote your heart fully to God, seek Him first ALWAYS; do not worry about money because He knows what is needed, and He will provide all of your needs, and more.

"... seek first His Kingdom and His righteousness, and all these things will be given to you as well." We either believe God at His Word and put it into practice, or we don't.

If we are constantly worrying about what's next, and what we need to do in order to accomplish a goal, leaving God out of the equation, or hoping He will bless us through our efforts as we busily build our own kingdoms, then we are incapable of serving Him with our whole hearts, fulfilling the purpose He designed us for (Ephesians 2:10). We are too busy clinging to our human understanding, having no idea what it means and what it looks like to trust that He will take care of all our needs PLUS bonus blessings!

Are we responding to the One who gave us life, or our own thoughts and ideas, spending more time creating plans for our comfort, building nets instead of dropping them and following Him?

I realize this is a challenge to most of us.

I believe we are genuinely trying to figure out how to navigate this life as Christians, and honor God.

On one hand, we have to work to live here. I mean, we gotta eat and pay the bills, and we can't walk around naked, right?

Thanks to Adam and Eve, we need to clothe ourselves!

On the other hand, we are believers in Jesus and truly desire to live for Him. What we need to activate, is a deep trust in God, believing that He will provide the resources for what we need, as we need it. If we are honest, we've really left trusting Him and seeking His Kingdom first out of the equation of our everyday lives. We trust ourselves, our education, our bank account, look around at what others have to see what we are missing, and then live in conflict with God's heart, clinging to earthly treasures for our comfort and happiness.

I have a feeling you're struggling a bit with what you're reading right now in fear that I'm about to tell you to sell all your belongings as Jesus said to the one who asked what it takes to follow Him.

We either BELIEVE GOD AT HIS WORD AND PUT IT INTO PRACTICE, OR WE DON'T.

Don't worry.

That's not where I'm going here.

For some, yes, God has called them to sell it all and go. He has an assignment for each of His children, positioning us in many different ways, and His grace will meet each of us.

God has planted you right where you are to be an extension of His Kingdom in your sphere of influence, and He will provide what you need in the places He's called you to. He knows the nets (idols) that each one of us has put in place, and what we need to release be all in with Him. Not everyone is bound by earthly riches. So, what He says to one, will not be the same as another.

What I am referring to is when we create life goals apart from God, and they become our driving force. When reaching man-made goals becomes the greater focus, we become slaves to the outcome and our master is getting to the finish line.

We ended up in bondage to the goal rather than freely living out the purposes God had planned for us. And feelings of defeat set in when life doesn't turn out the way we intended it to.

The gap between living our own way while also trying to maintain God's way (through works) is why it can be challenging to see ourselves the way God does and knowing our true value as a child of God. If we get with God and know that our value is not in what we do but in who we are in Him—chosen and marked with purpose, appointed and anointed to do the will of the Father—then we live an abundant life with purpose.

Dropping our nets becomes the goal.

If God has given you a position that feels lowly compared to someone else (if you need to go there) remember, God does not measure the way this world does; your value is still the same in the Kingdom of God. When we are living with our value system according to Him, we stop caring about worldly status ... we simply drop our nets and follow Him.

I'm not saying that creating goals is wrong. I create a lot of goals for my life. My "how-to" method (for myself and with coaching clients) is this: God is the One we partner with, and He is the One who downloads the vision. Seeking Him first, and His Kingdom, in each season, and checking in with Him regularly for the plan. Then, we pay attention to any course changes and submit to Him.

> **When reaching man-made goals becomes the greater focus, we become slaves to the outcome and our master is getting to the finish line.**

It's not our way, it's His.

This means He also directs our steps to the finish line of the projected vision.

God's will is not always the easier path, either. In fact, many of the ways the Lord has directed me have been met with roadblocks, twists, and unexpected turns that have really challenged my faith. But I knew with everything in me that it was the way He led me to go. I learned that stilling myself regularly in His presence, saturating myself in His Word, and submitting to His lead taught me to confidently know His voice and trust Him no matter what.

> *"Be still and know that I am God!"* — *Psalm 46:10[a] (NLT)*

We need to stop creating our own versions of what we think God wants to do in our lives and become firmly rooted in our faith, realizing that God desires to raise up solid warriors for the Kingdom of Heaven—He will provide all we need as we trust and follow Him! Through this process, He is also refining us, sharpening our discernment, and taking us on a tailor-made path to becoming like Him.

This is God's will for His children.

He desires us to become solid, faith-filled believers that aren't afraid of the challenges in life!

I will admit, sometimes I will fight with the step I am on and wish I was further along than I am, but I've learned the value of surrender and that God is doing something in me of great value that is ultimately preparing me for the more that He has ahead.

It's in our best interest to yield to His way and His timing, fully trusting that He's doing something that we cannot fully see.

We need to stop fighting for a way out, throwing in the towel, and giving up.

We need to learn to give in to Him and let Him lead.

When God is truly our lead, and we're living in rhythm with Him, we have a constant well of peace and joy, knowing that the vision may be slow in coming but it will come. When we begin to feel weary of the process, we can remember . . .

> *"This vision is for a future time. It describes the end, and it will be fulfilled. If it seems slow in coming, wait patiently, for it will surely take place. It will not be delayed." — Habakkuk 2:3 (NLT)*

His Word is our road map, and He speaks to us through His Word in such affirming ways if we read with the anticipation that when we seek Him, He will respond. I'm telling you, with eyes off of what's going on around us and our full attention on Him, we will not feel like we are missing out on anything in this life! We will never feel left behind, too late, or like we do not have enough. Our full focus on God *is* faith in action. We will experience total fulfillment when we drop our nets and follow him.

His plans will always far outweigh ours. I truly believe people are genuinely afraid to make faith-filled decisions and give room for God to make course changes. We plan out our course, make commitments, and when there is a nudge from the Holy Spirit for a course change, we dismiss it.

Faith is not seeing the whole picture but trusting in the One who does. Apply this Truth in your life. This is your game-changer to fully living in rhythm with Him.

> *In their heart's humans plan their course, but the Lord establishes their steps. — Proverbs 16:9 (NIV)*

God wants to dream with us and then build those dreams into our lives. This is not a prosperity gospel message; this is the abundant life Jesus paid for when we seek His Kingdom first and trust that He will add to it. Our life is abundant when we are faithful in the little things and are trustworthy. We become trusted with an increase in responsibility.

All too often we are building safety nets in our own strength, seeking a life of comfort, and success, instead of dropping our nets and fully trusting Jesus toward a fulfilling and satisfying life. In doing so, we might successfully build up one area of our lives, but at the cost of another area falling apart, from our home to our children to our relationships. We also completely miss out on a facet of God that can only be experienced when we fully obey, trust and follow Him.

Honoring Him in private is another key that will unlock the life that God is calling us into.

> *We will* EXPERIENCE TOTAL FULFILLMENT WHEN WE DROP OUR NETS AND FOLLOW HIM.

Remember my tiny apartment days when my children were small?

I shared with you that a deep-rooted desire birthed in my heart to take care of "my little" and get really good at it. I didn't take care of my little out of a need; I did it because I had a desire to care for what God had entrusted me with in that season. I was working as unto the Lord, desiring to honor Him in every area of my life, including when no one was watching. This is biblical and a call for each of us.

> *Whatever you do, work at it with all your heart, as working for the Lord, not for human masters, since you know that you will receive an inheritance from the Lord as a reward. It is the Lord Christ you are serving.* — Colossians 3:23-24 (NIV)

> *Whoever can be trusted with very little can also be trusted with much, and whoever is dishonest with very little will also be dishonest with much. So if you have not been trustworthy in handling worldly wealth, who will trust you with true riches? And if you have not been trustworthy with someone else's property, who will give you property of your own?* — Luke 16:10-12 (NIV)

I lived in rentals, tiny apartments, and other people's homes the majority of my adult years and cared for them as if they were my own property. I was also saturating myself in the Word regularly. I felt most satisfied sitting at the feet of Jesus, clinging to the words He was speaking to my heart, and from that place, taking care of my responsibilities did not feel heavy or overwhelming.

Yes, even during the turmoil and chaos of my previous marriage.

I felt the birth of honor in me to please God with everything. From my marriage and kids to my environment. There was a gentle nudge from the Holy Spirit whispering to my heart . . . *when I can trust you in the little, I will trust you with more.*

It was private.

It was personal.

It was not for public recognition.

It was a high honor to work as unto the Lord and care for the things and the people that He placed in my life in each season. This included my neighbors and beyond. Looking back, this is what developed the ministry I am living out of today, but I had no idea this was where God was leading. I just learned to drop each net that the Holy Spirit was showing me I was clinging to, and I realized that letting go gave me the light and free life that Jesus promises is available. This posture of letting go in order to receive everything Jesus says belongs to me came straight from the throne room of Heaven, creating an effortless ripple effect, impacting those around me.

As you learn to listen to the promptings of the Holy Spirit, putting one foot in front of the other, there will not be one area in your life that is negatively affected. God will keep adding and increasing as you become trustworthy and faithful. The peace, joy, and freedom that you will continually experience will be indescribable!

Could you imagine such a light and free life?

When we drop our nets and respond to the leading of the Holy Spirit, He shows us a perspective that is beyond what we can see on our own and uses hard, unpredictable seasons to strip us of any belief systems that are not of Him, shaping us and training us as He prepares us for what's up ahead. This life is available to each who is called according to His purposes. God has invited us into something greater than anything this world has to offer.

If I didn't experience powerful life-changing moments where His Word became alive in me, I would only have memorization of scripture and "talk" to give you, which does not bring revelation into your life.

My life has become a living message.

A testimony of the burden-free, light, and powerful rhythm of God that Jesus paid for, dropping my nets, and releasing the Kingdom of Heaven.

A testimony carries the power to change others. It is the release of what God has done in one's life and we say, "do it again Lord!" But first, we must learn to respond to Him and only Him, regardless of what others may think or say. This is the ministry that started when those who Jesus called chose to drop their nets and follow Him.

This ripple effect is meant to be ongoing.

Checklist Christianity has conditioned the church at large to believe that following Jesus is all about what we are doing at church and what others can see, blocking the simplicity and power of following Him. How much we are serving, how many ministries we are plugged into, how much we are giving that others can see. All good things, but oftentimes these actions make us believe we are following Jesus, but many are just following the church line, living totally disconnected from the Vine.

> I just learned to drop each net that the Holy Spirit was showing me I was clinging to, and I realized that letting go gave me the light and free life that Jesus promises is available.

Yep . . . I'm going there.

Why?

Because our faith-walk and all that Jesus paid for are at stake here.

The life that Jesus died for is being blocked based on human understanding and a generation of people who have been led to believe that this is what being a Christian should look like. Here's the thing: I have talked with hundreds of believers, and most of them desperately need a real touch from a real God who said, "I will never leave you," but they feel left by Him. They have become "burned out on religion." Some are still going through the motions, and some dropped out completely. Serving in ministry has replaced intimacy with God, blocking the ripple effect that was intended. We are too burned out on doing, believing that we are following Him. The ministry that started over 2,000 years ago was an overflow of a life-changing encounter with Jesus as they dropped their nets, gave freely, and walked with Him, releasing the Kingdom everywhere they went. It was a natural overflow of what they received from Him.

What's stopping so many of us today?

As a Church body, are we truly dropping our nets and following Him?

We are flooding into churches weekly. There are more ministries and activities for any category of life to plug into, drawing the masses in, but what is going on in between that leaves so many burdened and weary by life?

I was reading these familiar passages in Matthew:

> *"You are the light of the world. A town built on a hill cannot be hidden. Neither do people light a lamp and put it under a bowl. Instead, they put it on its stand, and it gives light to everyone in the house."*
> *— Matthew 5:14-15 (NIV)*

What the Lord whispered to my heart shook me. He said: "My church is like a bowl. My children are lighting up the inside of a building, but not the world."

Yikes! How did we get here?!

What we have is a generation of people who are struggling to understand what it means to truly drop their nets and follow Jesus. Without realizing it, many have built "safety nets" of false comfort, clinging to people, ministries, even the activities inside of a building. Then, they struggle even more when the perceived safety net does not provide the lasting comfort they need.

Serving in MINISTRY HAS REPLACED INTIMACY WITH GOD, BLOCKING THE RIPPLE EFFECT THAT WAS INTENDED.

The Holy Spirit continued to speak into this and showed me how His children don't really know how to drop their nets and follow Him, because, again, our faith walks are built around the projected checklist. This has cost us so much, including negatively affecting our ability to know what it means and looks like to live by faith, to follow Him, and to be bold enough to light up the world around us.

Church and community are highly important, but are we sharpening our ability to press in and hear God with a willingness to unashamedly follow Him?

Are we filled with the boldness to be a light to the world outside of the church, or is this church-way keeping us busy inside of the building and causing a barrier in our walks with God, limiting our "faith journey" to our perceived checklist?

More often than not, we go to church, do life with our small group, and drive straight into our garages.

> What the Lord whispered to my heart shook me. He said: "My church is like a bowl. My children are lighting up the inside of a building, but not the world."

I have even spoken to many who are genuinely afraid to talk to people with different belief systems in fear of what they will say or do. We shy away from allowing the Holy Spirit to use us in casual conversations with neighbors or in the workplace because we have been so busy building safety nets in our lives, building our kingdom, and compartmentalizing our Christian "faith" to only what we do within the church walls. From there, our church community becomes our safe place because we haven't learned that our true safe place is found in Jesus.

The church building has become our net.

We have to get past this wrong desire to surround ourselves with only like-minded believers and hide. The world is hungry and dying (literally) for what we have, and it was not meant to hide under a bowl, but to light the world up with eternal life and hope in Christ! We don't even know what it means to light up our neighborhoods, grocery stores, and playgrounds.

What we have done instead is form cliques (created nets) with the "like-minded." We are so uncomfortable with those who don't believe to the point that we remain silent, sometimes even harshly judging them rather than loving them and finding opportunities to share the good news. We are piling into church week after week, relying on the pastor to do it all, when we are disciples of Christ called to respond to Jesus, drop our nets and go.

Our pastor/pastors (or elders) are the Shepherds of the house called to serve and protect, teaching us biblical Truths. They encourage us to get away with Jesus, read our Bibles, be filled with the Holy Spirit, and then follow His lead in our lives. We have to put all we've been taught into practice, creating a ripple effect to those outside the church, lighting up the environments and territories that God has called us to:

Our homes.

Our workplace.

The playground where our kids play.

The sports field.

The grocery store, and everywhere in between.

My husband and I were out on a date recently when I noticed a woman sitting with a bandaged foot propped up on a chair. I casually asked her what she did and she shared the story of how she broke her foot, requiring surgery. She went on to share her disappointment because they had a family vacation coming up. I felt a boldness rise up in me that I knew was the Holy Spirit nudging me to pray. So, I told her we were going to pray healing for her foot! Her eyes were shocked and she welcomed the idea. She let me gently place my hands on her bandaged foot and I prayed a very simple prayer for healing in Jesus' name. After the prayer, I looked up to see tears in her eyes. She said the prayer made her cry. We both felt God's comfort come over us. I left her with my phone number so that I could get her updates and have more opportunities to share the love of Jesus with her. She was so moved that I took the time to pray with her and her husband voiced he was equally thankful.

This was such a beautiful opportunity to share God's love with them through a simple prayer of faith. I experience these divine appointments all the time. I just ask God to fill me with boldness and for opportunities to be a light in my daily life.

That's all it takes—asking the Holy Spirit to fill us with boldness and give us opportunities to be the hands and feet of Jesus in our everyday lives.

This is what it looks like when we drop our nets and follow Jesus.

I am not a bold person by nature. I had to drop the nets of shyness and fear of making a fool of myself. I had to become more aware of the Holy Spirit in me than the weird looks I might get from those around me.

You'd be shocked at how many strangers will say yes to your public prayers and how many onlookers smile when they witness these random acts of faith. Honestly, I'm not sure who is more blessed . . . me or the person I prayed for. It's a high honor to be used by God in this way.

All too often, being all in for Jesus looks like being all in with everything that is going on inside the building, not even considering what needs to be done in our daily lives that actually reflects God's glory because we haven't learned how to respond to Him. We have a bazillion churches that we are piling into week after week, but are we growing personally, thriving in our daily walks, filled with a contagious peace and joy, yielding to the Holy Spirit, releasing all we have found in Him to the world around us?

We are supposed to be freely giving away everything He has given us.

Heal the sick, raise the dead, cure those with leprosy, and cast out demons. Give as freely as you have received! — Matthew 10:8 (NLT)

For most, our Christianity has been boxed into a belief that if we are going down the checklist we are on track.

God has a much bigger vision in mind for His children.

God's design for His church is to be mobilized.

Churches are to be an equipping center for disciples to be taught what it means and what it looks like to have a personal walk with Jesus with a willingness to drop our nets, step into a life of bold faith, and light up the world around us.

You see, the perceived checklist gets in the way, convincing us we are doing it all right, missing out on the life that we were called into when we said yes to Jesus.

Instead, we have tried to create what I call, "cushy Christianity" where we are spending more time going down our checklist, keeping

Jesus mostly to ourselves, forming safety nets to keep us as safe and comfortable as possible, building our own kingdoms, convincing ourselves we are following Jesus, but we aren't.

Honestly, this cycle is why so many struggle when life gets hard. We've built a false belief system around what we are doing, believing it will help us avoid hardship, and when the storms of life come, we get rocked because we didn't learn to remain connected to Jesus.

> I had to BECOME MORE AWARE OF THE HOLY SPIRIT IN ME THAN THE WEIRD LOOKS I MIGHT GET FROM THOSE AROUND ME.

Have we been building a solid walk with Him to the point that we are anchored through life's most difficult storms, or do we somehow believe that following Jesus means He's going to make everything good and doubt God's goodness as soon as life gets hard?

When our plans don't go the way we want them to, our kids don't grow up loving and serving God, our careers take a plunge and we fall into a financial crisis, someone gets diagnosed with an illness that takes their life, our marriage is at risk and divorce is on the horizon . . .

Insert your devastation here.

They are endless.

Because we have spent so much time with our checklist Christianity, we do not know how to run to Jesus to carry us through the challenges. We haven't really learned to follow Him. The nets we were supposed to drop, we clung to instead, and we made them our safe place instead of Him.

We need to start asking ourselves: Am I building my life on the Rock of my salvation or on the sand?

> *So why do you keep calling me 'Lord, Lord!' when you don't do what I say? I will show you what it's like when someone comes to Me, listens to My teaching, and then follows it. It is like a person building a house who digs deep and lays the foundation on solid rock. When the floodwaters rise and break against that house, it stands firm because it is well built. But anyone who hears and doesn't obey is like a person*

who builds a house right on the ground, without a foundation. When the floods sweep down against that house, it will collapse into a heap of ruins. — Luke 6:46-49 (NLT)

We will experience life storms and devastations.

God never promised us the equation to a pain-free life. He promises to be with us always, catch all of our tears, heal our hearts, filling us with a peace that cannot be explained when our circumstances are saying otherwise, and He will comfort us continuously.

We have to understand what His promises are and make sure that we have not built our own safety nets in our lives apart from Him. These nets (idols) have been put in our lives in place of God and then when hard things come our way, we don't feel close to Him. For many, an underlying resentment, or feeling like God doesn't care about them begins to birth in their heart, and they either want to run away from God altogether or just go through the motions of life, carrying around a wounded heart that is bleeding inside. Resentment and life wounds are not God's heart for His children. Running away from God or believing He doesn't care will not lead us to the peace, freedom, and joy that is fully available here and now no matter what we face in this broken world!

> *"The Lord will guide you always; He will satisfy your needs in a sun-scorched land and will strengthen your frame. You will be like a well-watered garden, like a spring whose waters never fail."* — Isaiah 58:11 (NIV)

This isn't something to quote; this is something to live and experience. The only way we unlock the power of what these passages reveal to us is by responding to God and following His lead. As we learn to yield to the lead of the Holy Spirit, trusting Him in all things, we begin to see His goodness woven through devastation, and peace reigns in our lives.

The nets WE WERE SUPPOSED TO DROP, WE CLUNG TO INSTEAD, AND WE MADE THEM OUR SAFE PLACE INSTEAD OF HIM.

And we know that in all things God works for the good of those who love Him, who have been called according to His purpose. — Romans 8:28 (NIV)

I visited a church recently. The pastor

came out, opened his Bible, and began to preach. He was talking about the different types of people's responses to Jesus when He appeared to the crowds.

Good message, right?

I thought so.

Then he began to read the story of Mary and Martha. Mary being at the feet of Jesus, Martha being busy preparing "worrying about many things." Rather than teaching the actual point of the story, and how Jesus told Martha that Mary had found the most important thing when Martha complained to Jesus about her seemingly lazy sister, the pastor left that entire part out. I thought he was going to talk about the type of person who is too caught up in the worries of this life to sit with Jesus and how that is the most important, but he took the message in a whole other direction that left me speechless.

He stopped at Martha's inner struggle and trailed away from Jesus' actual reply to Martha.

Instead of sharing the message of these passages on how Martha is stuck in too many worries of this life, and that Mary has found that the most important is sitting at the feet of Jesus, clinging to what He has to say, the pastor flipped it. He placed the emphasis on Martha's "acts of service" gifting and began to tell the congregation the importance of plugging in and serving in a ministry at the church. He went on for several minutes making it seem that Martha was the one who had it right.

What's wrong with this picture?

We were just pointed to follow man and the checklist Christian way instead of sitting with Jesus.

Our lifeline.

While I do believe that God wants us to plug in and get involved, there are many other passages that he could've used to support this idea but didn't. Taking these scriptures out of context and using them as a call to action to go, serve, be, do, was not what Jesus said was most important. I promise you, your peace is not in the checklist.

Do the things on the list carry value?

Yes, of course!

But not at the cost of being at the feet of Jesus, clinging to His every Word that He wants to breathe into you, and following Him. His Words carry power! The power to fill us with exactly what we need when we need it.

We have gone off track, and it's time to get back to the Father's heart!

It's time to recognize what we are missing in our walks with Jesus: the pathway that was paved and paid for to get into His presence, sit with Him, hear His voice, drop our nets and respond to Him.

We are the bride of Christ.

Our marriage is to Jesus, not a church building, not to a pastor, or even our church community. It doesn't matter which church you go to, we are called to go and follow Jesus. This is the mandate. Not come in, stay and grow "roots." The only roots we should be establishing are with Jesus, the true Vine.

Is our church community vital?

Yes, absolutely!

The Word clearly teaches us not to neglect meeting together, but meeting in a church building was never meant to replace Him.

I'm reminded of Paul and His boldness to preach solid Truth, calling people out and pointing them to a higher standard of living. He was more concerned about spiritual maturity than He was in making people comfortable. He was more intentional with correcting the body of Christ than coddling them. He knew that coddling would not set anyone up to make it through this life with a boldness for Christ and a confidence that cannot be shaken by the hard things we will experience.

We do not like to be uncomfortable and we often avoid that nudge or call from the Holy Spirit who wants to lead us to greater depths of faith. We are all on a journey of learning and growing. None of us have arrived at spiritual perfection. We all have thresholds of fear and nets that we have clung to. Myself included! These nets are the borders that God wants us to let go of and respond in faith.

Let's decide today that we are done missing out on the facets of God Almighty that Jesus paid for by releasing our nets, and learn to run with bold faith!

The disciples were called, they dropped their nets, stepped into an abundant, fully satisfying life, and walked with Jesus. They went from a mundane and ordinary life to a life filled with awe and wonder. This life is the invitation of the Father's heart for each of us.

What's the Holy Spirit highlighting to you today?

What safety net have you built for yourself that God is asking you to drop so you can truly follow Him?

Take the time to release each one to God, open your heart wide and hear what He has for you.

> *"My sheep listen to My voice; I know them, and they follow Me."*
> *—John 10:27 (NIV)*

You have been called by name, drop your net, and respond to Him.

THE ONLY ROOTS WE SHOULD BE ESTABLISHING ARE WITH JESUS, THE TRUE VINE.

Pray with me:

> *Father, I have struggled to believe that You have the best intentions for my life. I have built my own kingdom, and I have been clinging to the nets of this world for my comfort, not to You. I have consumed myself with fear of judgment, criticism, worries of this life, and my sinful nature, realizing now that I have been following my own way and other voices instead of Yours. I have been afraid to miss out on something instead of trusting You with everything. Today I am dropping my net of false security and turning to You. I want to know You, know Your voice, and truly follow You with my whole heart. I desire that abundant life that Your Son, Jesus paid for. Show me what following You looks like in my everyday life. Help me take notice of the promptings of the Holy Spirit guiding me along the path that You have marked for me. In Your name I pray, amen.*

Chapter Seven
Releasing the Kingdom

"This, then, is how you should pray: 'Our Father in heaven, hallowed be Your name, Your Kingdom come, Your will be done, on earth as it is in heaven.'" — Matthew 6:9-10 (NIV)

What is God's will?

I think we spend a lot of time deciding what God's will is instead of reading the Bible with fresh eyes, so we can see what His will is through Jesus' ministry as well as the continuum through the apostles and beyond.

What's amazing to me is how many times I hear my Jesus family pray, "*if* it's Your will." But that is not how we are taught to pray according to the Word of God. There is only one time that I have read in the Bible where Jesus said, this is how you should pray . . . and this is the very first sentence: "Our Father in heaven, hallowed be Your name, Your Kingdom come, Your will be done, on earth as it is in heaven."

Jesus leads us to pray in a way that invites God's reign here on earth, lifting His name high above everything, inviting His Kingdom to come . . . today!

Not "if."

His Kingdom *is* His will, and it's up to us to partner with His will in our prayer lives. To grasp the mystery of what Jesus is saying to us as we read the prayer that He taught, we have to learn about the Kingdom, which means we soak in every single time Jesus states about the Kingdom of Heaven, understand what the Kingdom means, and realize the Kingdom is near.

The Kingdom of Heaven is perfect, with no sadness, no sin, no illness ... a perfect Kingdom is overwhelming to grasp through our minds because the world we reside in is filled with so much brokenness, heartache, and pain. Because of Jesus' death, burial, and resurrection, we have been given the ministry of the Kingdom of Heaven through the Holy Spirit. The same Spirit that brought Heaven to earth through Jesus is available to each of us, and it's for today.

Today we get to experience glimpses of what Heaven is like when we invite Jesus into our life circumstances, emotions, situations, and even the places we go; we can claim the ground we walk by inviting Heaven to reign. The Holy Spirit has to unlock this concept for us, igniting faith, allowing Him to take us deeper into what God has empowered us to accomplish. When we begin to understand what we have access to, we will become so rooted in confident trust, we will truly have nothing to fear.

> *"I am going to send you what my Father has promised; but stay in the city until you have been clothed with power from on high."*
> *— Luke 24:49 (NIV)*

This ministry could not start without the power and the presence of the Holy Spirit infilling the disciples, which is why Jesus told them to wait until He came. We have access to that same Spirit, releasing the Kingdom of Heaven everywhere we go. The flame that started through the Holy Spirit when Jesus went away to be with the Father was meant to be ongoing—we are clothed with power!

Wow ... can you even comprehend this invitation as we make Jesus Lord of our lives?!

Releasing the Kingdom of Heaven is the ultimate ripple effect of our Heavenly Father's heart. This is the assignment He has given to each of us who call upon His Holy Name. We have been invited into a lifestyle of bringing Heaven here on earth in the most natural yet supernatural way, and the work that He has been doing in us is meant to be a testimony of God's overwhelming love and power through us.

We are conduits of God's life-changing love and power.

Do you realize this?

Maybe you have been able to receive the love of God, but experiencing His power is not a norm in your life, and you reject the idea altogether. Don't let your experiences define the bigness of our God. There will always be a depth of God to be discovered as long as we're living on this side of Heaven.

No more boxing God in and telling ourselves that we have to wait for Heaven to taste it. When we read our Bibles, it should be increasing our faith and building excitement for what God wants to do, which is to bring Heaven to us right now. The foundation has been laid, which is Jesus Christ. The work has already begun. And we have been invited through the power and presence of the Holy Spirit not just to become changed ourselves, becoming more like Him going from glory to glory, but to release His glory to those around us.

> The flame that STARTED THROUGH THE HOLY SPIRIT WHEN JESUS WENT AWAY TO BE WITH THE FATHER WAS MEANT TO BE ONGOING—WE ARE CLOTHED WITH POWER!

We have been called.

Chosen.

Marked by Heaven.

Anointed and appointed for such a time as this.

Let's step into it!

In our home, when someone is sick or hurting, the first thing we do is declare healing in Jesus' name. We have watched fevers leave the body immediately, broken bones get healed, sickness' and headaches leave . . . this is releasing the Kingdom into the lives around us.

When my kids walk into a room and see me praying for someone, they immediately stop, extend their hands in prayer, and agree with Heaven to heal. We get to train our kids in this power. Engaging the Holy Spirit's power in our homes and beyond is what it means to raise our kids in the way of the Lord.

Now, there is a whole counterfeit movement that has spread through the church in regards to "manifestations and vibrations."

> **We are conduits of God's life-changing love and power.**

It's basically when you say what you want and believe it will happen by "releasing vibrations" out to the "universe" to "manifest." This is a New Age practice that twists scripture. With New Age practices trickling their way into the body of Christ (I've seen a lot over the years), I can see how one can reject the entire idea to lay our hands on the sick and declare healing.

But let's not confuse the two.

The enemy is a copycat.

He will come in and deceive people, twisting scripture and disguising himself as an angel of light.

> *For such people are false apostles, deceitful workers, masquerading as apostles of Christ. And no wonder, for satan himself masquerades as an angel of light.* — 2 Corinthians 11:13-15 (NIV)

I'm not sure if you realize that the enemy can mimic God. He is just limited as to what he can do. It is easy to be deceived by this power coming from the wrong source, being led to believe it's God when it's satan.

> *But the Egyptian magicians did the same things by their secret arts, and Pharaoh's heart became hard; he would not listen to Moses and Aaron, just as the Lord had said.* — Exodus 7:22 (NIV)

In Exodus 5-12, you can read the entire account of what the magicians were doing to prove that their god is equal to our God and that they did have limits when our God doesn't.

The enemy does this for two reasons and either one is a win for him.

One, he will make the Christians want to run away from anything similar to the work of Jesus so that we fear the ministry of the Holy Spirit. Or two, he will lead others away from the Holy Spirit, so that they are actually operating with a different spirit, and they think it's God when it's not.

This New Age practice is mimicking God, but it's satan disguising himself as an "angel of light." This movement, and all other ways the

New Age has blinded the body of Christ, is a wide-open door in one's life, partnering with the devil, giving him access in their life. New Age practices set people up to be their own god. It's self-focused and not seeking the Kingdom above all else. There is a dangerous trickle effect when we do not develop discernment and allow our fleshly desires to rule us; it leads us to operate with the wrong spirit in our lives. We are called to test the spirit that is operating:

> *Dear friends, do not believe every spirit, but test the spirits to see whether they are from God, because many false prophets have gone out into the world. — 1 John 4:1 (NIV)*

Testing the spirit is not a new concept.

If you read your Bible you can see that satan has been working to lead people away from God since Adam's fall. We need to make sure we are connected to the true Vine, Jesus Christ, reading our Bibles so that we are saturated in the Word with sharp discernment to know when the wolf in sheep's clothing is at work.

> *"Watch out for false prophets. They come to you in sheep's clothing, but inwardly they are ferocious wolves." —Matthew 7:15 (NIV)*

The people leading the New Age movement are either completely deceived, convinced they are connected to God and His power, or they are the false prophets, intentionally leading people away from Jesus, "servants" of satan.

I have watched New Age practices come into the church at large in so many ways, leading my brothers and sisters to believe they are experiencing the power of the Holy Spirit, when it's the kingdom of darkness at work, it's scary.

We need to always be paying attention!

False prophets will never mention or point you to a submitted life with Jesus. They do not talk about obeying and surrendering your life to God. They may even take certain scriptures and biblical wording that makes what they are saying seem biblical and godly, but it's only one part of the whole picture. You will notice a theme and it ain't about glorifying Jesus. It's all about glorifying "self" and gratifying their own personal agendas, teaching you that you can have this ability in your own life too.

Remember, satan told Jesus that he would give him everything Jesus saw if He would follow him and leave His assignment. The devil is still toying with us in the subtlest way, promising us the kingdoms of this world.

God's Kingdom is not self-seeking.

The devil attracts people through a selfish gain to "manifest" their own way and it's oftentimes desires of the flesh.

Remember Simon the sorcerer?

> *When they arrived, they prayed for the new believers there that they might receive the Holy Spirit, because the Holy Spirit had not yet come on any of them; they had simply been baptized in the name of the Lord Jesus. Then Peter and John placed their hands on them, and they received the Holy Spirit. When Simon saw that the Spirit was given at the laying on of the apostles' hands, he offered them money and said, "Give me also this ability so that everyone on whom I lay my hands may receive the Holy Spirit." Peter answered: "May your money perish with you, because you thought you could buy the gift of God with money!" — Acts 8:15-20 (NIV)*

We need to make **SURE WE ARE CONNECTED TO THE TRUE VINE, JESUS CHRIST, READING OUR BIBLES SO THAT WE ARE SATURATED IN THE WORD WITH SHARP DISCERNMENT TO KNOW WHEN THE WOLF IN SHEEP'S CLOTHING IS AT WORK.**

Money and selfish gain are not always the attraction, but this belief appeals to those who do not have a fully yielded life to Jesus, or discernment. Some genuinely just want to see power move in their lives, and others, and may truly have good intentions. The crazy thing about all of this is that I have seen how New Age leaders even use scripture with a slight twist that sounds like God, but it's twisting His Word to work for themselves.

There was a woman who purchased something from us recently. Through her random conversation with my husband she jumped on one of His replies about Jesus and said emphatically, "I am a healer!" She went on with a few more comments that sounded biblical, claiming to be a Christian. I'm not going to go into the whole conversation, but the key phrase that revealed she was operating in the wrong spirit was that *she* is a healer. She used some scriptures in her conversation, but then mixed some very New Age phrases that are not of God. This is where we learn to test the spirit.

A follower of Jesus who believes in the supernatural gift of healing, does not claim the power as their own. They know the Source in which the healing comes from—it's always Jesus!

We have to be rooted in the Word, connected to the Vine at all times so we are not led astray!

Back to releasing the Kingdom of Heaven ... I had a very dear friend in Colorado who had a young family like us. I knew God had brought her into my life to not just have a friend but to point her to Jesus. She was broken by religion and living a lifestyle that was far from God's heart.

He gave me such a special love for her.

I'm changing their names to share this story.

One day, Becky burst into our apartment (I had an open-door policy, and coffee was always ready for her, so this was not abnormal), but this time she fell to the ground in front of me. "Pray for John. He's in the hospital. The doctors don't know what's going on. An infection is taking over his body and he's dying. I know God hears you."

Without hesitation, I prayed: "Lord, I command the infection in John's body to go in the name of Jesus! I pray that not only will he live, but doctors will not be able to explain it and this miracle will all point to You."

I looked at her and boldly replied, "He's not going to die."

I will admit, inside I was terrified when those bold words fell out of my mouth. It was not me speaking. It was the Holy Spirit speaking through me. My whole body was trembling as those words dropped out of my mouth with a boldness I had never experienced before. I felt an internal push against what my human understanding did not want to say.

Becky called me later that day to tell me that she needed two witnesses to sign because the doctors said John was not going to make it. She needed to make sure she was in charge of medical decisions. I called my friend from church, filled her in, and we both continued to pray, believing he was not going to die but followed protocol. We went to the hospital; John was gray and lifeless. I wasn't hung up on what I saw. I knew he was going to live. If my memory is accurate, he was home three days later. And as soon as he had the strength, he and his whole family joined us at church. Becky left the lifestyle she was living and committed her heart to Jesus.

> We have to BE ROOTED IN THE WORD, CONNECTED TO THE VINE AT ALL TIMES SO WE ARE NOT LED ASTRAY!

This story is an example of releasing the Kingdom of Heaven in our daily lives when we are yielding to the Holy Spirit and available to those around us. This is the ministry that we have all been invited into. My simple walk with Jesus, living in rhythm with Him, filled me with a boldness that was the opposite of my "personality" or human wiring. This is the natural ripple effect that should be present in our lives on a regular basis when we are in sync with Him and His Holy Spirit within us.

I know many are afraid to pray boldly in fear of the opposite outcome.

I get it.

I've prayed many times, believing someone would be healed in Jesus' name, and they died. It's heartbreaking to watch someone (and myself) lose a loved one.

Does that mean I stop believing that God heals and stop praying for people in this way?

No.

I'm going to pray with bold faith every single time and trust God with the outcome!

This is where faith and trust will always override what I am experiencing and feeling. I believe God still heals today. Sometimes we see God show up through a creative miracle. Then there are times He shows up in other ways, and the fullness of healing comes when He completely restores our loved ones in Heaven. Faith is believing and trusting God with everything no matter what the outcome is.

I will not sway away from knowing my God can do anything—I will continue to contend, believe, and release the Kingdom of Heaven here on earth!

Because it's God's will.

There was a young gal who we moved into our house, becoming fused into our family for a season. She had been struggling with her job where she felt some serious warfare in the atmosphere, and it was becoming so heavy over her, she wanted to quit.

Before I go on from here, I want to invite you into a reality that you may not be familiar with.

Have you ever felt totally fine and then walked into a store, your workplace, or another situation, and all of a sudden you are just in a bad mood, depressed, anxious, or feel heavy?

There have been many times when I have talked with clients who experience this and think what they are feeling is in them, not recognizing it's actually coming from what's going on around them. We are spiritual beings, and we can feel things in the spirit realm that most of us cannot see. As I process with my clients about what they are experiencing and feeling, I bring them to biblical Truth, teaching them their authority in Jesus' name. They do not have to take in what they are feeling around them. This is one of the ways we live by the Spirit. Once they get a grasp of what God has given to them, they are ready to release something powerfully different into the atmosphere, lifting the heaviness off of them and others!

Exercising our authority in Jesus' name releases the Kingdom of Heaven into the situation. It is a su-

> I WILL NOT SWAY AWAY FROM KNOWING MY GOD CAN DO ANYTHING —I WILL CONTINUE TO CONTEND, BELIEVE, AND RELEASE THE KINGDOM OF HEAVEN HERE ON EARTH!

pernatural shift in an atmosphere that pushes back the work of the devil and his kingdom of darkness so that others can tangibly feel a change. Whether it be peace, healing, or a lightness in the atmosphere that wasn't there before, calling on Jesus' authority over dark feelings allows us to talk about how we prayed and called on Heaven, pointing people to Jesus.

Believe me, this is real and available wherever we go as change agents to the world around us.

The young girl who moved in with us wanted to quit her job. It was getting bad, and she was internalizing so much that she began experiencing serious physical ailments. Her perfect solution was to quit.

Makes sense, right?

Sorry to break the news to you, but quitting is the worst possible solution to the problem.

Unless God releases you from your position, you don't quit.

Period.

At this point in time, she was not being released from this job. She was being invited into a powerful opportunity for spiritual maturity as well as positioned for something greater for God.

Remember, James 1:2-4 shows us how to respond in these situations. *The Message* paints the perfect picture of what He is saying:

> *Consider it a sheer gift, friends, when tests and challenges come at you from all sides. You know that under pressure, your faith-life is forced into the open and shows its true colors. So don't try to get out of anything prematurely. Let it do its work so you become mature and well-developed, not deficient in any way.*

There are usually a few things going on when we are faced with tests and challenges:

1. God is doing something in us, and He's showing us where our faith life is not intact with Him, but rather in what we are feeling and experiencing, which is not faith.

2. He wants to do something powerfully amazing through us to those around us.

3. As our faith life begins to override what we are feeling, surrendering to the process, we become so spiritually mature, we aren't lacking anywhere.

We don't fully understand what this powerful transaction is accomplishing in us until we have faithfully walked through these hard situations rather than trying to get out of them. Culture gives us so many options and "ways out," that it's hard to comprehend the power we could experience in these moments with God.

I'm blown away at what He's done in me and through me during the most challenging seasons of my life as I yield to His way over mine, allowing Him to set my path straight. There is a depth of God that I've encountered in the "valleys" of life when I'm being pressed hard that the mountain tops do not reveal.

Keep in mind, this is a different concept than we discussed earlier—doing things we don't have God's grace for.

What I am referring to in this chapter is how often we bypass hard moments in life and leave positions that God has ordained for us because it gets hard. It is so important to develop discernment and hear what God is saying to us so that we can know the difference between something we should not have committed to, or a growth opportunity as we learn to live by the Spirit.

We both knew this young woman was placed in her work for a reason. God absolutely led her there. Her natural human response when it got hard was to "find a way out." This was a major test and challenge, and she could easily find an out by quitting.

As Jesus followers, we no longer evaluate things from a worldly perspective, recognizing that our battles are not of flesh and blood but the work of the kingdom of darkness. We need to take back some ground by releasing the Kingdom of Heaven in our everyday lives!

She was fully aware she was experiencing warfare because she had been taught this to be true, so this was not news to her. However, she was not walking in her authority, and she was allowing what she was feeling to have more power than the powerful presence of the Holy Spirit in her.

She wanted to retreat.

This was my starting point with her.

She needed to know that because she was internalizing and taking on the heaviness in the atmosphere through her flesh when she was called to live by the Spirit, the heaviness was actually attacking her body, causing some major medical problems. She needed to be open to the power she has inside her and what she has access to in these situations. As she began to recognize that she was called and placed in this work by God, not only for an income to provide for herself, but to be a light in this dark place—something shifted inside of her.

Let's connect with some things here . . . if we're consumed with the stress that our mortal bodies are not designed to carry, the stress will cause physical problems. In the Kingdom of Heaven, there is no stress. What we have in Jesus is peace. If peace is available to us no matter what, should we be overwhelmed with stress to the point that we are at risk for health problems?

Not in Jesus.

Remember, Jesus said that He paved the way for us to have an abundant life and that if we follow His ways, He will show us what it looks like and feels like to live light and free. The complete opposite of stress. When we are living from a limited understanding of what we have access to, we settle for what the world says is normal and try to manage it instead of calling on Heaven.

I'm not going to go any deeper into the concept of how stress causes sickness because this would be a whole other book topic crammed inside of this book. I encourage you to explore this reality with the Holy Spirit and go through the Word.

Recognize how many times the Bible talks about sicknesses that come from things that we have the power to overcome.

Here's one to start with. Many of us know these passages but may not have connected them with what they are telling us about health for our physical bodies.

> *My son, pay attention to what I say; turn your ear to My words. Do not let them out of your sight, keep them within your heart; for they are life to those who find them and health to one's whole body.*
> *— Proverbs 4:20-22 (NIV)*

Soak in this passage and read it prayerfully.

Ask the Holy Spirit to speak to you in the possible areas where you are struggling to turn to His Words and live by them in your everyday life. Areas where you are consumed with the stresses of this life, carrying loads you were not made to carry . . . maybe even areas you have some opened doors through sin. Check in with Him and your own heart. God wants to touch your body right here and right now!

I'm praying and believing that even as you read these words you feel His presence moving powerfully through you.

If you are reading this and feeling a shift in your body, pause. Press into Him and take the time to partner with the Holy Spirit. Pick up the book later when you are ready to keep reading.

Don't bypass this moment if you are experiencing the presence and healing power of the Holy Spirit!

When we are LIVING FROM A LIMITED UNDERSTANDING OF WHAT WE HAVE ACCESS TO, WE SETTLE FOR WHAT THE WORLD SAYS IS NORMAL AND TRY TO MANAGE IT INSTEAD OF CALLING ON HEAVEN.

Back to what God was doing in the young woman with the challenging work situation: Once she began to make the connection between what she was feeling around her to what she was taking on and how those things were leading her to anxious thoughts, panic attacks, and various other physical problems, she realized all this was the work of the enemy trying to hurt her and hinder her from becoming effective for the Kingdom of Heaven.

> *Cast all your anxiety on Him because He cares for you. Be alert and of sober mind. Your enemy the devil prowls around like a roaring lion looking for someone to devour. Resist him, standing firm in the faith, because you know that the family of believers throughout the world is undergoing the same kind of sufferings. — 1 Peter 5:7-9 (NIV)*

One: We have to recognize we are not alone in experiencing hardships. There is a lie that says our life is harder than what others are living, and then we look around comparing and believing that if we had a different life, we wouldn't feel these burdens. That is a lie from the pit of hell! Don't feed into these ideas because the problem becomes magnified rather than resolved.

Two: What we are feeling in the atmosphere easily leads us to a thought-life that is unsettled (the opposite of sober), creating anxiety. Then, we become a target to the enemy who wants to devour us and keep us ineffective for the Kingdom of God. Remember, the enemy and his dark principalities (demons) are literally, not figuratively, lurking for those with an unsettled mind.

We talked about how the enemy looks for people who are letting anxiety rule them instead of casting it to the Lord, and how she is a vulnerable target to the enemy by not washing her mind in the Word and standing firm in faith. Once this revelation took place in her mind and heart, she stepped into her position, buckling herself with Truth. She was ready for combat in the spirit; the peace that transcends all understanding enveloped her, panic attacks no longer had power, and her physical body got stronger.

> *Stand your ground, putting on the belt of truth and the body armor of God's righteousness.* — Ephesians 6:14 (NLT)

Her next shift was powerfully different.

Peace filled the atmosphere, and she was no longer in a cloud trying to crawl her way through the shift.

She was available for conversations with her coworkers, no longer bound with the heaviness that kept her silent. God could use her now as she learned to release the Kingdom. But first, she had to clear the pathway by recognizing that she was not meant to live with the anxieties she had been feeling.

How often do we go through this life paralyzed by what we are feeling?

This is 100% what satan hopes we continue doing. The enemy wants us to remain stuck in cycles of heaviness, getting pummeled by life instead of pulling from Heaven all that we have access to as children of God and carriers of the Holy Spirit.

Many in the body of Christ have spent much of their Christian walk trying to change themselves, creating their own prisons, living with God in a box, begging Him to change their circumstances, missing out on the fullness of life that Jesus paid for. The life that unlocks the Kingdom of Heaven in our every day ... God's Word reveals to us that we have been given access to His Kingdom through His power, and in the name of Jesus, we can go and change the world!

Jesus told us to "Pray like this ... 'Your Kingdom come, Your will be done, on earth as it is in Heaven.'"

Are you ready to activate what God has given us access to?

I hope by this point you are bursting inside and ready to do some serious damage to the kingdom of darkness that has had an upper hand in the body of Christ for too many generations!

I was having my quiet time with Jesus early one morning, curled up by my fireplace when God gave me a vision: There was a pasture with a flock of sheep casually grazing. They were safely in the fenced area. A hand from Heaven came and removed the entire fence. The sheep panicked. They began to huddle closer together, looking around in terror. And the Lord said to me: "Many of my sheep have created their comfort within the walls of the church building. They do not recognize my voice and struggle to follow Me ..."

The message was clear. The sheep represented you and me. Many are in the church grazing, and fearful of anything outside the protective walls. But like we've discussed, this is not real Christianity, or what the Bible paints for us to live by. We have become consumer Christians who have learned to rely on the church walls and what's available within the boundaries of the building,

> *The enemy wants us to remain stuck in cycles of heaviness, getting pummeled by life instead of pulling from Heaven all that we have access to as children of God and carriers of the Holy Spirit.*

expecting our pastors to do the work of a disciple.

He is calling us all into a rhythm of life with Him that defies the parameters we have placed on ourselves and on Him. He is calling us to rise up, step out, and release His Kingdom! It was never His will to build a physical church (temple) in the New Testament.

Again, this is not to say we shouldn't go to church; we have already discussed the value of being plugged into a community. This is where we become equipped to do the work of the Saints. Then we go, lighting up our homes, our neighborhoods, our workplaces, and beyond.

Wherever God has placed you, that is the territory that He has assigned to you.

The Lord gave me a Word for the church, He said, "My Church has been deployed." Not I'm *going to*, it has been.

Deploy means to position for battle, to spread out for a deliberate purpose.

God has dispersed His Church, you and me, all over the world. He has given us different territories and assignments, different positions, and they look vastly different from one to the next, but it's still the same call to action—Go and release the Kingdom ...

> *"The Kingdom of Heaven has come near. Heal the sick, raise the dead, cleanse those who have leprosy, drive out demons. Freely you have received; freely give." — Matthew 10:7-8 (NIV)*

The message has not changed.

We as the Church have changed the message.

Keep in mind, when God says deployed, we are living in the new covenant. The battle He is referring to is against the principalities in the spirit realm, not people. God is not telling us to go out and fight for land like much of what we read in the Old Testament; although, we can pull from the lives of many men and women who were placed in high positions within a palace of those who were not godly.

> *For our struggle is not against flesh and blood, but against the rulers, against the authorities, against the powers of this dark world*

and against the spiritual forces of evil in the heavenly realms.
— Ephesians 6:12 (NIV)

When someone does something hurtful to you or you are under a "government" that is oppressive from your workplace to the region you live in, recognize that there are spirits operating behind them. The spirits are the ones you stand firm against, and we do not wage war against them as this world does. We put on our armor of God's Word first and foremost so that when the battle is over, we are still standing. Not pushed down, oppressed, heavy laden, and burdened by the situation.

> The Lord gave me a word for the church, He said, "My church has been deployed." Not I'm going to, it has been.

Side nugget testimony of putting on our armor: My oldest son experienced depression for a season. Each time he voiced it to me, I would have him pray and repeat after me, "putting on his armor." We would call each part out and declare that he was putting it on. He would give me a hard time at first because it felt silly to him, but trusting me and choosing faith, he would. Instantly the heaviness would lift! By taking the Word of God, which is the only weapon of warfare we have been given, and all too often are not using, the battle that he was experiencing that was messing with him, left! Eventually, he learned to trust God for himself, and the tormenting spirits that were assigned to mess with him using depression and suicidal thoughts no longer had power over him.

Back to life battles . . . they are NOT against flesh and blood!

This means we have to stop fighting with our flesh and the "flesh" of others. When we are faced with people who are hurting us through their actions, those that seem like pure evil or just careless, Jesus died for them too.

Remember this truth.

Forgive like Jesus, out of obedience to God, recognizing that we are out of God's will when we withhold forgiveness.

> *"For if you forgive other people when they sin against you, your heavenly Father will also forgive you. But if you do not for-*

> *give others their sins, your Father will not forgive your sins."*
> — *Matthew 6:14-15 (NIV)*

One of the concepts that God helped me with so that I could genuinely release people who have hurt me, is recognizing that God never said I need to trust all people. He knows their hearts; He says trust Me and love them. When we are rooted in a trust walk with God, filled with His love, we are empowered to release those who have wronged us instead of keeping account of all that's been done to us.

Now, there are times where God has us move on.

We see this happening throughout the New Testament. Jesus knew when to move on from a certain people group, and so did the disciples. They listened to the leading of the Holy Spirit and went wherever they were sent. Sometimes, we are told to leave a certain situation because it is unsafe, or the heart is hardened completely. We have to trust God with those outcomes and move with Him while still forgiving people for their actions and behaviors.

Remember what Jesus said as He was being crucified?

> *When they came to the place called the Skull, they crucified Him there, along with the criminals—one on His right, the other on His left. Jesus said, "Father, forgive them, for they do not know what they are doing." And they divided up His clothes by casting lots.*
> — *Luke 23:33-34 (NIV)*

When we apply the scriptures as our armor, we are firmly rooted and cannot be taken down in the battle, recognizing that what we are experiencing has a demonic principality behind it. The enemy uses the weaknesses, hurts, and brokenness in others to attack us in our weak, unarmored areas. He uses people as pawns in his game to get us to fight the wrong source while he just sits back and laughs at the destruction going on.

We are not here to fight people.

We are here to love them and release the Kingdom of Heaven.

They are deceived and in bondage to the enemy. They are blinded by darkness and desperately need a touch from Jesus. Let's stop focusing on what the unsaved think, believe, their lifestyle, what they did, and everything that separates us from loving them fiercely into the Kingdom of Heaven!

> *I urge, then, first of all, that petitions, prayers, intercession and thanksgiving be made for all people—for kings and all those in authority, that we may live peaceful and quiet lives in all godliness and holiness. This is good, and pleases God our Savior, who wants all people to be saved and to come to a knowledge of the truth.*
> *— 1 Timothy 2:1-4 (NIV)*

If you are positioned alongside a leader who is not a believer, recognize that God has placed you there to be a light. We can see throughout the Bible the honor, respect, and humility of those God trusted with these positions. They had God's favor to walk out in obedience to the leaders without disobeying God, and they did it in a way that gained favor from the leader.

From Joseph to Daniel and even the three men that we know as Shadrach, Meshach, and Abednego who were put to the fire, and I want to highlight some things we can glean from them. Each one, as recorded in the Bible, did not fight for the king to change his ways. They just declined respectfully when it came to compromising their own personal beliefs. Let's take a look in Daniel:

> *The king assigned them a daily amount of food and wine from the king's table. They were to be trained for three years, and after that they were to enter the king's service. Among those who were chosen were some from Judah: Daniel, Hananiah, Mishael and Azariah. The chief official gave them new names: to Daniel, the name Belteshazzar; to Hananiah, Shadrach; to Mishael, Meshach; and to Azariah, Abednego. But Daniel resolved not to defile himself with the royal food and wine, and he asked the chief official for permission not to defile himself this way. Now God had caused the official to*

Let's stop FOCUSING ON WHAT THE UNSAVED THINK, BELIEVE, THEIR LIFESTYLE, WHAT THEY DID, AND EVERYTHING THAT SEPARATES US FROM LOVING THEM FIERCELY INTO THE KINGDOM OF HEAVEN!

> *show favor and compassion to Daniel, but the official told Daniel, "I am afraid of my lord the king, who has assigned your food and drink. Why should he see you looking worse than the other young men your age? The king would then have my head because of you." Daniel then said to the guard whom the chief official had appointed over Daniel, Hananiah, Mishael and Azariah, "Please test your servants for ten days: Give us nothing but vegetables to eat and water to drink. Then compare our appearance with that of the young men who eat the royal food, and treat your servants in accordance with what you see." So he agreed to this and tested them for ten days. At the end of the ten days they looked healthier and better nourished than any of the young men who ate the royal food. So the guard took away their choice food and the wine they were to drink and gave them vegetables instead. To these four young men God gave knowledge and understanding of all kinds of literature and learning. And Daniel could understand visions and dreams of all kinds. At the end of the time set by the king to bring them into his service, the chief official presented them to Nebuchadnezzar.* — Daniel 1:5-18 (NIV)

Notice the respect in asking, and the favor God gave them. They were not rude or demanding, and because of Daniel's respect, and the favor he had from God, he was trusted with more.

Then we have another example when Daniel was called in to interpret a dream no one else could give the king understanding to. Again he was not rude, but faithfully delivered the message from God, and this was the result:

> *Then King Nebuchadnezzar fell prostrate before Daniel and paid him honor and ordered that an offering and incense be presented to him. The king said to Daniel, "Surely your God is the God of gods and the Lord of kings and a revealer of mysteries, for you were able to reveal this mystery." Then the king placed Daniel in a high position and lavished many gifts on him. He made him ruler over the entire province of Babylon and placed him in charge of all its wise men. Moreover, at Daniel's request the king appointed Shadrach, Meshach and Abednego administrators over the province of Babylon, while Daniel himself remained at the royal court.* — Daniel 2:46-49 (NIV)

The result of Daniel respectfully going to the king and giving Him a dream interpretation positioned him for an increase under the king. He was trustworthy.

Then we see a crazy shift where the king now wants everyone to bow and worship him, and if one doesn't, they will be burned in a furnace. Fast forward to Shadrach, Meshach, and Abednego who do not bow down to the king. The king increases the heat, and we see how the Lord not only protected, but it caused yet another shift in the heart of one of the most evil leaders.

> *Nebuchadnezzar then approached the opening of the blazing furnace and shouted, "Shadrach, Meshach and Abednego, servants of the Most High God, come out! Come here!" So Shadrach, Meshach and Abednego came out of the fire, and the satraps, prefects, governors and royal advisers crowded around them. They saw that the fire had not harmed their bodies, nor was a hair of their heads singed; their robes were not scorched, and there was no smell of fire on them. Then Nebuchadnezzar said, "Praise be to the God of Shadrach, Meshach and Abednego, who has sent his angel and rescued his servants! They trusted in him and defied the king's command and were willing to give up their lives rather than serve or worship any god except their own God. Therefore I decree that the people of any nation or language who say anything against the God of Shadrach, Meshach and Abednego be cut into pieces and their houses be turned into piles of rubble, for no other god can save in this way." Then the king promoted Shadrach, Meshach and Abednego in the province of Babylon.*
> — Daniel 3:26-30 (NIV)

Notice they did not mock the king or others for falling in line. They just stood firm in faith and knew how to respond at the moment they were personally pushed to conform. Testimony after testimony from the Old to the New Testament we can read how God used so many faith-filled believers to serve under kings who were not even close to godliness, in regions that were filled with evil and sin. They were in their God-ordained position to release the Kingdom of Heaven.

I'm praying that no matter where you live, your heart is moved to compassion as you pray the heart of our Father in Heaven for those in authority, and if you are faced with a push to compromise, you can stand firm in the faith, rooted in love and humility as God helps you navigate whatever you may face.

It's up to us to partner with the Holy Spirit so that others' eyes may be enlightened to God's Truth and the Savior of the world. The Holy Spirit will give us the right words so we do not need to worry about what we will say. The Holy Spirit will equip and empower us with the wisdom of Heaven, releasing it to those around us.

> *You will stand trial before governors and kings because you are my followers. But this will be your opportunity to tell the rulers and other unbelievers about me. When you are arrested, don't worry about how to respond or what to say. God will give you the right words at the right time. For it is not you who will be speaking—it will be the Spirit of your Father speaking through you.*
> *— Matthew 10:18-20 (NLT)*

Many of us feel like we are on trial and being persecuted to a degree in our everyday lives whether it be with our own families, in our workplaces, or in fear that we will be if we say anything God-related. While these passages are talking about getting arrested, (there are parts of the world where this is actually happening, and we need to be praying) for many this has not been our experience. At least not in the American church. We can still get some valuable takeaway here when we find ourselves in situations where others want to cut us down for our belief:

- ". . . it's an opportunity to tell them about Me." Do you hear the heart of the Father here?

- "don't worry about how to respond or what to say. God will give you the right words at the right time. For it is not you who will be speaking—it will be the Spirit of your Father speaking through you."

Let the Holy Spirit lead.

Crucify the flesh that wants to fight or retreat (leave your God-appointed position or remain silent), and press into the Father's heart.

Let Him give you His eyes to see what He sees.

Train yourself to look past what you are experiencing and feeling. God sees the treasure and He wants us to call it out. Realize how God wants to position each of us and use us in the most unconventional ways, pointing the masses to the love of the Father.

It's in our human wiring to want to make our fight against people who live or believe differently, but fighting makes us ineffective for the Kingdom. The people who do not have the same values as us are not going to agree with a godly lifestyle, so let's not make our fight about the lifestyle they are living when they haven't met God yet. Instead, trust that when they experience God's love through us, the same Holy Spirit that is at work in our life, will work in theirs, too!

How are they going to meet God through us if our focus is on getting them to agree or obey biblical fundamentals that are not their belief, yet?

You see?

Ineffective.

Counterproductive.

We end up with the Church against the world instead of lighting up the world. Not only that, but if we check in with our own hearts, we are most likely in turmoil and not in peace. Heaviness and stress can form knots in our gut, revealing to us that we are probably fighting a battle that was not ours, no longer living within the parameters of God's grace. Not every battle is our battle. We have to trust that the Lord will fight for us, as we remain in step with Him.

When we release God's love and power, pointing the world to a life-changing encounter with the Creator of the universe, allowing the Holy Spirit to draw them to Jesus, we see lives changed and that change shifts culture . . . and "kings."

We are called to be peacemakers:

> *"Blessed are the peacemakers, for they will be called children of God."*
> *— Matthew 5:9 (NIV)*

Do you see how all this ties together?

When we understand how passionately God loves us, and that nothing can separate us from that kind of love, we are no longer living in fear of the evil going on in our world or what may come because of hardships.

God sees THE TREASURE AND HE WANTS US TO CALL IT OUT.

> *Who shall separate us from the love of Christ? Shall trouble or hardship or persecution or famine or nakedness or danger or sword? As it is written: "For your sake we face death all day long; we are considered as sheep to be slaughtered." No, in all these things we are more than conquerors through Him who loved us. For I am convinced that neither death nor life, neither angels nor demons, neither the present nor the future, nor any powers, neither height nor depth, nor anything else in all creation, will be able to separate us from the love of God that is in Christ Jesus our Lord.* — Romans 8:35-39 (NIV)

Everything that Jesus has done for us, and then in us, pours out of us without hesitation. We can't help but radiate. It doesn't matter what position God has given us in life; we are naturally radiating a glory so authentically rich, people see and feel it. We are living testimonies of the living God. It's not about doing church, or what it looks like to "be a Christian" but about becoming, forming, transforming, and going from glory to glory—becoming the purified bride of Christ. Our life becomes His message: the message of Jesus Christ, Savior of the world.

I love the picture Paul paints for us in 1 Corinthians 9:

> *Even though I am free of the demands and expectations of everyone, I have voluntarily become a servant to any and all in order to reach a wide range of people: religious, nonreligious, meticulous moralists, loose-living immoralists, the defeated, the demoralized—whoever. I didn't take on their way of life. I kept my bearings in Christ—but I entered their world and tried to experience things from their point of view. I've become just about every sort of servant there is in my attempts to lead those I meet into a God-saved life. I did all this because of the Message. I didn't just want to talk about it; I wanted to be in on it!* (19-23 MSG)

What Paul shows us is powerful! Living in sync with God's heart empowers us to build bridges to all people, in all places, at all times. We get to be in on what God wants to release on the earth today!

The light we carry from Jesus is pure and simple, yet powerful, uncomplicated and attainable.

God's love revealed—

Rooted in our true identities as children of God, citizens of Heaven—

Receiving and believing like that of a child—

Living from a renewed mind, the mind of Christ—

Responding to Him, fully surrendered—

This is the ripple effect of our Father's heart.

We get to be in on what God wants to release on the earth today!

You have been invited into a powerful rhythm, a lifestyle that is beyond your ways and thoughts.

> *"For My thoughts are not your thoughts, neither are your ways My ways," declares the Lord. "As the heavens are higher than the earth, so are My ways higher than your ways and My thoughts than your thoughts." — Isaiah 55:8-9 (NIV)*

Release the Kingdom of Heaven.

About Jillian Ahonen

Jillian Ahonen, founder of Jillian Ahonen Ministries, has been serving the body of Christ for over a decade through coaching, mentoring, speaking, and writing. She is as real, relatable, and passionate about seeing lives transformed through God's overwhelming love and power.

Jillian is a committed wife to Rolf and mom to her five kids first, but her heart's desire is to see her family of faith living out the freedom and victory that belongs to them through Jesus, and then lighting up the world around them. When Jillian teaches, she combines her transparent, no-nonsense and humorous story-telling style with her spiritual insight to teach biblical messages of truth and hope. Jillian is a lover of Jesus, a Kingdom bringer, and a faith igniter; she is the definition of an overcomer and her life is a reflection of the words she speaks.

When Jillian is not speaking or writing, you will find her out on her daily run while catching up with a friend on the phone, or relaxing on her front porch watching all the kids in the neighborhood, including her own, create a skatepark in the cul-de-sac. She looks forward to gathering with her kids, son-in-love, and grandbaby Oliver for weekend barbecues, and enjoys the simplicity of being home with her family.

Weekly dates are a must for Jillian and her husband, which includes their favorite local sushi restaurant, where everyone knows their name. It's not uncommon to find them off-road somewhere, sitting in the back of Jillian's Suburban with their take-out picnic dinner.

Jillian will be the first to admit that she has somewhat of an obsession with buying and selling used furniture and she feels designing and re-furnishing different rooms of her home is her much-needed creative outlet. While her husband Rolf sees a livable room, Jillian sees a canvas ready for another masterpiece. He has finally given in to his wife's ongoing "issue" and is now a full participant when she finds another "treasure" to add to their modern-farmhouse-themed home.

Her favorite place is, and will always be found, in the stillness of her quiet mornings with Jesus and a good cup of coffee.

www.anchor.fm/notjusttalkwithjillian

Let's Stay Connected

Be on the lookout for Jillian's new podcast,
Not Just Talk with Jillian Ahonen,
coming April 6, 2022!
www.anchor.fm/notjusttalkwithjillian

You can also check out Jillian's previous book, *Life is Muddy*, through her website, Amazon, or your favorite online bookstore.

Stay connected with Jillian daily on her public Facebook page (*www.facebook.com/JAhonenMinistries*) and on Instagram (*www.instagram.com/jillianahonen/*) to get a sneak peek into life with the Ahonen's as well as daily words of encouragement.

Learn more about Jillian and her ministries on her website, www.JillianAhonen.com.

 Don't forget to download the Jillian Ahonen Ministries mobile app (*www.apps.citybyapp.com/m/jillianahonen/*) for free and receive direct notification of everything we have going on, daily encouragement, scriptures, and more!

Or scan the QRC to get started!

About Life is Muddy

What if the "mud" of life no longer had the power to take you down?

Jillian takes us on a revolutionary journey to freedom through what she calls, "the mud pits of life." Not only do we get to relate to her raw emotions because of her willingness to be transparent, she helps us adopt a new and life-changing perspective through the mess. Applying Biblical truths, she teaches us practical ways of how we can learn to work with the mud rather than allowing it to harden us or hold us back, keeping us a victim to life's unsuspecting circumstances. She shows us that the mud pits of life do not get to determine who we are or where God wants to take us as she points us to God's ability and our full authority, because of Jesus and the ever-present power of the Holy Spirit to completely redefine life's mud. Jillian helps us peel off the mud, layer by layer, through cultivating an intimacy with God, establishing a trust relationship with Him through the mud, and the powerful stance we can take while facing the pits of life head on.

It's time to unleash the warrior that God has designed us to be and establish an unshakable foundation that sets us up for complete and total victory!

Honest … Relatable … Life Changing!

Life is Muddy is a transformational book that will inspire you to take your place as a victorious Child of God, igniting a faith so deeply rooted in who He is, you will be empowered to slay your way through the mud of life no matter what pit comes your way!

"Life is Muddy is freedom in print! Jillian writes with such wit and care as if she's your personal encourager and cheerleader. Her very transparent and candid insight into what it takes to get through the muddy waters of life reveals a heart that desires to champion you until you are victorious in every area of your life. As you read this book you will pause, ponder, chuckle, laugh out loud and even shed a few tears, but the feeling you receive as God peels back the layers will be an unforgettable delight! Jillian believes 'taking the time to nurture your heart will make you stronger emotionally and spiritually.' This is a must-read!"

Leila Johnson
Founder and Executive Director, Just Us Girls Women's Ministry
and Author of *A Worship Experience*

**Available at www.JillianAhonen.com,
Amazon, and your favorite online bookstore.**

www.ingramcontent.com/pod-product-compliance
Lightning Source LLC
Chambersburg PA
CBHW071234070526
44583CB00017B/2180